The Gifting Logos

The Gifting Logos

Expertise in the Digital Commons

———

E. Johanna Hartelius

UNIVERSITY OF CALIFORNIA PRESS

University of California Press
Oakland, California

© 2020 by E. Johanna Hartelius

Library of Congress Cataloging-in-Publication Data
Names: Hartelius, E. Johanna, 1979– author.
Title: The gifting logos : expertise in the digital commons / E. Johanna Hartelius.
Description: Oakland, California : University of California Press, [2020] | Includes bibliographical references and index.
Identifiers: LCCN 2020010006 | ISBN 9780520339637 (cloth) | ISBN 9780520339644 (paperback) | ISBN 9780520974449 (epub)
Subjects: LCSH: Knowledge, Theory of. | Creation (Literary, artistic, etc.)—Social aspects. | Knowledge economy—Social aspects. | Expertise. | Digital communications.
Classification: LCC BD161 .H295 2020 | DDC 303.48/3301—dc23
LC record available at https://lccn.loc.gov/2020010006

29 28 27 26 25 24 23 22 21 20
10 9 8 7 6 5 4 3 2 1

For Zander
For Elin

You fill my heart.

CONTENTS

Acknowledgments   ix

    Introduction   *1*
1. The Commons Aggregate and the Gift   *10*
2. The Infrastructural Commons   *43*
3. The Archival Commons   *70*
4. The Popular Commons   *101*
5. The Gifting Logos   *131*

Notes   147
Bibliography   193
Index   209

ACKNOWLEDGMENTS

Analyzing the rhetoricity of the gift, it seems imperative to acknowledge one's gratitude. And indeed, I am intensely grateful for the various kinds of support that made this book possible.

First, I appreciate the gentle efficiency of Lyn Uhl, executive editor at the University of California Press, and the anonymous reviewers. I wish to thank the University of Pittsburgh Department of Communication, especially Caitlin Bruce, Paul E. Johnson, Brent Malin, Calum Matheson, and Gordon Mitchell, and the University of Pittsburgh Humanities Center, who funded my research with a faculty fellowship in 2017. For giving me a new home and cheering me on as I carried the book across the finish line, I thank the faculty of the Department of Communication Studies at the University of Texas at Austin. Hook 'em!

I am grateful for friends and colleagues who create intellectual community across the country: Jennifer Asenas, Vanessa Beasley, Jon Carter, Jay Childers, John Durham Peters, Katya Haskins, Kevin Johnson, Bryan McCann, Mari Lee Mifsud, Jessica Moore, Annie Laurie Nichols, Tom Oates, Ned O'Gorman, Angela Ray, Tim Steffensmeier, Mary Stuckey, Mary Anne Taylor, Jaime Wright, Amy Young, and many others.

For championing this project with unyielding confidence, I am grateful to my friend Damien Smith Pfister, who provided encouragement even when I was losing steam. For word swapping among logophiles, I am forever grateful to JP. And for teaching me new aspects of the Logos, I am grateful to Jason Micheli.

I am grateful to my parents Lena Hartelius and Göran Larson, who remain inexhaustibly enthusiastic from afar. Finally, my deepest thanks to Zack Fogelman and our kids for all the most important gifts.

Introduction

Expertise has never been more ubiquitous than in the present moment of information superabundance, nor has it ever raised more complicated questions: What does it mean to have *expertise*? What kinds of experiences, and interpretations thereof, qualify as expertise? How is it made, and by whom? What are the effects of defining social and political relations via this value-laden term? Marcus Boon, author of *In Praise of Copying*, suggests that humans are conditioned to repeat and imitate. Through *mimesis*, or cultural copying, we learn how to be creative on our own. What troubles Boon is the contemporary moment of ambivalence; digital technologies allow easy reproduction, but reproduction itself is often associated with inauthenticity or even a vague sense of guilt. Boon reflects on his students' plagiarism conundrum:

> They are encouraged to learn through the act of repeating information, quoting, appending citations, in the traditional academic way; but with access to the Internet, to computers that can copy, replicate, and multiply text at extraordinary speed, they are also exhorted not to imitate too much, not to plagiarize, and to always acknowledge sources. They are ordered not to copy—but they are equally aware that they will be punished if they do not imitate the teacher enough![1]

Boon's students are like many of us, in that they are expected to absorb information and learn by repeating but are penalized if they go too far. The prospect of expertise pins them between the norms of repetition and the impetus to be original, in both cases in the interest of acquiring and producing knowledge. Pairing formal knowledge with creativity, then, Boon uses the example of improvisational jazz. He understands this art form as striving for a fully "depropriated" event, a moment that cannot be identically restaged. Boon describes "the erosion of the line that separates performer and audience, accompanied by a destabilizing of notions of profession and expertise that produces a new (but hardly unknown) type of collective; and the challenge of a 'being-with' based on a dynamic, immanent sense of relationship to what's going on."[2] Improvisational musicians, much like Boon's students, repeat and innovate, encountering each other through interdependent productivity. And as I highlight, copy, and paste quotes from an electronic version of Boon's book, hoping to gather insights and learn, his argument reverberates.

If asked to define *expert*, most people characterize a person who has extensive knowledge and competence. This definition is not inaccurate so much as it is incomplete and potentially misleading. Expertise, as I have argued elsewhere, is the function of persuasion.[3] It is contingent on the rhetorical situation, with its exigencies, participants, and constraints. For this reason, expertise depends on continuously ongoing rhetorical invention. On a global scale, the invention of expertise has accelerated exponentially in the last three decades, enrolling many of us in the coordinated and contested production of *stuff*, a term that I take quite seriously and later define in detail. Connected by microelectronic technologies and infrastructures, we produce digital materials and imprints, inventing ourselves as we engage with one another. Thus, while pundits on television may be experts in whatever subject they are asked to comment on, they are not the only ones who constitute their lived experiences as an information resource to define themselves relationally. Many if not most of us do so. An understanding of expertise as the rhetorical invention of everyday hermeneutics recognizes that "expertise" may be used as a critical lens even when no one in the room has used "the e word." Expertise, in short, is knowledge living its rhetorical life. What, then, is the character of this life in the present moment? What are its outcomes?

This book provides a rhetorical analysis of what it means to know things and to make things in the digital commons, which for my purposes is an active aggregate of three components: humans, networks, and cultural resources. Later in the introduction I explain each of these components, having first introduced the natural and cultural commons for historical and theoretical reference. First, however, I want to drop anchor by noting that the codependence of knowing and making has long been a subject of interest to rhetorical theorists. For the fifth-century Sophist Protagoras, for example, the homo mensura thesis asserts that humans are the measure of all things, and even more fundamentally, that all things that humans recognize as measurable (or, indeed, knowable) are invented in the moment of recognition.[4] In this moment, the thing to which the experiencer attributes the experience is made, as is knowledge of it. Similarly, for the Enlightenment thinker Giambattista Vico, the *verum factum* principle establishes that what is true is invented rather than, as the Cartesians would have it, discovered. The invention itself, according to Vico, produces knowledge that might be called "true."[5] Thus, when we have "knowledge," we have the substance of our own rhetorical productivity. With a leap from eighteenth-century Naples into the United States of the late 1970s, when the epistemic functions of rhetoric became the center of disciplinary attention, we find a conversation about the productive discourses of knowing that still continues. We recognize, too, looking back at the many years between Vico and Robert L. Scott, that compared to classical and premodern studies of rhetoric, modern theories are in general less emphatic about the connection between knowing and making, or epistemology and invention[6]—that is, until the discourses of scientific inquiry again become an object of rhetorical analysis. To wit, rhetoricians have long been intrigued by the symbolic activities through which experience becomes knowledge, knowledge gets authenticated as true, and true knowledge bestows authority in a way that might be labeled "expertise."

As I begin this book with the great theorists of rhetorical epistemology, I am compelled to offer a slightly different point of view as well, one that also informs my thinking. Protagoras and Vico, however potent their theories of productive knowledge, must be read as partial rather than sufficient. As anthropologists and ethnographers know, there are numerous examples from around the world of how knowledge and experiences are created, literally woven into cultural artifacts. They are made into tangible knowledge through creative activity. When a tapestry or a basket tells the story of a people's struggles and triumphs, this, too, is an iteration of the *verum factum* and homo mensura theses. Those who weave them have expertise, not only in the procedures of making crafts but also in the subject of their collective history. They *make* the truth as far as their communities are concerned. I would hardly be the first to call them the people's historians. Attending to their productivity, their epistemic methods, and their cultural function is imperative for contextualizing networked expertise. With these creators in mind, it becomes possible to ask questions about how, where, and by whom expertise is generated, not far away and long ago but here and now, in the technological paradigm that Manuel Castells calls "informationalism."[7] And it becomes possible to look not only to baskets but also virtual artifacts. My point—which is simply to set the contours for the introduction—is that in the contemporary moment, analyzing the productivity of expertise requires a willingness to consider capaciously not only the scientific and professional but also the amateur and quotidian. I also examine how common(s)-ality is an outcome of networked living and the artifacts that this living generates.

The purpose of this book is to offer the concept of the gifting logos to account for how expertise in the digital commons integrates three rhetorical practices: knowing, making, and gifting. What follows are three case studies: first, a study of the infrastructural commons, specifically the Creative Commons suite of licenses; second, the archival commons, specifically the Internet Archive and the Wayback

Machine; and third, the "Pirate Party," which rose to prominence in Sweden in 2006, and which I refer to as the popular commons. Through these case studies I demonstrate that expertise functions as, and indeed *is*, a gifting logos, and that the gifting logos makes three rhetorical practices inextricable:

- the invention of cultural materials such as text, music, film, photography, software, and computer code;
- the imbuing or encoding of the materials with the creator's lived experience, interpretations, and knowledge; and
- the constitution and dissemination of the materials as gifts.

These rhetorical processes are arranged sequentially in analog theories of cultural production. For example, someone with extensive knowledge of penguin habitats might make a film about it, then give that film to the Public Broadcasting System. A person with knowledge of computer science might write a program and then give it away in the spirit of open source ethics. From a slightly different angle, we might imagine someone with firsthand knowledge of chronic illness who composes music about the experience, and then, again, gives the music away. What I am proposing with the concept of the gifting logos is to conceive of the three rhetorical processes as one practice. The making, the knowing, and the giving are all constructed by participants in the digital commons as a complex activity, specifically one that is identifiable as expertise, or, more awkwardly, "expertising."

Digitally networked expertising is different from the sequential models previously mentioned. In those models, expertise is a finished product that is transmitted through channels that keep it intact. The product moves from an expert to laypersons, consumers, clients, or audiences. Continuous productivity is not in focus in these conventional models, nor is the infrastructure that facilitates productivity or the common life of which productivity is a feature. Traditional analog models of expertise are constrained in their ability to understand individual agents in terms of multiple functions, experiences, and investments. They see expertise as distinguishable from ordinary life and everyday habits, and they tend to define expertise almost exclusively as a market commodity aligned with purchasing power. From this point of view, expertise operates through formal binaries: having and not having, being and not being, selling and buying. By contrast, digital expertising places the meaningful aspect of expertise on various knowing activities in the participle form, which is to say as continuous. Rhetorical activities of knowing and making are inseparable from one another, and even though their products may be bought and sold (as in the analog case), they may alternatively be constituted through the logos of gifting. My intention is to illuminate how these activities work rhetorically and what their outcomes are. Put simply, my contention is that there are things about expertise in a digital context that we cannot recognize without considering knowing-making-gifting as integrated, including and especially in the networked life of an emerging commons. The famous gifting theorist Lewis Hyde argues that analyses of scientific collaboration must recognize "the emergence of community through the circulation of knowledge as gift."[8] My ambition is to extend the idea of "knowledge as gift" to include not only the scientific community but also the multitude of active participants in the digital commons. What is at stake in this book is the question of what we might learn about the digital commons if we consider expertise as the production and circulation of gifts.

The gifting logos as a pairing links two terms that are notoriously difficult to define. In chapter 1 I survey the theorists of gifting that inform the analyses to follow, noting how differently they invest the term with various ideals. The other term, *logos*, likewise requires an introduction that identifies major influences by name. For my purposes, the most fitting approach to logos is pre-Socratic. It predates and in my assessment exceeds the Aristotelian understanding of logos that prevails in rhetorical scholarship: dialectical engagements, technical discourse, and particular modes of persuasion. And unlike the Platonic understanding of logos, which appears less in argumentation textbooks than in theology, a pre-Socratic approach does not look for a transcendent truth beyond the particular iterations that necessarily betray its value. Personified in the Socratic method and dramatized in dialogues that end with the triumph of philosophy over rhetoric, Plato's logos is the truth that few seek and even fewer find. With a pre-Socratic approach, attending to both practices and principles, I am afforded an integrative approach wherein logos carries multiple meanings at the same time without one of them usurping another.

Among the pre-Socratics who took on the concept of logos, Heraclitus is especially compelling. In his fragmentary accounts, logos begins as an existential principle ordering the natural world, including the elements' relation to one another. Dominating these relations is a self-sustaining energy source, constantly "kindling itself by regular measures and going out by regular measures."[9] By extension, Heraclitus's logos principle orders the sociocultural world as a function of humans' fundamental, natural orientation. Here, logos is something like the immaterial material we humans move around in, experiencing its texture variously as constraining and enabling. The word *system* is not quite right; neither is *culture*, *paradigm*, or *framework*. But somewhere among these words is the meaning of logos as a condition. Within this conditional Logos (with a capital "L"), we engage one other wielding logoi (with a lowercase "l") instrumentally. These individuated engagements, arguments, and claims, reflecting logos as a nominal version of *legein* (to say, speak, or tell), are "languaged" in singular episodes. As Martin Heidegger explains in a beautiful essay on Heraclitus's logos fragment, *legein* originally meant to lay things in patterns, to "place one thing beside another."[10] The particular logoi are intelligible, meaningful, and valuable in the context of the Logos. To express meaning, then, is to gather things such that they reference one another, laying and being together. Logos, Heidegger writes, is "the Laying that gathers."[11] At the point when individuated engagements revert to the conditional Logos principle, they congeal as an account, or theory; they synthesize as sense making. In sum, I turn to Heraclitus so that I can use logos to mean (1) a sociocultural condition or context, (2) the principles that order it, (3) particular rhetorical actions within it, and (4) the theories generated by actors in that context about their rhetorical action. Moreover, a Heraclitean logos allows for an analysis that assumes principles but does not require praxis to be rational and an analysis that assumes the continuous indeterminacy of a network in flux.

As the book's central concept, the gifting logos is both a principle of operation within the digital commons and the hermeneutic with which I study this principle's instantiations. It is a language and structure that coordinates the activities of digital commoners. As such, it is variously implicit and explicit in the artifacts of those activities. And digital commoners may be more or less critical in their orientation toward the rhetorical processes in which they are engaged. By comparison, in my use of the gifting logos as a hermeneutic, my ambition is to analyze the productivity, artifacts, and life-forms of the digital commons. As a rhetorical critic, I am attuned to the assumptions that certain language practices make evident, including, for example, the idea that expertise is captured in digital materials and generatively distributable in a network infrastructure that connects people and experiences.[12]

As is evident throughout chapter 1, my analysis of the digital commons as an active and productive aggregate is informed by the extensive interdisciplinary literatures dedicated to the natural and cultural commons. My intention is to offer the reader a rich and historically grounded perspective on life in the commons, especially the centrality of expertise and authority. It is to highlight the connectedness and situatedness of cultural invention and proprietary powers. My intention is not to participate in the idealism that characterizes much scholarship surrounding the natural and cultural commons.[13] On this point, I take a different approach. My interest in the commons is primarily conceptual. I make a methodological recommendation to a specific group of scholars, suggesting that those who study digital rhetoric would be well served by the concept and theory of the commons. I do not advocate for a commons of a cultural or ecological kind or argue that the commons were, or would be, a more ethical or democratic arrangement of people and resources than other regimes.

In chapter 1, following the sections on the natural and cultural commons, I detail the components of the digital commons, specifically working with Paolo Virno's idea of the multitude and Manuel Castells's and Yochai Benkler's theories of networks. After the section on the digital commons, I introduce prominent theories of the gift. This section begins with Friedrich Nietzsche, Marcel Mauss, and Martin Heidegger, moving on to Lewis Hyde and Jacques Derrida. Focusing then on studies of gifting within rhetorical studies, I review the works of Michael J. Hyde and Mari Lee Mifsud. I direct attention to the rhetoricity of gifting, indeed to the potential of the gift for rhetorical scholarship. The subsequent section on the gifting logos foreshadows the final chapter, specifically the five characteristics and functions of the gifting logos itself that the conclusion explicates.

Chapter 2 situates the gifting logos in the discourses of the Creative Commons, a nonprofit organization primarily associated with a suite of licenses that make cultural content accessible beyond the constraints of copyright. The chapter begins with a historical survey of copyright, highlighting especially significant moments, including the English Stationers' Company royal charter from 1557, the Statue of Anne in 1710, the copyright clause of the US Constitution, the Copyright Extension Act of 1998, and the emergence of the Free Software Foundation and the open access movement. This section is intended to contextualize how the Creative Commons articulates, reinforces, and/or subverts certain long-contested assumptions of copyright, authorship, and the common good. The analysis, then, focuses on primary texts, including the 2015 Creative Commons memorandum "State of the Commons," a series of success stories titled *The Power of Open*, documents from the organization's website, and a set of academic articles and popular books by Creative Commons founder Lawrence Lessig. Examining these texts, I analyze how the Creative Commons defines and constitutes expertise via the gifting logos. The question of the chapter is: How is the interplay of knowledge and experience that happens in the making of cultural artifacts like texts and music accounted for by those who participate in the digital commons, specifically through the Creative Commons infrastructure? Explicating the gifting logos's rhetorical functions, I focus on creative individuation, timing, networked accretions of value, the ideal of abundance (or *copia*), reproduction, and gifting intent.

Chapter 3 turns to the gifting logos as archival, exploring how the digital commons invents and curates its history. How, I ask, is the past *made known* and *given* to the digital commons? I analyze discourses by and about the Internet Archive (IA), a massive storehouse of digitized collections of literature, music, photography, and film, and its most famous initiative, the Wayback Machine, a retrieval technology for past versions of hundreds of billions of web pages. As in chapter 2 I begin with a contextualizing section that surveys archival theories and practices. From a rhetorician's point of view, I introduce specific aspects of "the archive," including the historical connection between institutions of curated knowledge and public authority. Orienting archival theory in relation to expertise, I examine both processes and contents of archiving and archival research. To transition from brick-and-mortar archiving to digital archiving, I bring along a cluster of topics, including the public-private dialectic and the paradox of bureaucracy and mystery. In the analysis of the IA and the Wayback Machine, I trace several themes of archiving as an inventive practice of knowing, connecting them to the discourses of gifting that circulate through the IA and that identify founder Brewster Kahle as a heroic benefactor. I demonstrate how the inventions of the gifting logos emerge in the context of data loss and how this urgency rhetorically deploys the familiar ideal of archival preservation, in which productive knowledge forecloses the limits and gradual disappearance of the commons.

Chapter 4 examines the gifting logos's political implications for the digital commons. It extends the preceding two chapters' analyses of expertise by explaining how a loosely affiliated group sought recognition and authority by *making* itself and the moment of its emergence *known* to potential supporters, *giving* them a policy agenda. In other words, the chapter approaches the gifting logos as the gift of a political construct for the common good. It focuses specifically on the campaign discourses of the Swedish Pirate Party, an organization that in 2006 grew out of an internationally known file-sharing community called The Pirate Bay. The first half of the chapter contextualizes and situates the Pirate Party with reference to the theoretical and historical motifs of populism. In so doing, the chapter introduces both what I call "digital populism" and the parliamentary climate of Sweden at a time when confidence in traditional parties had waned. Against this foil, I ask: With what rhetorical strategies does the Pirate Party articulate itself, its politics, and its prescription for a prosperous polity? What is the character of the political construct that the Pirate Party gives to the commons? I analyze the Pirate Party's enactment and use of populist rhetoric, in particular antagonism toward the state and corporate institutions, an articulation of "the people" and its inherent potential, and a model of political representation and access. Throughout the chapter I demonstrate how the open access ideals that sustained the Pirate Party, which have garnered international support since the 1990s, were especially resonant in Sweden, where networked access is rhetorically associable with a legal and cultural custom known as *Allemansrätten*, the right of commons access. I suggest that by linking access to digitized cultural content with access to natural resources and territories, the Pirate Party made a compelling case for its concept of good governance.

In the aggregate of the digital commons, rhetorical influence, knowledge, and invention concur. In order to theorize this concurrence, my intent is to closely examine how productive expertising functions. I direct attention to a networked multitude of cultural inventions in a space managed by its inhabitants. I also demonstrate how, especially for scholars of networked and digital rhetoric, the commons might serve as a useful complement to rhetorical theory's more familiar concepts, such as "public" and "audience." And though this book is addressed primarily to scholars of digital rhetoric, my hope is that others will find it valuable as well. For scholars of epistemic rhetoric, my hope is that the book will indicate new venues for studying the inventive aspects of expertise and its mediation of lived experiences. I believe the concept of the commons, informed by interdisciplinary literatures, will help to transcend the insularity of projects devoted to peer production, exchanges between specialists and laypersons, knowledge communities, and so on. For scholars of rhetoric and public address generally, I hope that the book will offer a resourceful perspective on human networks, situatedness, and the constitutive functions of material and continuous circulation, indeed on the very notion of address. From chapter 4 especially, I hope that the political implications of digital culture and networks emerge, along with insights about representation, access, and advocacy. Finally, I hope that my engagement with both logos and the gift will offer readers a theoretical and critical resource to energize invention.

1

The Commons Aggregate and the Gift

A commons, generally speaking, is a living arrangement wherein humans interact via social, technical, and material networks to manage vital resources. It is a "paradigm [that] consists of working, evolving models of self-provisioning and stewardship that combine the economic and the social, the collective and the personal."[1] According to historian Peter Linebaugh, "*commons*" is a widely misapplied term: "From the quaint village commons to the cosmic commons of the electromagnetic spectrum, from the medieval subsistence economy to the general intellect, no term has been simultaneously so ignored and so contentious."[2] *Natural commons* refers to relatively unbounded resources such as water and aquatic ecologies; forests, jungles, and the animals that inhabit them; air and space; plants, seeds, and grain and their genetic makeup; wind that may be used for the harnessing of energy; and so on. By analogy, the cultural commons are customs, traditions, inventions, and the "vast store of unowned ideas [...] that we have inherited from the past and continue to enrich."[3] As David Bollier underscores, however, "commons are not just things or resources. [...] A commons is a resource + a community = a set of social protocols."[4] This composite definition is especially instructive for my project, which uses theories of the natural and cultural commons to build a critically viable concept for studying the digital commons. Thinking with Bollier and others, I define a commons as a rhetorical aggregate comprised of three components: the commoners, the sites and networks of encounter, and the cultural resources with which the encounters are coordinated. With the phrase "rhetorical aggregate" I invoke a coordinated dynamic roughly akin to Lloyd Bitzer's rhetorical situation. As in the rhetorical situation, attention is directed toward rhetors' responses to a contextual urgency.

Rhetoric in an aggregate may be defined as the exertion of influence through the production and application of symbols. What the commons contributes conceptually is a sense of a continuous lived experience of cultural invention in a situated space.

THE NATURAL COMMONS

The context and management of the natural commons are best explained by telling the story of the English land enclosures.[5] Since well before the Norman invasion, English commoners lived off the bounty of land that they did not own. They sustained themselves by grazing livestock, hunting and fishing, collecting firewood, and harvesting fruits and grains. As custodians of a natural, inhabited network, they were dependent on generally accessible goods, which they used according to specific privileges. Beginning in the early sixteenth century, modern commodification gradually turned common land into private property, segmenting the land for the emerging gentry class. An especially noteworthy moment occurred in 1532, when Henry VIII dissolved a number of monasteries, displacing the commoners who lived on the monasteries' land. Throughout the seventeenth century formal law took over common law, and between 1725 and 1825 four thousand enclosure acts appropriated six million acres of land; many of those who had been commoners of the land became the laborers of burgeoning industry.[6] In 1845 the General Inclosure Act affirmed the privatization of England's land and natural resources, necessitating a redefinition not only of ownership but of social hierarchies and ways of life. Those who had kept themselves and their families alive by applying the knowledge they had of how to use the resources around them had to acquire other kinds of knowledge; they learned skills that were different from those that their communities had transmitted generationally for centuries. In short, the expertise of the commons networks was at least in part replaced by the expertise required by the new networks of industry.

Contrary to the often Edenic picture of village life is the dismal prognosis presented by Garett Hardin in 1968. His essay, "The Tragedy of the Commons," inspired by an 1832 pamphlet written by amateur mathematician William Forster Lloyd, argued that nothing trumps human greed. Hardin summarily rejected the idea of sustainable governance beyond private ownership. The tragedy, according to Hardin's dystopia, is that rational choice is selfish. In his widely cited pasture example Hardin writes,

> Picture a pasture open to all. [sic] A rational being, each herdsman seeks to maximize his gain. [sic] Therein is the tragedy. Each man is locked into a system that compels him to increase his herd without limit—in a world that is limited. Ruin is the destination toward which all men rush. [sic] Freedom in a commons brings ruin to all.[7]

Hardin's point is that relying on self-restraint is irrationally self-destructive in the long run. The commons is unsustainable as a way of life because individuals cannot be trusted to tend to the interests of others as well as their own. The common good has no sincere proponents. And despite the endless refutations with which Hardin's polemic has been met, it continues to prompt discussion, perhaps because Hardin-type individuals and their grubby hands are ubiquitous. If you tell someone that you are writing a book about the commons, what most will respond is, "Oh, as in the tragedy of the commons?" The phrase accompanies the idea.[8]

Of the scholars who have critiqued Hardin and attempted to disarm the notion of a looming tragedy, the most prominent is the Nobel prize-winning economist Elinor Ostrom. Ostrom, whose legacy is "the Bloomington School" of commons scholarship, identified a set of design principles that distinguish the successful management of common pool resources. Having studied commons in fisheries and pastures in various places in the world, Ostrom's response to Hardin and other proponents of privatization is that a custodial model is empirically viable. In *Governing the Commons*, she calls this model "Game 5," wherein participants develop a contract of resource usage that is enforced by an appointed arbiter.[9] Those who depend on the resources reach an agreement based on the information available to them. As Ostrom notes, lamenting the widespread support for a coercive government or corporate authority:

> Unfortunately, many analysts—in academia, special interest groups, governments, and the press—still presume that common-pool problems are all dilemmas in which the participants themselves cannot avoid producing suboptimal results, and in some cases disastrous results. [. . .] Instead of presuming that some individuals are incompetent, evil, or irrational, and others are omniscient, I presume that individuals have very similar limited capabilities to reason and figure out the structure of complex environments.[10]

Ostrom's work demonstrates that the notion of unmanaged commons, as Hardin might call them, is misleading, even oxymoronic.[11] The pasture is never entirely open. Common pool resources are governed by rules and norms that are enforced by variously elected community leaders. They are "stinted."[12] The authority of leaders is assured by consent, which naturally entails conflict and continuous negotiation.[13] The networks of the commons are maintained by the participants' adherence to explicit and implicit codes; this adherence assures the endurance of the networks. Codes are in effect even when the networked interactions and the products thereof seem chaotic. When this is not the case, the commons falters and requires repair.

Because the Norman Conquest was a long time ago, and the Alanya inshore fisheries of Ostrom's research are remote, it is helpful to bring the natural commons closer to home, connecting it to my project here and now. Specifically, before proceeding to the next section on the cultural commons I highlight a few ways in which the natural commons directly informs my analysis of digital rhetorical networks and processes. First, it is significant that the boundaries of ownership and access in the natural commons are negotiated continuously rather than through a one-time purchase, and that this negotiation happens through the symbols and practices of the commons rather than through the markers of official authority. As Linebaugh explains, undeterred English commoners persisted with their customs for centuries after the enclosure movement. Indeed, the example of so-called perambulations illustrates this point: long after the privatization of English common lands had begun, the commoners would ceremoniously walk *along* the perimeters of their territories, walk *through* the invisible lines dictated by parchment maps, and walk *on* the grounds where their families had long lived.[14] These perambulations were a rhetorical negotiation of ownership and access. They entailed potentially hostile conflict and an enactment of rights, expectations, and motives through spatial and generational networks. To fully appreciate this practice, we might envision a group of commoners walking through the damp chill of spring and coming upon a fence in the middle of a field, a limit that previously was not there. What do they do? What should they think? As Hyde notes, the annual tradition of the walkabout did not become subversively defiant until legal edicts began to inscribe the land with property regulation.[15] At that time, the physical act of moving through a network (of fields) was a way of establishing belonging: what belonged to whom and who belonged where. In the networks of the natural commons (as in the networks of the digital commons, which I get to later in the chapter), proprietary rights are not managed by a single buy-and-sell transaction, despite the best laid plans of mice and kings. Rather, the relationship between commoners and ownership is constituted through living habits.[16]

Second, it is significant for my study of the commons that the distinction in the natural commons between labor time and not-labor time is indeterminate, as commoners are continuously engaged in some form of production. One may think of it this way: in a village, commoners work continuously to make the things that sustain life, such as shelter, tools, and food. There is no "on the clock" or "off the clock" in terms of labor, nor are there clearly distinguishable places of labor and leisure. The products that are made in the evening hours (such as knitted socks or sharpened knives) are not worth less than the products that are made between nine in the morning and five in the afternoon. All production is part of the livelihood of the commons. By contrast, laborers in an industrial setting may only be said to be working per se when they are *at work* in the factory, plant, or office. In this context, not-labor is the activity that happens in the not-workplace, which is to say at home or in establishments of social pleasure. Moreover, the indistinction of labor and not-labor in the natural commons must be correlated with governance. As Bollier explains with reference to historical industrialization,

"One of the lesser-noticed aspects of enclosures was the separation of production and governance. In a commons, both were part of the same process, and all commoners could participate in both. After enclosures, markets took charge of production and the state took charge of governance."[17] I underscore this point about productive labor, time, and access to governance in the natural commons to explain that when we think of the continuous labor of village commoners from centuries ago, we might also think of today's digital commoners, whose productivity is similarly continuous. The latter are engaged in digitally organized labor not just from nine to five but most of the time. This labor takes place not only at the office but in domestic and social venues: on the couch or at the coffee shop. Thus far, the analogy make sense. What is perhaps more complicated, and receives more attention in chapters 2 and 4, is the issue of managerial control. Bollier argues that productive commoners of the pre-enclosure time were involved actively in the governance of the commons. In later chapters I explore the extent to which this may apply to the decision-making procedures and power negotiations of the digital commons.

Third, the natural commons are relevant to my study of the digital commons insofar as they thrive on a rhetorical tension between the familiar and the unfamiliar, the mundane and the mysterious. Put differently, the commons are conditioned by a dialectic of what is readily known and what is potentially knowable. This is so in the past and present, and in the natural as well as the digital. Regarding the familiar, perhaps it goes without saying that the commons are common. They are routinized and dependent on predictability. In the natural commons, village life contains few surprises and plenty of well-worn habits. In the digital commons, routines are both mathematical, which is to say algorithmic, and human; most of us execute the chores of everyday life through communication technologies. At the same time, however, the natural commons are liminal, shaped by a boundary separating cultivated space from wilderness.[18] In the uncharted, unmapped territory of the forest, ocean, and outer space, there is no telling what mysteries may dwell, exceeding or resisting human control. We the commoners watch these knowable phenomena from our windows, looking into the deep woods, the dark sky, or the World Wide Web. The commons and their unboundedness thus stimulate the imagination and beckon rhetorical invention. In the digital commons the mystery hides somewhere deep in the machine. In the inaccessible paths of the electronic networks, certain functions exceed the knowledge of most digital commoners. We who know precious little about the networked machines and their impenetrable languages are as mystified by them as the village commoners were by the idea of wood nymphs and krakens.

This dialectical feature of the natural commons is important for my analysis because delineating what is familiar and what is unfamiliar, or moving the line such that what was unfamiliar becomes familiar, is a rhetorical act of expertise.

It is to *make* something known or knowable, to invent something in such a way that it is intelligible. It is to explain something, such as the movements of stars or the binary code of a computer program, so that we commoners understand: to make known and to give. This is a process of invention designed both to demystify and to maintain enough mystery that the expert remains necessary for the common good; for without some measure of mystery, the commoners would not need explanation from an authority figure. The mystery that exists at the periphery of the commons, like a horizon against which the commons may know itself, is significant not only for the commoners' experience of everyday life but also for the identification and appointment of authority figures, the function of which is to make things known.

THE CULTURAL COMMONS

Reflecting on the vast concept of the cultural commons, it is helpful to begin with something concrete. In 1963 the Walt Disney Corporation released an animated film titled *The Sword in the Stone*, loosely based on the legend of King Arthur and the sword Excalibur. The film depicts a young boy, a wise old wizard with a pet owl, and a critical moment in which the boy rises to a challenge to fulfill his destiny. In short, the film is generic. Its narrative is familiar even to those who have not seen it. With this film as a starting point, my introduction of the cultural commons could go in various directions. For example, I might treat the film as a specific fixation of a perennial idea and discuss the implications for commercial copyright; this discussion would address how long Disney's exclusive privileges ought to last, the value of the public domain, and where art and commerce meet for the good of society. These matters, which reappear throughout the book, are not the place to begin with the cultural commons as such, particularly when the issue at stake is expertise. Instead, my consideration of what constitutes the cultural commons and where they might be found begins with the notion of inspiration. Despite the unsettling sentimentality of the word, the metaphor itself of *in-spiration* helps me make my point. The cultural commons are, among other things, in the air. That is precisely why questions of property sometimes get awkwardly stuck. *The Sword in the Stone* is indeed copyrighted material, but it is also an iteration of a deeply rooted and pervasive myth. The myth of a noble hero, a fated journey, and the powerful object that only the hero can wield—sometimes it is a sword, but it might just as well be a ring (Frodo Baggins), a lamp (Aladdin), or a wand (Harry Potter)—is remade again and again. It hovers in the space of inspiration. Thus, it is misleading to speak of the cultural commons primarily as a question of who owns what.[19]

The most readily graspable and widely used definition of the cultural commons relies on analogy with the natural commons, comparing air and land to traditions, customs, and inventions. This way of thinking, which preserves the notion of inspiration and its centrality in cultural life, indicates how the natural and the cultural commons both consist of commoners, resources, and networks or sites. Or, as I explained with reference to Bollier, "Commons = resources + community + the rules and norms for managing them."[20] On each side of the analogy are resources that belong to no one in particular but are vital to all and must be governed sustainably if they are to remain common. Otherwise they become the private possessions of whoever is in charge. Ownership thus enters the conversation not solely via property, including the relatively young concept of intellectual property, but as a structure of governance. Governance and property together make it possible to think of enclosures as applicable to both the natural and cultural commons. As I explained in the preceding section, the natural commons globally have been and continue to be enclosed, which is to say privatized. This is the case not only for land but also increasingly for scientific discoveries, species (including plants with pharmaceutical properties), and biological materials (including components of the human genome). In terms of the cultural commons, the much-cited argument of legal scholar James Boyle is that presently a "second enclosure movement" is under way. With respect to the distribution of cultural content, Boyle argues that intangible resources like ideas and facts are being enclosed as the English moors once were: "Things that were formerly thought of as common property, or as 'uncommodifiable,' or outside the market altogether, are being covered with new, or newly extended, property rights."[21] In Boyle's view, the second enclosure movement is driven by a "deep pessimism about the possibility of managing resources that are either commonly owned or owned by no one."[22] Like Ostrom, Boyle is convinced that those who see privatization as the only way to manage common pool resources are cynical, and that cynicism limits opportunities to develop commons governance.[23]

When scholars and activists analogize the cultural and natural commons, the distinguishing feature that is most often mentioned is "nonrivalrous" resources. These are resources that are not diminished by use. They are difficult to contain, or "nonexcludable," but there is no urgent need to contain them because they are not at risk of depletion. As Hardin's pasture example illustrates, natural commons are finite, at least when they are not managed sustainably; where one sheep has eaten all the grass, less grass remains for others. If I fish all the cod out of the North Atlantic, precious little remains for future fishermen. By contrast, if I teach a song that I have composed to a friend, my song is not depleted. This comparison of fish and songs is, of course, complicated by market value, which I address in later chapters. For now, the point is that comparisons between the natural and cultural commons often hinge on the issue of what is finite and valuable. As Michael Hardt and Antonio Negri, who compare "the air, the water, the fruits of the soil, and all nature's bounty" with "knowledges, languages, codes, information, affects," write, "When I share an idea or image with you, my capacity to think with it is not lessened; on the contrary, our exchange of ideas and images increases my capacities."[24] This is the leitmotif of the open access movement and, in a larger historical context, the Enlightenment. At stake in nonrivalry is whether a resource multiplies and migrates from its point of origin or stagnates and dies. Most commentaries on the cultural commons, especially those that encourage resistance against "the second enclosure," emphasize that ideas thrive when they are accessible to all, when commoners breathe the open air of inspiration, as previously suggested.

It is remarkable, however, that alongside the concept of the cultural commons as nonrivalrous is the recurring, albeit suppressed, suggestion that the cultural commons may be threatened from within, indeed by the commoners themselves. From the outside, enclosures threaten natural and cultural commons insofar as they turn shared resources into privately owned commodities. Commoners cannot gain access to what has been bought up by a private entity, whether it is land or copyrighted music. Further, natural commons are threatened by excessive use because they are rivalrous. When the fish are gone, they're gone for good. But in discourses about the nonrivalrous cultural commons and the generative effect of sharing ideas, there is often an implied urgency to organize and protect. Not everyone is thrilled about the idea of the cultural commons as a repository from whence everyone may draw and into which anyone may make a deposit. The concern is quality control, and the risk that the cultural commons may, as Hardt and Negri fear, be "drained."[25] Marxist historian David Harvey cautions that while the cultural commons "cannot be destroyed through use, it can be degraded and banalized through excessive abuse."[26] What, one wonders, does he mean by abuse? What interests are served by the argument, which extends far beyond Harvey, that even in the cultural commons there are, or should be, standards and order, or by the argument that even in the cultural commons not "everything goes"; rather, someone is in charge? Framing this line of inquiry in terms of expertise allows me in later chapters to analyze how value and authority (or authorship) are managed via a logic of gifting, the gifting logos.

In rhetorical theory, the cultural commons enter through the concept of commonplaces. Most simply, we may think of the aforementioned stuff of the cultural commons—the ideas, artifacts, inventions, and knowledges—as necessary equipment for any persuasive effort. The cultural commons as Boyle defines them, in other words, supply rhetors with strategies for making arguments. Classically conceived, commonplaces, or *koinoi topoi*, are general resources for discovery and creativity, wherein rhetors formulate messages with regard to audiences' "habits of thought, value hierarchies, forms of knowledge, and cultural conventions."[27] Aristotle famously lists twenty-eight of them in the second book of the *Rhetoric*, noting how speakers' effectiveness depends on their capacity to innovate within the structure of what is well established. The trick to persuasion is to turn the common and obvious toward a novel insight; here we get the notion of a trope, which turns an argument as needed. In the process of innovation, the commonplaces give rise to rhetorical artifacts and performances. They are productive methods, indeed forms that continue to be useful for as long as they are relevant. Put another way, the forms of the commonplaces are nonrivalrous. Aristotle's inventory of general topics demonstrates how rhetors might persuasively mobilize the audience's sense of consequences, antecedents, and various dialectical relationships such as more and less, past and future, possible and impossible. Commonplaces are the rhetorical opportunities of the cultural commons.[28]

Another term in classical rhetorical theory that instructively connects the cultural commons with commonplace arguments is *doxa*. In Plato's scornful definition, *doxa*, from *dokein* (how something appears), refers to the superficial beliefs of the public. It is indeed the purview of rhetoric, but to Plato, this is a bad thing. *Doxa* is distinct from *episteme*, or knowledge that is absolutely true rather than popular or common. From the beginning, thus, the commonness of *doxa* presses against questions of epistemology and what commoners may be said to know. Aristotle rehabilitates *doxa* with *endoxa*, which in his study of the *Topics* extends beyond the fickle whims of the people to more enduring beliefs and consensus.[29] Because I am concerned with commons expertise, Mari Lee Mifsud's treatment of *doxa* in terms of cultural "givens" is especially instructive, and I turn to it in the case studies that follow. As Mifsud explains, *doxa* are the givens of a particular community; references to *doxa* pass without critical reflection.[30] *Doxa* are the assumptions that are taken for granted, the knowledge or wisdom that is smoothly, even imperceptibly transmitted. We might think, for example, of a garden variety idiom and how it contains a kernel of common epistemology: "Don't count your chickens before they hatch!" says the wise elder to the impatient youth. And the idiom proves him right. To say that idioms are commonplaces is to note that they are places in which one might discover the knowledge of the commons. What is commonly known may then be referenced among commoners, prompting us to say to one another, "There goes that guy who counted his chickens," when we see the man who bought a Tesla at the first indication that his start-up company was going to take off. *Doxa*, put differently, constitute the theoretical context for studying the rhetoric of expertise in the commons, digital or otherwise. They are nimble, productive, effective, and as subtle or brash as they need to be.

As I take certain insights from the preceding sections on the natural and cultural commons, transitioning with them to the following section on the digital commons, I am compelled to emphasize emplacement. That is, the cultural commons are situated in particular places in the world. These places shape the cultural commons in fundamental ways. My own experience illustrates this, but in offering it anecdotally, my assumption is that the reader will supplement my story with his and her own. I grew up in Sweden, where traditions that reference light and dark are synchronized with seasonal rhythms. Advent, for example, falls at a time of year when most waking hours are wrapped in deep darkness. In this circumstance, lighting candles that signify hope and life against death and placing them in the liminal space of windows, where a thin glass pane separates cold and dark from warmth and light, is a way of culturing nature. Or, we might say, the cultural and natural commons interlace. Likewise, in the summertime the Swedish Midsummer pagan rituals play on the meanings of light and darkness, specifically the endurance of light. Midsummer is a major holiday that incorporates the natural commons, casting certain characters like the forest in myths and songs. Reflecting historically on the cultural commons of Midsummer, it is easy to imagine how, before electrical lighting, celebrants might spot fairies in the midnight haze against the tree line. Less romantically put, the living practices of commoners connect the natural and cultural commons in networked forms. What remains to be seen in the next section, and throughout the book, is how digital sites constitute these forms.

THE DIGITAL COMMONS

The term *digital commons* carries an idealistic connotation. It prompts many of us to think of the open access movement, or academic and public institutions that make their holdings publicly available. In order to critically complement rather than oppose this perspective, I align the digital commons with the natural and cultural commons, not because the three are neatly analogous or distinct but because significant conceptual insights may be drawn from multiple disciplines in order to examine the aggregate form of the digital commons. My contention with this alignment is that, when we study the digital commons from the point of view of commons theory generally, we are able to see certain facets of the aggregate that are important for rhetorical analysis. Thus, I define the digital commons in terms of three components: humans, networks, and resources. The humans, articulated via the formation that Paolo Virno calls "the multitude," populate and constitute the networks. The networks are both electronic and social; they are, as I demonstrate in chapter 2, infrastructural. In the networks, the multitude engages in productive interactivity, inventing digital artifacts, or stuff, for circulation. In so doing, the multitude governs itself and its resources. In the following paragraphs I explain this definition of the digital commons with respect to the three key concepts.

Multitude

Paolo Virno's theory of the multitude is an illuminating way to think of social being in the digital commons. For Virno, the multitude is a network that produces individuals rather than the other way around. Or, as he writes, singularities are the point of arrival following a process of individuation: "The individual of the multitude is the final stage of a process beyond which there is nothing else, because everything else (the passage from the One to the Many) has already taken place."[31] Taking this position on the individual and the network, the singular and the multitude, Virno begins by recasting the contention between Spinoza and Hobbes on political structures. Hobbes rejects the multitude, Virno explains, because it fails to achieve the unity of a single will.[32] For Spinoza, "the multitude indicates a plurality which persists as such in the public scene, in collective action, in the handling of communal affairs, without converging into a One, without evaporating within a centripetal form of motion."[33] The multitude remains politically and socially networked, not foregoing individuation but also not taking it as a prerequisite for collective action.[34] For this reason, the multitude is appropriate for analyzing the "associative life" of digital commoners. As I demonstrate in the case studies, the multitude convenes and disperses in productive pulsation through networks, less like the languid motion of a jellyfish than like the rapid flutter of an embryonic heartbeat. In this pulsation, the multitude functions as a name for the digital commoners. I turn to Virno's theory because it affords a useful vocabulary for rhetorical analysis. As he notes, "an entire gamut of considerable phenomena—linguistic games, forms of life, ethical inclinations, salient characteristics of production in today's world—will end up to be only slightly, or not at all, comprehensible, unless understood as originating from the mode of being of the *many*."[35] In the digital commons, "the coupling of the terms public-private, as well as the coupling of the terms collective-individual, can no longer stand up on their own [;] they are gasping for air, burning themselves out."[36]

As Virno explains, the multitude coheres around "formal and informal knowledge, imagination, ethical propensities, mindsets, and 'linguistic games.'"[37] It meets on common ground, in other words—specifically the common ground of language itself, which belongs to everybody.[38] Thus, the multitude functions through what Virno refers to as the "general intellect" and what I might describe as the cultural commons within the digital commons. With this description, I am drawing attention to how the aggregate of the digital commons (humans, networks, and resources) encompasses the cultural commons, as well as to how the cultural commons exceed the structure of digital networks. The cultural commons necessarily establish the context for what happens in the digital commons. In addition, the cultural commons are called upon in the particular rhetorical actions of digital commoners, as *endoxa* is instantiated in particular appeals to rhetorical commonplaces (see previous discussion). Virno writes, "The unity which the multitude has behind itself is constituted by the 'common places' of the mind, by the linguistic-cognitive faculties common to the species, by the general intellect."[39] Thus he connects the multitude with the commons. Using the notion of a general intellect,

Virno identifies a central resource with which the multitude may rhetorically constitute itself (or, its "selves"); this creates the possibility for a rhetorical invention of the multitude in common practice. The informal knowledge and mindset of the multitude are the digital substances of networked life. Moreover, Virno indicates how the rhetoric of the general intellect animates the multitude. The general intellect is, in a word, the stuff of the commons.[40]

Resources, or "Stuff"

The resources of the digital commons are like resources of the natural commons and the cultural commons in the sense that they sustain life, connecting commoners to one another. The resources are a heterogenous stratum layered on top of digital networks, which I address later in the chapter. As we think of land, air, and fish in the natural commons and ideas, artifacts, and traditions in the cultural commons, so may we think of resources in the digital commons as digitized "stuff." The stuff, the material and symbolic artifacts of everyday life, is generated by digital commoners. Indeed, this productivity and its buildup of content and imprints are effects of the digital commons. The stuff is infrastructural and immersive, as webs are to the spiders who make them. As I demonstrate in chapter 2, the Creative Commons suite of licenses is designed to structure and tag creators' stuff, such as music, text, photography, and software code. The licenses are the infrastructure of commons stuff. Similarly, chapter 3 explains how the archiving of digital stuff preserves a historical treasure for future generations, foreclosing the loss of culture. In chapter 4, the main campaign promise of the Pirate Party is common access to digital stuff. To be sure, the word *"stuff"* is rather colloquial and lacking in academic authority. Nevertheless, it is suitable for an analysis of the digital commons. Its polysemy makes it user-friendly. *Stuff* could refer to personal property (as in "My basement is full of stuff") or a performance (as in "I like to strut my stuff"). Stuff can be stacked on shelves, but it can also be immaterial. As Boyle puts it, focusing on an internetworked context, "If you can make it somehow into the public consciousness, then you can be paid for allowing the world to copy, distribute, and perform your *stuff*."[41] Similarly putting the emphasis on material impact, Brian Ott explains, "It *matters*, in every sense of that word, that digital data and information is made up of bytes rather than atoms, that it is comprised of binary code, that traditional modes of communication (sound and image) can, regardless of medium (radio, television, newspaper, book, music, etc.), be converted to digital form."[42] Digital form, in a word, is stuff; the form is binary, distinguishable in two states of either off or on, 1 or 0.[43]

Employing Virno's concept of the multitude's general intellect and the notion of digitized stuff as the resources of the digital commons, Boyle's aforementioned concern about a second enclosure becomes salient. It is a matter not only of privatizing knowledge, mindsets, and languages, but also of technically restricting the networks of the digital commons as lands might be restricted by fences. In the digital context, the cultural commons are bound not only by copyright laws but by the technologies that enforce them. As prominent scholars of intellectual property have argued, the same technologies that enable cultural creativity and innovation are used by the legal interests of copyright holders to enforce monopolies, threatening the vibrancy of the digital and cultural commons. According to "free culture" advocate Lawrence Lessig, "Technology, tied to law, now promises almost perfect control over content and its distribution. And it is this perfect control that threatens to undermine the potential for innovation that the Internet promises."[44] Lessig argues that the content industry, what we might think of as pop culture media, has abused its political influence to legally erase the divide between regulated commercial use of copyrighted material and private noncommercial use.[45] This is relevant for my study of the digital commons in the same way that any appropriation, regulation, or enclosure would constrain other kinds of commons. At stake is the prospect of producing life-sustaining things and circulating them, or *making* them part of the commons network, the multitude's connectivity.

Networks

The infrastructure of the digital commons is a network of networks, what Manuel Castells defines as a "set of interconnected nodes [. . .] powered by microelectronics-based information and communication technologies."[46] Although this infrastructure may be partially identified with the global network of shared protocols known as the internet, it also, more particularly, connects situated content and practices. (For example, I later characterize the Creative Commons licenses as a commons infrastructure for the copyright negotiations of the World Wide Web.) In theory and practice, the purpose of a network is to sustain itself by carrying out a program that systematizes norms and codes. Because this is so, networks have an important function in any commons (digital or natural). In the natural commons of Ostrom's fisheries, a central objective is the longevity of the fish colonies. Networks coordinate the resources (the fish) and the participants. In the digital commons, the network's purpose may be more nebulous. Castells writes, "The culture of the global network society is a culture of protocols of communication enabling communication between different cultures on the basis, not necessarily of shared values, but of sharing the value of communication. This is to say: the new culture is not made of content but of process."[47] The question, then, is how the process may be understood. My intention is to demonstrate that the networked process of the digital commons may be understood as a productive epistemic habit. This habit, in which making stuff and knowing stuff are integrated, is identified by the networked participants as expertise. Furthermore, in this logic (or logos) of expertise, gifting is essential. As Castell notes, "The culture of the network society is a culture of protocols of communication between all cultures in the world, developed on the basis of a common belief in the power of networking and of the synergy obtained by *giving* to others and receiving from others."[48] Network theory supports attention to the rhetorical processes of expertise as knowing, making, and gifting.

One of the most important aspect of the networked structure of the digital commons is that the electronic network itself is built for accreting exchanges between peripheral nodes. It is built for production among peer participants.[49] Thus, the digital commons, like the natural and cultural commons, depend on the ingenuity and rhetorical invention of the commoners. This aspect of digital networks is elucidated well by Yochai Benkler, whose widely cited analysis of the information economy traces "the emergence of nonmarket individual and cooperative production."[50] Benkler claims that after 150 years of an industrial paradigm, two features now distinguish the advanced economies of the twenty-first century: a shift toward the production and manipulation of information and an extensive communication network with high computational capabilities.[51] As he assesses the long-term prospects of this cooperative production, Benkler argues that the network society "provides a platform for new mechanisms for widely dispersed agents to adopt radically decentralized cooperation strategies other than by using proprietary and contractual claims to elicit prices or impose managerial commands."[52] For my purposes, Benkler is informative in his attention to the habits with which "individuals pool their time, experience, wisdom, and creativity to form new information, knowledge, and cultural goods"—in other words, the networked habits of knowing and making.[53] Moreover, while Benkler's interest in economic mechanisms differs from my interest in rhetorical practice, his discussion of nonmarket agents opens rich possibilities for studying goods and the management of value beyond the industrial paradigm. He indicates ways of exploring how people make things and how things acquire value through logics that may, without the concept of the network society, be elusive.

A few words of clarification are appropriate at this juncture. First, the network society is not synonymous with the digital commons as I understand it. The infrastructure of the digital commons functions as a network, but the digital commons exceed this infrastructure. By comparison, it would be odd to reduce the natural commons to the infrastructure of space, spatial relations, and physical movement. Relatedly, the internet, which is a network of networks, is not the digital commons. It is not, in its current form, a commons in any effective sense, including though not limited to the sense of shared property and governance. From the early years of the 1990s, the policies that determined internet expansion and access were dictated largely by the private sector. As Benkler notes with reference to the Bill Clinton administration's telecommunications programs, corporate interests shaped the internet into a market structure from the beginning, in which "property-like regulatory frameworks" were strengthened while "various regulatory constraints on property like rights" were eased.[54] Whether this history is good or bad is beyond the scope of my project; the same goes for the question of whether the internet or the World Wide Web could, in terms of ownership structures, become a "real" commons in the future. It seems, to me, unlikely. What I am concerned with as a rhetorical scholar are the habits of language, which in the case of the digital commons invent a form of being together digitally. In part, my reason for drawing conceptual insights from the natural and cultural commons is that doing so allows me to study the digital commons not solely as a function of property, but as a living arrangement. As a living arrangement, the digital commons are constituted by the commoners, the cultural productivity in which they are engaged, and the networks through which they are connected.

For rhetorical scholars, digital networks have in recent years acquired a new inflection and prominence. According to Damien Smith Pfister, "The changing conditions of mediation merit the development of a 'new rhetoric' capable of guiding public advocacy and deliberation in contemporary times. *Networked media* spur *networked rhetorics*."[55] In his study of the blogosphere, Pfister explicates a historical "shift in sensibilities as people participate in, make sense of, and enact new modes of thinking, feeling, and being."[56] As he carefully notes, however, the network has long been "rhetoric's key metaphor," connecting rhetors and audiences via paths of influence.[57] In terms of the value of the concept of network for the study of digital rhetoric, Pfister and I agree. What is especially compelling is how he mobilizes the rhetorical tradition to study "how the affordances provided by networked media change practices related to the invention of public argument, the role of emotion in public life, and the exercise of expertise."[58] And yet the network concept on its own is necessary but insufficient for a study of digital rhetoric; that is, it is insufficient to function without a framing concept such as commons.[59] One of my reservations about the network as self-sufficient is that it tends to orient one's imaginary and focus toward utilitarianism.[60] Networks function with a purpose, designed to execute. With some exceptions, networks have a greater potential for efficiency than commons do, and a higher aspiration for efficient processing, specifically information processing.[61] It is difficult to conceive of a network in which figurative litter is simply lying around. Compared to the commons, networks have nodes rather than textured destinations. In the commons, including the digital commons, the multitude of commoners live with each other's cultural residues. Networks do not necessarily contain a tradition or the products thereof. Commons, however, do.

As is by now evident, this book belongs in an interdisciplinary literature dedicated to digital rhetoric. As a rhetorical scholar rather than, for example, a media literacy critic, I take the term "*digital rhetoric*" to designate the practice and study of persuasion in the activities, objects, and sites of digital information technologies.[62] Specifically, as my point of view is informed by theories and grammars of the classical canon, I join the conversation that Kathleen Welch pioneered twenty years ago, Collin Brooke mapped ten years after that, and many others have contributed to richly.[63] I wholeheartedly agree with Michele Kennerly and Damien Smith Pfister, who introduce their innovative collection of essays by noting, "Returning to ancient texts from new technocultural vantage points shakes up accepted interpretations, produces readings with different nuances, allows old terms to be revivified and reinhabited in new ways, and generates theoretical resources to guide critics, theorists, and publics in negotiating continuity and change."[64] Further, I appreciate Aaron Hess and Amber Davisson's dialectics of theory and analysis, whereby they emphasize that "the concept of digital rhetoric requires sustained attention to the ways that rhetoric changes in a technological era *and* how technology is shaped by human expression both about and through the technology itself."[65] As Douglas Eyman notes, "Digital rhetoric should be viewed as a field that engages multiple theories and methods rather than as a singular theory framework."[66] Responding to Barbara Warnick's germinal work, Eyman explains that scholars of digital rhetoric "need to align theories and methods of classical and contemporary rhetoric to networked texts and new media as objects of study, but we also need to develop new theories and methods to account for gaps in these more traditional approaches."[67] By inventing and deploying the concept of the gifting logos to examine discourses of expertise in the digital commons, I respond to the invitations extended by these scholars.

Scholars of digital rhetoric, as well theorists like Castells and Benkler, are explicitly wary of being charged with technological determinism, and for good reason. And because I, too, could be indicted on this charge, a comment is warranted. As the word "*determinism*" suggests, the idea is that mechanical, industrial, and communication technologies constrain and enable human habits and perspectives in ways that we ourselves do not control. To a point, this seems a fairly obvious assessment. A commuter train allows me to go faster than a car, but not as fast as a rocket ship. A telephone allows me to hear my friend's voice, while a letter does not. The reason that the point of view known as technological determinism is so often rejected or even derided is that extreme versions of it tend to elide the human origins of technology. In scholarly analyses as well as popular discourse, technology at times is talked about as though it appeared out of nowhere, enveloping and dictating human life. This point of view is especially prominent at historical moments of innovation, such as at the introduction of the printing press, the steam engine, the incandescent light bulb, microprocessors, and the internet. In terms of information technologies and media specifically, tales of origin are often fervently optimistic, marking a moment of ingenuity after which people were brought closer together and communicated better than ever before.[68] The way the tales get recounted obscures not only the social context in which a technology is invented but the historical precedents thereof: the moments in the past when old technologies were new and characterized with the same enthusiasm as that with which the most recent technological invention is hailed.[69] To critics of technological determinism, the phrase "*new media*" and the revolutionary impact that enthusiasts predict allow a presentist interpretation of media and human practices.

Although I obviously agree that all inventions and technologies are produced in a social context, that "history matters," and that hope springs eternal until it gives us amnesia, I submit that a brusque rejection of technological determinism sometimes exaggerates human agency and control over machines.[70] Of course we did not wake up one morning inside microelectronic networks and begin to produce culture there, conditioned by the technologies of the network and the machines in our midst. Instead, the networks were installed and continue to change, shrink, and grow as humans do things to them. But now that the networks are here, they do in fact shape life in the digital commons: not all the time, or in all matters, but significantly. To underestimate this process of impact is to overestimate the authority that humans exercise over the technologies of our lives, communicative and otherwise. As I look around my office, my home, and my city, it is evident that technology in some measure "determines" me. As Castells writes, "Our society is characterized by the power embedded in information technology, at the heart of an entirely new technological paradigm."[71] My concern is with the language in which that power is vested and with which it is negotiated in particular moments. Thus, I am cautious with my own tendency to reinforce the perspective of technological determinism, but because of what my project demands, I am compelled to recognize the rhetorical indicators of determination.

Before I proceed, it may be helpful to take stock of the chapter's major points thus far. First, the digital commons are an aggregate of three components. The *humans*, articulated as a multitude of networked individuals, convene in the practices of rhetorical constitution; the immersive *resources*, or digital stuff that connect them, are incorporated in networked interaction and governance; and the *networks* of governance supply the infrastructure for productivity. Second, analyzing the digital commons with reference to the natural and cultural commons brings to light certain qualities of the aggregate that demand scholarly attention, specifically from rhetoricians. These qualities include situated experience in particular sites, the importance of inventive knowledge and lived experience in social relationships, and the boundary between the familiar and the unfamiliar. Third, rhetorical scholars, who have long studied commonplace argumentation and networked persuasion, have much to gain by deploying the commons as a critical concept for productive sociality. Doing so allows us to complement more familiar terms, such as *public* and *audience*. This opportunity is essential for scholars of digital rhetoric and also potentially useful and significant for others.

THE GIFT

Gifts are messages. That is to say, gifting is a rhetorical practice. It is an engagement between a giver-rhetor and a recipient-audience, mediated by a third substance. The gift-message may be as petty as "I did not forget to bring a gift" (see, for example, all birthday parties for children under five years old) or as vital as organ donation. In each case, the gift communicates. In this section I introduce five prominent thinkers who have responded to either the question "What is a gift?" or the slightly different "What functions does a gift serve?" In chronological order I highlight recurring themes in the works of Friedrich Nietzsche, Marcel Mauss, Martin Heidegger, Lewis Hyde, and Jacques Derrida. These thinkers' commitments lie in the interstices of anthropology, sociology, philosophy, art, and economics. And insofar as they have shaped the very concept of the gift as we know it, one cannot write about gifting without giving due space and attention to each of their perspectives. I survey them here in order to identify certain insights that inform my rhetorical position on gifting. It is thus important that I begin with a declaration of my own assumption: gifts are messages. As I explain in the next section, which deals directly with the gifting logos, my concern is with the rhetoricity of gifting and with the presence of gifting rhetoric in activities that are typically thought of as unrelated to gifts. Operating from this position, I am relieved of the burden of determining whether there *really* is such a thing as a gift or whether one can *really* give or receive a *true* gift. Because gifts are messages—because gifting is a rhetorical practice—the determination must depend on the event of the message rather than on a transcendent, absolute standard.

Friedrich Nietzsche: The Curse of Wisdom (1883–1885)

In the parable of Zarathustra, Friedrich Nietzsche theorizes the gift in two forms. From Zarathustra himself, who leaves his mountain and "goes under" to impart wisdom to humans, the gift of wisdom is unreceivable.[72] Humans do not understand.[73] In response to Zarathustra's unintelligible message, the people laugh; hating him, they treat him like a jester.[74] Lamenting this, Zarathustra asks himself, "They receive from me, but do I touch their souls?"[75] By definition, Zarathustra's gift cannot be received. That this is so is reflected in the failure of his project, which ultimately does not generate a cohort of "overhumans." The humans are unable to receive the gift they really need. They are incapable of grasping Zarathustra's insight that gifted wisdom cannot be wisdom in any true sense. With reference to the tenth and sixteenth chapters of the Gospel of Matthew, Zarathustra exhorts his followers to "lose me and find yourselves."[76] Nietzsche insists that the gift of wisdom cannot be received when wisdom is understood as a perspective on the folly of the social world.[77]

Within the social world—this is the second form in which Nietzsche theorizes the gift—gifting is self-interested manipulation, driven by pride and shame. Giving gifts is a selfish drive in pursuit of the "gift-giving virtue" that puts in the eyes of the gifter a "goldlike gleam."[78] That humans stuff themselves (with material or symbolic goods) so that gift-giving love can flow out of them as from a well is deeply selfish.[79] To help a person out of pity by bringing her a gift brings her only shame. Such charity turns into a "gnawing worm" of indebtedness.[80] In other words, regarding gifts within the social order, Nietzsche aligns with theorists who emphasize the political dictates of gifting. The saint who appears early in the story underscores the sociality of gifting, explaining to Zarathustra that people do not believe that hermits bring gifts since their "steps sound too lonely through the streets."[81] Givers of gifts are not lonely but belong in society. Important to note here, of course, is that to Nietzsche this belonging is deplorable, even nauseating.[82] The overman might value friendship, but he does not stomach the collective.[83] And the gifts with which humans administer their pity and persuasion are efficacious only there.[84]

Nietzsche's theory of the gift in both forms explicated here posits desperation as a motive. Zarathustra's impulse to give away his wisdom reflects how, as a cup that overflows, he "wants to become empty again," which is to say that he "wants to become man again."[85] With his gift still intact, he is something other than a man. His gift (of wisdom) is onerous, setting him aside from the humans. He is like a bee burdened with too much honey. The gift is a compulsion, however, and Zarathustra discovers that his wisdom cannot be received. He complains that his "happiness in giving died in giving."[86] The humans' system of gifts, as demonstrated in Zarathustra's lectures, is inextricably tied to the meanings of virtue, which entail punishment, justice, and reward—all of which are learned from fools and liars.[87] Those who give do so in an effort to control the actions of those whom they pity. Those who receive begin to resent the experience of obligation. Givers and receivers alike, Nietzsche intimates, are drawn to and trapped in sociality. There, humans can actually wield gifts in a symbolically coherent way, in contrast to the wisdom-gift that Zarathustra offers. The trouble is that the ways in which they wield the wisdon gift only recommit them to good and evil.[88]

Marcel Mauss: In Praise of the Noble Expenditure (1925)

In the most widely cited ethnography of gift exchange in "primitive"/"archaic" cultures, Marcel Mauss identifies the functions of gifting for the social order.[89] He examines gifting habits as the "total social phenomena" of the Samoan, Maori, Andaman, and Melanesian peoples, encompassing religious, moral, economic, and legal institutions. To trace the history and cultural force of these social phenomena, he relies on the concept of "prestations," which indexes a proto-economic arrangement "between clan and clan in which individuals and groups exchange everything between them."[90] Within prestations, material objects circulate "side by side with the circulation of persons and rights."[91] Geographically distant cultures, Mauss demonstrates, rely on institutions that "reveal the same kind of social and psychological pattern. Food, women, children, possessions, charms, land, labor, services, religious offices, rank—everything is *stuff* to be given away and repaid."[92] As gifted stuff circulates, power is managed as "property and a possession, a pledge and a loan, an object sold and an object bought, a deposit, a mandate, a trust; for it [the gift] is given only on condition that it will be used on behalf of, or transmitted to, a third person, the remote partner."[93] Gift exchange cultures, according to Mauss, depend on a circulation system that produces social capital.

The social capital generated by gift exchange may be understood in Mauss's analysis as agglutinating and manipulative. The agglutination happens as prestations form internal and intergroup bonds. In addition, it happens as a function of the symbolic relationship between a gift and a giver, or donor. Mauss notes that in Maori culture, an object that is given away "still forms a part of" the donor, affording him or her "a hold over the recipient."[94] Regarding the Brahminic law of Hindu cultures, Mauss explains, "Nowhere is the connection between the thing given and the donor, or between property and its owner, more clearly apparent than in the rules relating to gifts and cattle."[95] Social hierarchies emerge through an exchange of gifted stuff, and participants articulate identities as a function not only of their relation to each other, or their efficacy within the exchange, but also of their personal relationship to stuff. Gift exchange, according to Mauss, allows prestations to manipulate one another in societies that "have not yet reached the stage of pure individual contract, the money market, sale proper, fixed price, and weighed and coined money."[96] He writes, "The agonistic character of the prestation is pronounced. Essentially usurious and extravagant, it is above all a struggle among nobles to determine their position in the hierarchy."[97]

Notwithstanding the description of gift exchange as a struggle, Mauss's project is optimistic, animated by what seems like either exoticism or nostalgia. He claims that modern societies, if they take heed of the lessons of a simpler place and time, may be on the precipice of realizing "a dominant motif long forgotten."[98] Thankfully, we are not yet full fledged as "*homo oeconomicus*."[99] Indeed, writes Mauss, "It is our good fortune that all is not yet couched in terms of purchase and sale."[100] In a call to repentance, he insists, "We should come out of ourselves and regard the duty of giving as a liberty, for in it there lies no risk."[101] "We should return to the old and elemental," he asserts, and rediscover "those motives of action still remembered by many societies and classes: the joy of giving in public, the delight in generous artistic expenditure, the pleasure of hospitality in the public or private feast."[102] Mauss's study, which set the tone for twentieth-century ethnographies of nonmonetary value systems, idolizes gifting. He places it in cultural systems that, for the reader, are impossibly far away. Still, he nostalgically orients those cultures toward the reader, making them exemplary rather than unintelligible.

Martin Heidegger: The Ereignis of Being (1962)

Martin Heidegger's treatment of the gift appears in a publication that he completed late in life, having more or less abandoned the metaphysical ontology of his famous *Being and Time*.[103] In a 1962 lecture titled "Time and Being," while "groping his way out of metaphysics," Heidegger emphatically rejects the Western tradition that starts with Plato's distinction between ideational forms and phenomena.[104] He critiques the idea of Being as presence, insisting that nowhere around us—nowhere around the lecture hall in which his audience is gathered—can Being be pointed to. Heidegger asks, "*Is* Being at all?"[105] To this grammatically constrained question, he responds that if matter is a thing that is, then neither time nor Being is matter.[106] So instead of saying "Being is," which would characterize Being as a kind of situated, human matter, Heidegger lands on "There is Being."[107] In the following paragraphs I rely on Indo-European semiotics to draw a path from Heideggerian Being to gifting.

In German, the phrase "there is" (*es gibt*) translates literally to "it gives." For example, *Es gibt eine Katze auf der Strasse* means, "There is a cat in the street," or more literally "It gives a cat in the street." That the "it" that gives is not identical with the cat is indicated by the genus: neuter for the "it" and feminine for the cat. In Latin, Heidegger notes about two-thirds of the way into his lecture, the predicate *pluit*, the present-tense third-person singular of the verb "to rain" (*pluere*), takes no subject.[108] In Latin, it isn't that "It rains," in other words. There is no "it" that rains. There is only "Rains!" This expression in English, however, is unintelligible to the point of being obscure. The question is, What is it that rains? What rains? The reader who is thinking "Rain rains" is on the right track. This insight is helpful in the following transition from weather to Being. In Heidegger's phrase "There is Being," the "there is" (*es gibt*) must be translated as "it gives." "There is Being" and "It gives Being" are synonymous. "It gives Being" is the statement that brings gifts and gifting into Heidegger's lifelong project.

The three-pronged assertion that "It gives Being" raises at least three questions. First, what "it" is the subject? Who or what is acting in the phrase? In pursuit of this question, Heidegger cautions his audience not to resort to the implied divinity of a metaphysical supposition. There is no higher "indeterminate power" that bestows life upon humanity and then sits back to observe.[109] Second, what is given? What is the substance of the gift? In response, Heidegger brings together the first and second questions, suggesting that we stop thinking of "Being as the ground of beings," and instead focus our attention on the giving.[110] It is not that Being as some immaterial substance (such as God) gives life on the planet (i.e., being with a lowercase b) to humans. Rather, what gives *and* what is given is Being. Heidegger writes, "As the gift of this It gives, Being belongs to giving. As a gift, Being is not expelled from giving."[111] Or, to reference the earlier grammatical excursion of "Rains!" (as opposed to "It rains"), "Gives!"

Developing the idea of "Gives!" and asking a third question—Where, or how, does the giving take place (or time)?—I turn to the concept that Heidegger discusses toward the end of the lecture: appropriation. With this concept, Heidegger suspends the term that is "simply too bogged down with metaphysical connotations" and offers what editor and translator Joan Stambaugh calls an "activity."[112] Appropriation is an event (*Ereignis*); it is not *an* event or *the* event of a singular occurrence so much as it is *that* occasion is a possibility. When Heidegger explains appropriation as allowing time and Being to "belong together," he characterizes appropriation as a condition of "eventing."[113] This eventing, specifically, is a gifting event: "Giving and its gift receive their determination from Appropriating."[114] The "it" in "It gives Being" is appropriation, which is to say that the "it" is not a presence but an event that enables "the realm in which presence is extended."[115] In appropriation, then, Being "vanishes."[116] Again, there is no "it" that like an immanent divinity watches its gift from afar. "It" is neither revealed nor remnant after the giving. Indeed, "after" the giving misconstrues the event as such. Heidegger notes that in the giving, "the sending source keeps itself back and, thus, withdraws from unconcealment."[117] He concludes by discarding the idea that appropriation either "is" or "is there"; instead, "appropriation appropriates."[118] Or indeed, "Rain rains." In English, it would make no sense to say that Being "be's." The present tense, the realm of what is present, demands that a translation move "to be" into the realities of "is." But if we were to tentatively permit the phrase "Being bes," then a way to explain the nature of that act or event would, in reference to Heidegger, be as gifting. To Heidegger, the gift is the event of Being. Moreover, this event must by necessity concern us beings. It gives all the "There is" around us, as we are the "constant receiver[s] of the gift given by the 'It gives present.'"[119]

Lewis Hyde: Artistic Talent (1983)

Lewis Hyde uses the notion of a gift to theorize the relationship between art and artists and between artists and their audience. He embraces the gift's affordance of social connectivity and authenticity, referencing various gift-exchange cultures, including the ones studied by Marcel Mauss.[120] To Hyde, art begins with inspiration, the "initial stirring of the gift."[121] The individual inspiration to make art is "a gift [that] we do not get by our own efforts."[122] Art, then, depends on the artist's gift both in the sense of artistic talent and in the sense of a core substance from which art emerges. Hyde writes, "All artists work to acquire and perfect the tools of their craft, and all art involves evaluation, clarification, and revision. But these are secondary tasks. They cannot begin (sometimes they must not begin) until the *materia*, the body of the work, is on the page or on the canvas."[123] The gift involved in artistry, in other words, is "stuff"; the gift-stuff is molded and perfected in accordance with the artist's gift-as-talent.[124] This inventive process, to Hyde, is enigmatic and excessive. He notes, "A gift—and particularly an inner gift, a talent—is a mystery. We know what giftedness is for having been gifted, or for having known a gifted man or woman. We know that art is a gift for having had the experience of art."[125] Through the experience of art, artists' gifts circulate in a community, wherein "the spirit of a gift is kept alive by its constant donation."[126] Hyde prescribes, "Whatever we have been given is supposed to be given away again, not kept."[127] On this point and throughout his analysis, Hyde dictates a gifting ethic, distinguishing between true and false gifts.[128]

Gifted art in Hyde's romanticizing theory is described in terms of erotic "fertility."[129] Gifted works, he writes, "circulate among us as reservoirs of available life."[130] With this pregnant metaphor, Hyde foregrounds the production of art as continuously generative, motivated by eros. Art multiplies; gifts beget more gifts. As with biological reproduction, at least in its most romantic interpretation, the "sentiment" of the transaction is vital to the result.[131] In the transcultural gifting myths that Hyde analyzes, the abundance of gifts ceases as soon as the gift's value is calculated. After the calculation, self-interest and greed undermine the spirit of the gift, stunting its generativity. Moreover, the characters involved in gifting narratives are drawn into dramas in which a gift multiplies itself with the help of human interlopers. In other words, the gift, as Hyde presents it, assumes its own agency, reproducing copiously with the help of human bystanders. He explains, "Wherever property circulates as a gift, the increase that accompanies that circulation is simultaneously material, social, and spiritual; where wealth moves as a gift, any increase in material wealth is automatically accompanied by the increased conviviality of the group and the strengthening of the *hau*, the spirit of the gift."[132] In this process of increase, the gift is the central force (as spirit) and the outcome, in Hyde's case primarily as art. Increase is a function of the virtue with which participants engage the gift.

A central tenet of Hyde's gifting ethic is that true gifts are entirely distinguishable from commodities.[133] This is an illustration of his highly idealistic view of the gift's function in creativity. To Hyde, art that is intended for market value does not remain a gift.[134] The artist who "hopes to market work that is the realization of his [sic] gifts cannot begin with the market. He must create for himself that gift-sphere in which the work is made, and only when he knows the work to be the faithful realization of his gift should he turn to see if it has currency in that other economy."[135] Whether art that is *not* a realization of any gift within the artist may begin with the market is unclear. Plausibly, such art is neither true nor a gift. To Hyde, the gift sphere and the market are incommensurate. Indeed, he characterizes this dichotomy along the distinct lines of eros and logos; the former is "unanalytical and undialectical," whereas the latter is predicated on value assessment.[136] Logos is "the money of the mind [that] destroys the gift."[137] Using Mauss's notion of gifting in a circular exchange but rejecting the value management of its economic logic in a way that foreshadows Derrida (see next section), Hyde writes, "The gift is lost in self-consciousness. To count, measure, reckon value, or seek the cause of a thing is to step outside the circle, to cease being 'all of a piece' within the flow of gifts and become, instead, one part of the whole reflecting upon another part."[138] The moment when an artist reflects cerebrally on a work of art in progress, the gifted *materia* is jeopardized, just as a gift loses its giftedness in the moment when market value is estimated. Awareness of the gift in art forecloses the possibility of both art and gift. In critical response to Hyde, my contention about the gifting logos is that it is possible to define logos as a "principle of differentiation," as he does, but, instead of rejecting it, I insist on a connection between logos and gifting. Doing so enables an investigation on how symbolic differentiation brings together rhetorical invention and gifting.

Jacques Derrida: Always Already Annulled (1992)

To study the gift, if such a thing there be, Jacques Derrida deals in absolutes, wholly rejecting what most of us would call a gift. He offers an account that, perhaps consistent with Derridean deconstruction, contains much more information on what gifting is not than it does on what the true gift is. Most emphatically he argues that "gifts" in ordinary life are trapped by "common language and logic" in a structure of three: "A gives B to C."[139] This structure, Derrida announces, is what produces "the annulment, the annihilation, the destruction of the gift."[140] As soon as something is identifiable as a gift, the "giftedness" of that thing is destroyed.[141] In that moment, debt dominates the exchange and the relationship of the parties. Expectations and norms of reciprocity creep in and destroy the purity of the potential gift. Writes Derrida: "From the moment the gift would appear as gift, as such, as what it is, in its phenomenon, its sense, and its essence, it would be engaged in a symbolic, sacrificial, or economic structure that would annul the gift in the ritual circle of the debt."[142] The circle symbolizing the economics of the gift is anathema to Derrida's gift, which must be understood as "aneconomic."[143] Put another way, Derrida understands the gift as invaluable: infinitely precious but beyond evaluation. This makes his theory of gifting open to alternative definitions of value, which becomes useful in my later chapters.

In his essays on the gift, Derrida responds directly to Mauss, whom he accuses of "speak[ing] blithely" about gifts in a circle of exchange.[144] Mauss, he claims, "never asks the question as to whether gifts can remain gifts once they are exchanged; [nor] does [he] worry enough about this incompatibility between gift and exchange or about the fact that an exchanged gift is only a tit for tat, that is, an annulment of the gift."[145] In Derrida's view, all of Mauss's ideas are complicit in the annulment of the gift: the potlatch, the transgressions, and the surpluses that manage the social hierarchies of "prestations."[146] Derrida first addresses the complications of syntax and then the moment when Mauss "excuses" himself, which Derrida uses to pivot the argument to "the triple and indissociable question of the gift, of forgiveness, and of the excuse."[147] With reference to syntax, Derrida asks, simply put, how a single word (such as "*give*" or "*gift*") could mean so many different things.[148] Giving one's word in the form of a promise, he suggests, cannot reasonably be grouped with other symbolic acts like giving a ring.[149] Relatedly, Derrida questions the extent to which the verb of giving actually couples with the noun gift in an intelligible way.[150] Finally, deconstructing the premises of Mauss's project and targeting the argument that "evolved" societies ought to return to the gifting ethics of archaic societies, Derrida aptly characterizes Mauss's agenda as a "Rousseauist schema."[151]

The gift, a Derridean impossibility, takes place only on the condition of the exchange circle's interruption.[152] Derrida writes, "A gift could be possible, there could be a gift only at the instant an effraction in the circle will have taken place, at the instant all circulation will have been interrupted and *on the condition* of this instant."[153] In this interruption, the madness of the gift sends nomos and logos into "crisis."[154] Logic and reason, norms and culture, are infinitely exceeded when a gift is given that does not forge a structure of expectation and debt. With the notions of effraction and interruption, Derrida pursues something other than simple humility or altruism. He notes, "If there is gift, the *given* of the gift (*that which* one gives, *that which* is given the gift as a given thing or as act of donation) must not come back to the giving (let us not already say to the subject, to the donor)."[155] Derrida considers the possibility of a gift wherein giver and receiver are radically remote, separated from one another in anonymity. The gift is not recognized as such by either participant, and both forget the whole thing as soon as it happens.[156] Such a gift is not only boundless and immeasurable but impossible and untheorizable.[157] With the help of Heidegger, Derrida presents the gift as a giving event that overtakes all.[158] Doing so, he discounts those human practices in which participants interpret what they are doing as gifting, disallowing those practices as not-quite-good-enough-to-be-gifting, or worse, as delusional simulations. Nevertheless, his conclusions leave open the possibility that a gift could be a submission without expectation and without gratitude, rhetorically constituting a social form.

The Gift in Rhetorical Studies

The notion of a gift has long been subtly present in rhetorical studies, not only because gifts are messages, as I have noted, or because some rhetors are described as especially *gifted*, but because rhetoric, in Aristotle's words, may be defined as discerning the available means of persuasion in any *given* situation. With this tacit acknowledgment of preexisting conditions in which events take place (or time—remember, "Rain rains"), rhetoricians are scholars of the gift, albeit implicitly. Moving toward a more explicit model, I submit that by rendering insights from the five thinkers discussed here, it is possible to build a specifically rhetorical theory of gifting. What I am interested in is the question, What happens rhetorically when a cultural practice is constructed by participants through the motifs of gifting? When rhetorical agents refer to something that they have or something that they are making as a gift, what does this mean? What about when they describe sharing their experiences as gifting, or when they talk about knowledge as a gift? This line of inquiry, as the reader will discover, runs through the three case studies of this book. Before proceeding to the section on the gifting logos and to the case studies themselves, however, I address directly two scholars whose works make the concept of the gift viable in rhetorical scholarship: Michael J. Hyde and Mari Lee Mifsud.

Rhetorician and bioethicist Michael J. Hyde offers an interpretation of acknowledgment as a life-giving gift that bestows upon another a dwelling place of ontological significance. Acknowledgment, Hyde writes, is "a form of consciousness that transforms time and space," creating "a moral place of being-with-and-for-others."[159] In *The Life-Giving Gift of Acknowledgement*, Hyde traces the Judeo-Christian creation story alongside the scientific theory of a "big bang" explosion, claiming that both events extend a kind of "acknowledgment to Being."[160] The first phase of the gift of acknowledgment, then, is to make room. From this initial moment, all subsequent, smaller-scale acknowledgments are possible. On this point—the idea that originary acknowledgment (from a divine or cosmic power) enables acknowledgment as gift giving among human beings (in the context of Dasein)—Hyde gets more compelling fodder from the Bible than from scientists. He references the creative function of language, noting that God "called us into being with a 'Word' [Logos] of acknowledgement that brought forth the truth of all that is. By way of this most glorious gift, God created the place wherein all other such gifts could be given by creatures with the capacity to do so."[161] This inaugural giving returns in chapter 4 in my analysis of how the Pirate Party, emerging in view of the commons, gives a political construct. The original gift of acknowledgment, according to which subsequent ones are modeled, begins with making.[162]

The notion of the gift, as Hyde explains, reveals how "rhetoric and acknowledgement go hand in hand."[163] In the study of public address, audiences are not remote variables of the rhetorical situation but must be "acknowledged, engaged, and called into the space of practical concerns."[164] Hyde's rhetor offers acknowledgment as a gift that he or she is able to give against the odds of being, which is always already precarious. Hyde writes:

> Acknowledgement is a moral action that in its most positive mode is dedicated to making time and space for the disclosing of truth. Appropriateness helps to facilitate this action by lending itself to the rhetorical task of creating dwelling places wherein people can collaborate about and know together matters of importance. Human

beings are gifted with the potential for developing the capacity to perform such an artistic and moral feat.[165]

Here the gift is not just an acknowledgment extended by the rhetor to another person but the potency that the rhetor possesses. Via the notion of a gift, Hyde identifies "rhetorical competence" as "essential for our social well-being."[166]

Mari Lee Mifsud in *Rhetoric and the Gift* likewise interprets the gift as presented by a call from something Other and adds to this the more mundane habits in which gifts are human necessities. Mifsud's theory of the rhetorical gift, in other words, is dual, at once profoundly excessive and pragmatic. First, rhetoric as a gift that exceeds figuration is "outside the system of exchange altogether, beyond exchangist figures."[167] The call demands a response, which gives rise to figuration and to rhetoric. It is a gift to be called, Mifsud argues, as Aristotle was called by Homer. The former's works are full of invocations and references to Homeric poetry; these references, cataloged by Mifsud in a sort of re-performance of Homer's and Aristotle's gifting, amount to *poesis* in *rhetorike*. Second, on the more technical level, the "level of the artful response," rhetoric concerns itself with gifts more readily understood as cultural inheritance.[168] Aristotle's theory relies substantively and stylistically on such inheritances, as does any ordinary exchange between friends that starts with "Well, you know what they say." The elegance of Mifsud's project is how she traces the movement of the gift from the pre-techne call to the "art-full" system of figuration. She is explicitly set on how "the gift we get on the other side of the gift's having gone through the technical apparatus is something quite different than the gift had been" under circumstances "not amenable to figuration."[169]

In Mifsud's analysis of Aristotle's rhetorical theory, the deliverer of gifts is Homer, who "gives the sublime to the civic."[170] As a function of his gift giving (i.e., the call from the "imaginative, inventive, and ingenious" muse-cum-patriarch), Aristotle is capable of formulating the precepts that still nourish rhetoricians.[171] Further, the Homeric themes of gift giving that structures human relationships and interactions inform Aristotle's poetic scenes and dramas.[172] Homer's gift is settled into Aristotle's text topically and metaphorically. Further still, Aristotle's Homeric references make manifest the givens of the cultural history that unites the two Greeks and the givens of the cultural context to which Aristotle's audience belongs. As Mifsud explains, "By 'givens,' I mean to call attention to the performance of the Homeric gift transformed into the *doxa* of Aristotle's *Rhetoric*. The *doxa* are 'generally accepted principles' derived from the beliefs of a people that all or a majority or the wise accept."[173] These principles are *taken* for granted—a potent phrase in this context—as appropriate and self-evident without further explanation. As gifts, they are, Mifsud argues, *haplous*, or without the need for qualifying remarks.[174] In order to mentally conflate doxastic principles and gifts, readers might think both about whatever "truths we hold to be self-evident" and whatever presents are handed over pro forma at a dinner party (flowers, a bottle of wine, etc.). They are simply that they are; they are a given. Being able to wield them competently, in Mifsud's words to practice them as a rhetorical art, is a sign of cultural viability.

Within Mifsud's framework, gifts are both material and "animistic" in a way that obligates recipients to respond.[175] To describe gifts as material, Mifsud emphasizes how "aggregation guides relations in the gift economy."[176] Gifts tend toward their own multiplication and reproduction. Mifsud oscillates back and forth across the line that separates one gift from another, or a gifted *symbol* from a gifted *thing*, or an initial gift from a reciprocal one, noting "multiple and divergent things can be seen as touching."[177] The "animistic quality," then, is an indication that the given material that tends toward its own aggregation "is not inactive" but indeed active and effectual.[178] The gift, to simplify, must be understood as both tangible stuff and intentional in its own right. Reflecting on this insight, Mifsud's reader might turn to her conclusions about Aristotle's relation to Homer, which deploy the aforementioned dual notion of the gift and posit a sacrifice. Aristotle sacrifices Homer, Mifsud argues, insofar as he gives up on gifting ethics in favor of the prudential rhetoric of the polis. As the epic dramas of Homer's world are translated and condensed for the managerial purposes of everyday life, *poesis* is dehydrated into civic judgment.[179] The polis demands rhetoric as a techne; song has no business in the polis, Mifsud laments. And although Mifsud insists that she is not attempting a corrective on Homer's behalf, her sanguine gifting theory of rhetoric suggests otherwise. Refusing to sacrifice Homer as though on a patricidal pyre of political necessity, we "need not continue to make the same choices" as Aristotle does in his appropriation of the gift.[180] Mifsud promises an alternative, a theory and praxis of the rhetorical gift that supplies "resources for resisting tyranny."[181] More than a call (of conscience, as Hyde would have it), the gift is full of potential; the recipient's task is to manage the proliferation of the gift's materiality without squelching the animus of excessive generosity with which the gift arrives.

Both Hyde and Mifsud provide ways of understanding the gift as rhetorical; in so doing, their work is indispensable to my project. And yet I am troubled by the way that both scholars isolate the gift from the complications of human conduct. To them, the gift is principally an a priori circumstance, expressed by the grace (or call) of God, Homer, or Aristotle. By extension it may be given among rhetorical agents in particular actions, but only insofar as these agents are capable of something as existentially noble as responding, "Here I am!" Neither Hyde's nor Mifsud's insightful work dedicates attention to the human practices that situate gifting inside ordinary experience. My ambition is to present a theory of the gifting logos, relying via Heraclitus on the multilevel meanings of logos to examine not only the noble but the quotidian. Conceptually adding logos to gifting in this way allows me to approach the gift as rhetorical, as integral to symbolic practices. By now I have sufficiently emphasized my assumption that gifts are messages. Specifically, the gifting logos accounts for the production and circulation of epistemic materials in the networked context of the digital commons. By arguing that digital commoners engage with discourses of expertise via the gifting logos, I am grounding Hyde's and Mifsud's works in everyday rhetorical life.

A distinctly rhetorical perspective on the gift does not buckle under the weight of romantic idealism. I am convinced that this perspective is valuable insofar as it is more attuned to what people claim to be doing than what they may be said to be doing according to an absolute standard. Most gifting theory is full of absolutes. In Ralph W. Emerson's poetic imagination, for example, "The gift, to be true, must be the flowing of the giver unto me, correspondent to my flowing unto him. When the waters are at level, then my goods pass to him, and his to me. All his are mine, all mine his. [. . .] Thou must bleed for me."[182] As beautiful as Emerson's portrayal is, I am compelled to ask whether the kinds of gifts that he describes are the only ones that count, and if so, why. What insights might be gained by choosing not to disqualify nonbleeding instances of gifting as inadequate? Christina M. Geschwandtner suggests:

> While a kenotic and self-sacrificial love, a purely gratuitous and entirely unselfish gift, a devoted and pure appreciation of art, or a profound sense of the utter uniqueness of each historical and cultural event may be the ideals, surely they cannot be the exclusive paradigms for all love, all gifts, all art, all events without thereby implying that all less extreme versions immediately collapse into objectivity and certainty.[183]

Sharing Geschwandtner's interest in gifts and events beyond the "purely gratuitous and entirely unselfish," I might add that mundane gifting is not necessarily trivial. Gifting may be, as I suggest, a rhetorical way of making sense of something, a logos. John McAteer, positing a "third kind of gift" in between absolute grace and a stick of gum, proposes that "we think of gift as communion where what is given is the gift of being-with-the-other."[184] This Heideggerian tack has considerable potential, even if McAteer's Christian ethics are bracketed. From this vantage point, we might see the event of being-together as a given, indeed a condition of what is common.

THE GIFTING LOGOS

The gifting logos is the epistemic rhetoric of the digital commons whereby knowing and making become integrated practices of everyday life, thematized as gifting. The purpose of this book is to present a theory of how this logos functions as expertise. At the beginning of this chapter, I stated that expertise is knowledge living its rhetorical life. In the present historical moment, this life is intensely focused on the production of interpretations of everyday experiences. Expertise is thus the production of digital stuff that captures the lived experiences of networked commoners. The gifting logos affords the commoners a rhetorical activity that configures them as a networked multitude. In a continuous process of invention, the knowledges and experiences of the multitude are digitized, and through the continuous process of circulation, the digitized stuff is constituted as a gift. The making and knowing of the multitude are inextricably linked, and the language of gifting supplies the link. To be clear, the issue at stake in my project is not whether the digital multitude is *really* giving away knowledge, art, or other materials free of charge, nor is it whether digital commoners are authentically generous or altruistic. Instead, the question is: What are the characteristics and functions of the gifting logos as a rhetorical habit? As a rhetoric of expertise, how does it integrate making, knowing, and gifting? I foreshadow the conclusion chapter by briefly introducing here five prevalent features of the gifting logos; I return to these in more detail following the case studies.

The gifting logos assumes participants' awareness in order to function.

The gifting logos places significant emphasis on the intentionality of those who engage one another through the message of a gift. Its ordering of knowing-and-making activities in the digital commons becomes most distinct when commoners articulate a kind of informal theory of what they are doing. As is evident in the section on gifting theory, the motives of those who give and receive gift-messages are central not only to their relationship but also to the health of the social system around them. Successful gifting happens in the context of mutual recognition. In rhetoric, the counterpart of intent is agency, a fraught notion that questions how rhetorical agents intervene in particular situations so as to exert influence over the behaviors and beliefs of others. Rhetorical agency and intentionality are recurring points of scholarly contention precisely because they push the question of humans' impact on their context, indeed their awareness thereof. With respect to this contention, I offer additional nuance to this feature of the gifting logos in chapter 5.

Emphasizing intent, the gifting logos makes entry into the networks of the digital commons a matter of active participation. Moreover, awareness of one's participation in the gifting logos becomes a strategy for maintaining the integrity of one's network node with respect to future uncertainty. The productive interactions of the digital commoners are predicated to some degree on the idea that their fully conscious decisions lead to a future for the digital commons that is consistent with individual choices and that those choices may be fixed in digital form. This is not to say that the gifting logos never makes room for those who produce and circulate cultural materials without active use of the gift concept. Circulating material can function as epistemic gift-stuff to some degree even without gifters' or receivers' explicit recognition of their materials' impact. Still, the contours of the gifting logos emerge most visibly as digital commoners construct their knowing and making practices as expertise-as-gift.

The gifting logos derives rhetorical potency from tensions between artifice and nature.

The gifting logos thrives on the tension between, on the one hand, the idea that knowing-making-gifting happens naturally in the commons, and, on the other hand, the idea that commoners must intentionally codify this practice. So it is that the resources of the digital commons, the stuff that the commoners use and invent, are constructed through the gifting logos as both natural and artificial, or, as I demonstrate in chapter 4, as both a matter of access to nature and a state of political governance. Relatedly, in the rhetorical processes of expertise, the natural and artificial are oriented in relation to the familiar and the unfamiliar. Expertise is the *making sense* of something for others to consider. To make something unnatural seem necessary and natural (such as access to a broadband infrastructure or digitized music) is to *make* it natural or to rhetorically give it over to an audience in a natural form. To transform something mysterious into something familiar is to make it knowable. Conversely, to make something like silicon and metal wiring into a mystery is a matter of rhetorical epistemology. The gifting logos as expertise thus wields the rhetorical tension between nature and artifice.

The gifting logos is abundant.

The gifting logos as a rhetoric of expertise values quantity and the promiscuous replication of "stuff." "Lots and lots" is the motif of the gifting logos; to have lots is to know lots, according to the discourses of expertise in the digital commons. The bigger the data, the better the expertise. In the abundant digital networks of the commons, delivery and access are thus fully wedded; any and all things that circulate in the networks to which commoners have access are entirely assessible (access-able) to them. Expertise, measured in bulk, functions such that the more of it that is delivered to nodes in the network, the more of it the nodes can absorb. On this point, the gifting logos aligns with the history of rhetoric in which *copia* has been associated with expertise and knowledge, specifically how expressions may be multiplied so that a subject may be fully understood. A subject is made knowable through repetition that produces an abundant result. In digital networks, the scale and speed of *copia* are distinguishable from more traditional forms of repetition. With speed and scope operating in tandem, the abundance of digital "stuff" effectively becomes immersive, a substance mediating between digital commoners.

The gifting logos is time sensitive and progressivist.

Because it is a rhetorical practice, the gifting logos is necessarily time sensitive, attuned to kairotic moments of appropriate intervention. Further, because it is a gifting practice, timing is everything; timing enables a meaningful gift. For example, as I demonstrate in chapter 2, time variously constrains the gifting logos as productive expertise via the structure of copyright, which dictates that the ownership privileges of expertise are contingent on time. The basic tenet of copyright is that those who create materials are entitled to enjoy the benefits of their creation for a limited time. Expertise as content is thus timed. Adding another layer, the gifting logos manages time-as-history, indeed makes time, through the retrieval technology of digital archiving. The Wayback Machine, as I demonstrate in chapter 3, gives the past of the digital commons to the commoners, making digitized history knowable. Finally, the time sensitivity of the giving logos is set to "urgent"; digital commoners are called, for example by the Pirate Party in chapter 4, to act quickly in order to ensure a happy and prosperous future. Via the gifting logos, expertise refers both to making history knowable (accessible via a screen) and to the historical progress of technologies that serve networks of the commons.[185]

The gifting logos assumes a rhetorically playful posture toward its "others."

Unlike the serious affect that characterizes traditional expertise, enabling experts to be taken seriously as such, the gifting logos often operates in a playful and irreverent mode. It is a rhetorical epistemic habit that distinguishes itself from other epistemic habits and hierarchies by being un-serious. In so doing, it facilitates critique of these others via comic subversion and parody. Whereas traditional politicians are serious, for example, the Pirate Party is deliberately unconventional and, for lack of a better word, cool. Whereas copyright law is dull and antiquated, the Creative Commons is agile and cutting edge, giving the commons access to information and pop culture. Whereas brick-and-mortar archives and archivists are dusty institutional holdovers from another era, the Wayback Machine is a whimsically named technology for time travel. In each case, the rhetorical posture of not taking oneself too seriously frames expertise, allowing it to function in ways that traditional conditions would preclude. This posture, I argue in the conclusion, disarms two sets of questions that confront expertise in the twenty-first century. First, are the habits that function as expertise in the digital commons recognizable by that term from a traditional perspective on productive epistemology? Are they *really* expertise? Second, does rhetorically constructing an activity as a gifting activity make it so? Can knowing and making be effectively integrated with gifting, or is the latter a façade for something else entirely? The networked expertise of the digital commons depends on that of the gifting logos' to critique but also to destabilize traditional expertise and its authority.

2

The Infrastructural Commons

While writing this chapter, I took my four-year-old son to see a theater production of the folktale *Stone Soup*.[1] A connoisseur even at his modest age, he loved the play. So the next time we went to the children's library, I picked out *The Real Story of Stone Soup*, thinking it would be received with the same enthusiasm.[2] I was wrong. The boy who had loved the live performance wholly rejected the book, which prompted a conversation about what "version" means. In the spirit of an educator parent, I tried patiently to explain that a single story can be told in different ways. Some stories, I suggested, may not be owned by anyone in particular, but instead tinkered with and adapted to suit various needs. My son was having none of it. Nevertheless, through our discussions of narrative play and transcultural myth, something emerged: important questions about artistic interpretation, situatedness in particular places and times, ownership of the human drama, the transmission of privileged knowledge, and engagements between community insiders and outsiders.

Although not about fairytales or soup per se, this chapter explores the kind of experiential, inventive, communal practices that the legend's culinarian stranger enacts, wherein to know is to make and to make is to gift. The man who comes to town possesses the knowledge not only to make soup, but to live a precarious life defined by the making of soup. His expertise is inextricable from his situatedness in the world, a condition that depends on the invention and delivery of a substantive gift; the man's knowledge and experience—his gift to his ever-changing hosts—*are* soup. For my purposes, the soup corresponds roughly to what copyright law calls "expressive content": music, photography, film and video, text, design, and imagery in digital form. This kind of content is the reification of what its producers experience and know within the context of their lives. The expressive content, for the purposes of this chapter, may be thought of as what I define in chapter 1 as "*stuff*." As noted there, "*stuff*" is a handy term for digital cultural content, reflecting both ubiquity and a smudged line between what is material and immaterial. It refers at once to tangible things and symbolic currency. Further, it captures a performative dimension, as in the phrase "to strut one's stuff." In the digital commons, stuff is both the products and processes of invention that demand an integration of knowing and/as making and/as gifting.

My study of the gifting logos turns in this chapter to the Creative Commons, a nonprofit organization primarily associated with a suite of licenses that negotiates copyright.[3] Challenging the legal and technical mechanisms of copyright, the Creative Commons licenses supply makers of digital artifacts with a structure for distributing their "stuff" beyond the "all rights reserved" default premise. A simple example is a musician who attaches a Creative Commons license to a song, making that song freely accessible to anyone who might want to listen to it, slice it up into beats and riffs, make new music, and license the new music likewise. Another is a graphic designer and software programmer seeking publicity and membership in a professional network that coheres around collaboratively produced content. Of primary interest to my analysis is the question: How is expertise rhetorically managed in this process? How is the interplay of knowledge and experience that happens in the making of cultural artifacts like text, code, and music accounted for by those who participate in the digital commons, specifically via the Creative Commons infrastructure? What *is* expertise in this infrastructure?

In response to these questions, I offer the notion of the gifting logos as expertise. To demonstrate how the gifting logos functions in the Creative Commons, I analyze a set of discourses: (1) the 2015 Creative Commons memorandum "*The State of the Commons*," with appended data sheets; (2) *The Power of Open*, the Creative Commons's self-published collection of success stories; (3) the history, vision statement, and general user instructions published on the organization's website; and (4) three academic articles and two popular books authored by Creative Commons founder Lawrence Lessig during the initiative's early stages.[4] I argue that the production and circulation of cultural "stuff" is framed by the Creative Commons as expertise that subsumes gifting. I argue further that the Creative Commons texts construct an account of what knowing, making, and gifting are *as one*, and that, in their efforts to challenge traditions of expert ownership, they establish an alternate logic, or logos.

The first section of the chapter is an introduction to copyright history, theory, and policy. It provides a selective rather than chronological account of copyright, directing attention to certain theoretical assumptions and pivotal moments.[5] In the analysis that follows, I begin by describing the Creative Commons licenses as the imposition of order on cultural invention and the individuation of creative efforts. Second, I discuss the management of value, a complicated notion in gifting theory, by distinguishing between the declarative and subjective conditions for gifts. Third, the discussion of value is followed by an analysis of how the Creative Commons conceptualizes both itself as a program and its participants' inventions as gifts. I offer an interpretation of this duality of what gifting means in the Creative Commons infrastructure by analyzing assumptions about intentionality and digital action. Fourth, I examine how gifting and the notion of inheritance together complicate intent. Fifth, I examine how the gifting logos accounts for productive abundance, the massive quantity of digital cultural production. Sixth, I examine how copiousness may be thought of in relation to time and the rhetorical sensitivity to timing marked by the concept of kairos.

COPYRIGHT, "STUFF," AND STRUCTURES OF CONTROL

Copyright codifies the idea that a person who creates a cultural artifact ought to be allowed to control that artifact's public life, particularly the making of duplicate copies. The right to exercise such control is grounded either in the creator's personal connection to the artifact or in the assumption that control, especially over profit, incentivizes creation. Expertise is a dimension of copyright, in other words, either because expertise is what characterizes the expert herself or because it has a certain market value. Since the 1990s the emergence of user-friendly digital technologies and the World Wide Web, enabling the global production, reproduction, and circulation of cultural content, has made copyright exceedingly complicated. These technocultural developments, and their fraught relationship to legal tradition, are duly noted in every treatment of copyright and digital culture. Such notations are merited and important but ought to be qualified with at least two comments. First, technological determinism as a perspective warrants critique, which I offer in chapter 1. Second, and more important as I proceed in this chapter, copyright was always complicated. The notion that a particular symbolic form can *belong* to a legally empowered individual is on some level preposterous. Hardly anyone would deny that knowledge and art are products of inspiration. As Boon, whom I cite in chapter 1, notes, imitation is integral not only to learning but to being human. How then could a person possibly put particular words or images in her or his pocket and claim to own them? Yet powerful legal institutions and cultural precepts, including labor, capital, originality, and personhood, reinforce copyright. This chapter must be read, in short, in the context of complexities that predate the internet.

As an exclusive commercial privilege, copyright was from the very beginning associated with the production of stuff. In Venice in 1469, the five-year printing privilege extended to the German printer Johannes von Speyer was not different in kind from the contracts extended by the Venetian authorities to other craftsmen.

Like them, Speyer made and sold a material product. The exclusivity of the process by which the product was made ensured profit. Joanna Kostylo describes how "makers of soap, of gunpowder and saltpeter, of glass" petitioned for trade monopolies on "every imaginable subject, from devices for draining marshes to windmills and poisons, or culinary experiments such as special kinds of lasagna in an Apulian style and new types of dumplings filled with meat and fish."[6] Using the screw press, Speyer made text just as others made wine and olive oil. In the Speyer story of copyright origins, the text content itself is beside the point. Of far greater importance is the manufacturing technique that produces stuff, specifically text in Speyer's case. When two hundred years later another entrepreneur named John Usher secured an ad hoc discretionary grant to publish the laws of the colony of Massachusetts, his relationship to the local authorities was similar to Speyer's, insofar as he, too, sought primarily to make stuff for profit. Usher's printing privilege was indistinguishable from those extended in Massachusetts to industrious men who made salt or operated ferries.[7] Speyer and Usher in their own times manufactured text as a commercial object.

Origins and Regimes of Control

As copyright from the beginning was about the production of stuff, so were the ancien régimes of copyright about exercising institutional control. In the Venetian case, mercantile guilds of printers and booksellers served as a mechanism for oversight.[8] The same structures that were put in place in the early sixteenth century to retain commercial advantages for Venice's prosperity, preventing craftsmen's individual entrepreneurship, effectively enabled state-sanctioned censorship.[9] As copyright historian Mark Rose notes, the Venetian system was exported to several European countries, including England. There, a royal charter in 1557 authorized a guild of book binders and publishers called the Stationers' Company to oversee published materials, moderating the circulation of anything that might be construed as "illicit, antigovernment publishing."[10] The powerful company's "monopoly on the British book trade" was solidified a few years later with the Licensing Act of 1662, which made it illegal to publish any text without special permission.[11] This law also restricted the import of published materials and limited the number of active presses and printers. For five decades, the Stationers' Company policed libel, sedition, heresy, and treason, managing the commercial as well as the ideological aspect of the British book industry.

The Stationers' Company's authority and usurpation of profits drew the ire not only of booksellers and printers excluded from the royal arrangement but also of authors. Not unlike in the twenty-first century, creators of cultural content resented the state and corporate powers that constrained them. Amid the late seventeenth century's general prosperity and increased literacy, what Rose describes as an "emergent ideology of possessive individualism" prompted authors to critique the fundamental presumption of the Stationers' Company.[12] Questions arose: What rights to the creative accomplishments of an especially gifted individual should a commercial guild have? To whom do ideas belong? Prominent literary figures made their case for the cause: in the polemic *Areopagitica* in 1644, English poet John Milton extolled the benefits of books and condemned the royal licensing system. To Milton, censorship, although it may prevent infectious material from corrupting the public mind, obstructs discovery and truth. Likewise, John Locke, a staunch critic of the Licensing Act, argued in *Two Treatises of Government* in 1690 that a person's natural right to the property that results from his (or her) labor is inviolable. The social order's first task, according to Locke, is to protect individual property. Notes Rose, "The representation of the author as a creator who is entitled to profit from his intellectual labor came into being through a blending of literary and legal discourses in the context of the contest over perpetual copyright."[13] The British Parliament did not renew the Licensing Act in 1694.

What happened next is the watershed moment in any historical account of copyright: In 1710 the Statute of Anne went into effect. The two most significant consequences of the statute, whose full title was "An Act for the Encouragement of Learning, by Vesting the Copies of Printed Books in the Authors or Purchasers of such Copies, during the Times therein mentioned," were that authors could be designated as the proprietors of their texts and that the privileges associated with such proprietorship, including those enjoyed by the Stationers' Company, were time limited.[14] The implications of the statute for the Stationers' surveillance powers and their relationship to authors is the topic of some scholarly dispute. What appears to have been a definitive victory for authors and a recognition of individual author(ity) may have brought with it some unintended consequences. Prior to the passage of the statute, policing authors was an elaborate task that required cunning and guile. Jody Greene describes how Sir Robert L'Estrange, frustrated with the Stationers' impotence and lack of commitment to penalizing authors, invented an intricate intelligence-gathering system that implicated not only those who wrote illicit books but also those who, when discovered in possession of them, refused to provide information about the author. The Statute of Anne, Greene argues, expedited almost universal regulation: "It did so not by inventing new means of tracking down authors but instead by encouraging authors, in effect, to give themselves up voluntarily."[15] When the statute was later used as a model for other copyright legislation, including in the United States, this precarity of authors' rights remained.

Property and the US "Copyright Clause"

The significance of material property in the history of copyright—what I have discussed as a close relationship between exclusive rights to manufacture text and exclusive rights to produce stuff (such as windmills, dumplings, or salt)—is evident not only in certain colonial arrangements, including those that benefited John User of Massachusetts, but in the original language of the US Constitution. As an outcome of the Constitutional Convention's deliberations in the summer of 1787, much of which centered on strategic protections of individual property, the so-called copyright clause connects copyrights with patents. Article 1, section 8 of the Constitution affirms that "Congress shall have Power [...] to promote the Progress of Science and useful Arts, by securing for limited Times to Authors and Inventors the exclusive Right to their Respective Writings and Discoveries." Not surprisingly, the exact meanings of "promote," "progress," "useful," and "limited times" have given legislators heaps of trouble. The latter is especially vexing, and later in this chapter I discuss the continual extension of copyright terms throughout the twentieth century. Suffice it to note here that the language recommended by the Congressional Committee of Detail not only links science (including knowledge and inquiry generally) with useful arts, which in that time must be thought of as artisanal and craft based, but also contextualizes the protection of material property (such as land) alongside the protection of what would later be called "intellectual property."[16] When Congress acted on its constitutional authority by passing the 1790 Copyright Act, it protected individuals' rights to such useful intellectual property as "maps, charts, and books." Simply put, making stuff and knowing stuff are protected by the same constitutional clause, which emerged in a discussion of property as a source of power.[17]

During the politically and culturally formative years of the United States from 1790 to the Civil War, copyright was relatively small in scope. Many of the printed works that circulated did so without copyright. In some cases the texts were translations of English or French works, to which the 1790 act did not apply. Other texts were adaptations or abridged versions of a more well-known story or play, which were likewise permissible. Some authors simply did not seek copyright for their works since, as Meredith McGill notes, restrictions on the already difficult distribution of printed text were imprudent for authors wanting to reach a wide audience.[18] In other words, copyright was subordinate to the goal of publicity. In her study of "reprinting" culture in the antebellum period, McGill argues that the circulation of unauthorized reprints stimulated a culture consistent with the nationally budding republicanism. She explains that a "belief in the inherent publicity of print and the political necessity of its wide dissemination [...] stressed the interests of the polity over the property rights of individuals."[19] This point sets the stage for my analysis in important ways, dissociating proper name authorship and ownership from the motives of a circulation network. In the context of decentralized production of print and a general commitment to public access (including a free press and public education), McGill suggests, the proprietary connection between authors and their works was secondary. The link between a text and its identified owner was less important that the impact that the text's circulation might have on an emergent community with text at its center. Successful authors sought exposure more than exclusive rights.

In the twentieth century the link between authorship and private ownership became the center of copyright policy debates, particularly in efforts to establish appropriate time periods of privilege. A series of copyright laws gradually extended the reach and duration of copyright. In the original 1790 act, the term of recognized privilege was fourteen years, with a single renewal option for another fourteen years. The 1909 revision of this act doubled down, extending the term to twenty-eight years with the option to renew for an additional twenty-eight. The major revision in 1976 extended the term to cover the life of the author plus fifty years. Furthermore, that this act protected "unpublished works" meant that producers of content need not register their creations with a central agency. Any idea captured in fixed form is covered by copyright. This automatic proprietary status still applies. In 1998 the Sonny Bono Copyright Extension Act changed the length of time to be added to the author's life from fifty years to seventy years. In the same year the Digital Millennium Copyright Act, inspired by the World Intellectual Property Organization, sanctioned so-called digital risk management tools that control access to copyrighted materials.[20] Criminalizing any attempt to circumvent such tools, Congress confirmed the legality of organized efforts to police copyright infringement using integrated digital mechanisms.[21] A year later Eric Eldred, who had been publishing literary works from the public domain in an online library called Eldritch Press, filed a complaint contesting the constitutionality of the Sonny Bono Act. As a result of the Sonny Bono Act's extension of copyright terms, Eldred's press would not be able to publish anything more recent than 1923 until 2019.[22] In 2003 the Supreme Court ruled against Eldred, confirming the constitutionality of the 1998 act. After this major statement regarding the Court's interpretation of congressional authority to secure authors' rights, a decade of intellectual property legislation followed that buttressed the legal ownership of text.

A Confluence of Developments

When studying on the one hand the legal regulation of copyright and, on the other, the idealism of digital activists like Eldred, one is prudent to consider three developments in confluence from the 1970s onward: first, the passing of laws and rendering of judgments that protect private ownership, the most important of which I have previously chronicled; second, the development of information infrastructure and technologies, including the end-to-end design of the internet, the popularization of the World Wide Web, and eventually low-entry platforms for creating content (including blogs and social media); and third, the commercial governance of software in the 1980s, resulting in a movement for open access.[23] The last of the three merits a bit of commentary here insofar as it served in the late 1990s as inspiration for Lessig and the Creative Commons team.

As a language that allows people to communicate with computers, source code can be either opaque or transparent. The reason to keep it opaque, or secret, is generally commercial; proprietary code may be thought of as a trade secret. Transparent code, or open code, means that anyone can peek inside the machine. The peeker can not only discover the code that operates a program but take parts of it, modify them, and use them for new purposes. Richard Stallman, a legendary coder at the Massachusetts Institute of Technology, founded in 1985 the Free Software Foundation, whose agenda was to advocate for open software.[24] The foundation developed the general public license (GPL) as a way to enable open code to remain open in multiple iterations. Simply put, use of a code covered by the license was required to be, reciprocally, open. If I peek into your code and turn it into something new for my own purposes, I have to render that new code open, just like yours. "Free" enters the picture as a consequence of the license's insistence on openness in perpetuity. Open code is free insofar as it remains open.[25] And free does not mean "available at no cost." Stallman's much-quoted adage is helpful here: "Not free as in free beer, but free as in free speech."[26] Of lasting importance within the digital commons, and for my purposes here, is that the GPL contained an ethic of use. Out of the open access software movement grew a public argument favoring free access not just to programming code but to cultural, artistic, and scientific content. This more general open access movement, in which the Creative Commons is a vocal participant, mobilizes concepts like "copyleft" and "free culture" politically.[27] The open access movement's advocacy must be seen in light of the theory of authorship and creative invention that the movement endorses, as well as that theory's historical competitors.[28]

Copyright Conflicted: Two Models and Two Moments

Theories of copyright tend to be organized according to two models, both of which are grounded in assumptions about the author's and the community's claims to the material: the Anglo-American model and the French-European model. The former is utilitarian, prioritizing social instruments that ensure the greatest good for the greatest number of people. In this model, copyright incentivizes authors to create texts with economic rewards. As a result of these incentivized creations, the community as a whole advances. And when the specified copyright term runs out, the community advances by having access to the text directly. The second model relies on the ideal of individuals' natural and moral rights (*droit moral*), which are thought to exceed the community's right to text and culture, even as text and culture are generated in a shared environment of inspiration and influence.[29] A person has the right to benefit financially from her or his labor. Moreover, a person who writes words on paper imprints the writing with a sort of indelible essence; that connection between author and text cannot be violated by the assignment or denial of legal rights. To the utilitarian model, and the laws that codify it, this belief that texts are imbued with their artist's personality, and that the connection renders certain rights onto the artist, is dismissible as "intuitive, unanalyzed feeling."[30] The natural rights model and the utilitarian model, in short, reflect two different ways of thinking about authorship.

In scholarly exchanges about authorship, particularly those that center on the relationship between authors and texts, two disputes in twentieth-century intellectual history are rehearsed repeatedly. They demand inclusion here because their implications are especially pertinent to scholars of digital culture and technology, who are invested in both critical theory and the emergence of collaborative networks and fragmented artifacts. The first is the publication of Michel Foucault's 1969 essay "What Is an Author?"[31] In this essay Foucault argues that even though literary criticism and cultural theory generally may have accepted the "death of the author," individual authors' names still mark off "the edges of the text, revealing, or at least characterizing, its mode of being."[32] There is no understanding or theory of the text, what Foucault calls a "work," that is free from "the millions of traces left by [the author] after his [sic] death."[33] The "author function," Foucault explains, saves readers and scholars from the intolerable condition of literary anonymity. Far more dispersed than the real writer himself or herself, the author function "operates in the scission" generated by the deconstruction of singular authorship.[34] Beyond literary and cultural assumptions, Foucault's essay interrogates how power is appropriated and wielded discursively with or without the individual author(ity) of a name.[35] His writings on these processes of power became especially influential among poststructuralist scholars in the United States in the late 1970s, when authorship and ownership were emerging as at once political and technical matters.[36]

The second momentous dispute is between Jacques Derrida and John Searle, debating the legitimacy of authorship as a convention of textual ownership. To Searle, authorship is an extension of the kind of intentional communication that a speaker effects when putting thoughts into words.[37] Words belong to their utterer insofar as they represent his or her intentions. Derrida insists, simply put, that no such alignment of words and intentions is possible, and that ownership marked by copyright is a fantasy. Searle and Derrida's legendary kerfuffle is sometimes characterized as a historical engagement between French-German and American-English philosophical traditions.[38] It began in 1977 when Derrida's essay "Signature, Event, Context" was first published in English in a volume of *Glyph*.[39] The second volume of the year featured an article by John Searle, in which he critiques what he considers to be Derrida's misreadings of J. L. Austin's linguistics. In his published reply, "Limited Inc abc.," Derrida deconstructs his own as well as Searle's status as owners of their words and texts. He notes, "the difficulty I encounter in naming the definite origin, the true person responsible for the Reply: not only because of the debts acknowledged by John R. Searle before even beginning to reply, but because of the entire, more or less anonymous tradition of a code, a heritage, a reservoir of arguments to which he and I are indebted."[40] To illustrate that all writing exists in reference to other writing—that is, in quotation marks, or as a copyright violation—Derrida puts "copyright © 1977 by John R. Searle" first in quotation marks, then in another set of quotation marks, and then another.[41] Copyright laws and theories notwithstanding, the text is always "separated at birth from the assistance of its father."[42] No use of language, no authorship, no relationship between a text and its author, Derrida insists, is free from the complications of contagion.

As a binary distinction, the two models of authorship and copyright (natural rights and utilitarian) are somewhat artificial. They belie the cultural histories that unify transatlantic thought. The two are neither straightforwardly distinct nor wholly incompatible. Legal scholar Jane Ginsburg complicates the matter by identifying instrumentalist agendas in French legislation and natural rights ideology in early American copyright law. She notes that French "revolutionary legislators, courts, and advocates perceived literary property primarily as a means to advance public instruction."[43] In the French case, Ginsburg writes, "a strong current of Enlightenment thought objected on instrumentalist grounds to any assertion of property rights in idea-bearing works: individual proprietary claims would retard the progress of knowledge."[44] In the American case, the public's right to knowledge and the individual's property interests are, in Ginsburg's assessment, given equal protection. She argues, "If U.S. copyright's exponents sought to promote the progress of knowledge, they also recognized that the author's labors are due their own reward."[45] Moreover, as Deazley and his coeditors note, the idea of moral rights connecting texts and writers via personality continues to influence US copyright praxis. Forecasting a public attitude change toward copyright, they find in twenty-first-century legal discourses the "metaphysical concept of the copyrighted work as an intellectual essence."[46] To put it directly, and in so doing orient the two models to my project, the question of *why* someone would have copyright to cultural stuff necessarily raises questions of value: What value do copyrights secure for creators and their audiences? Are copyrights about the past or the future? Are they about the relationship that was established in creation, or are they about the benefits that the creation might have for the creator or audience eventually?

Value and Incentivized Creativity

If "*incentive*" may be thought of as a more pleasant word for "*control*," then the notion of an incentive to creativity, the product of which is copyrighted, is poignant. Copyright experts have long debated whether financial incentives make sense in the context of creativity, whether texts and cultural artifacts that are created as a result of incentives are any good, particularly when compared to artifacts that are created, as it were, for their own sake. The challenge for my purposes is to discern whether copyright or something else is the mark of value that incentivizes in the digital commons. In the context of print and the production of tangible stuff, the incentive notion has the same kind of intuitive merit as the idea that intellectual property is comparable to other material property. If I whittle figurines so that I can sell them for profit, there is no point at which my figurines leave my possession to become part of the public domain. Without incentive, would I whittle? Jeremy Bentham insisted that no one would do anything without incentive; no one would sow where there is no hope of reaping. And to be sure, traditional market economics has a firm grip on commerce in the digital environment; it would be silly to suggest that digital culture upended profit as a motive. But what are the *other*, or simultaneous, kinds of incentives, beyond the valuations of offline economics, that drive invention in the digital commons? What kinds of value sustain the gifting logos? If cultural stuff is not principally produced because creators are financially incentivized but because creating cultural stuff is what people *do*, then a lack of financial incentive would not impede production. The scope of the issue might be expanded to say that if articulating lived experience into a form of knowledge by making cultural stuff is what the participants in the digital commons *do*, then offering those articulations as gifts is about something other than economic value.

The two most recurring truisms in conversations about copyright and digital culture are that core legal principles of copyright are not well-understood by lawyers, experts, or practitioners, and that both the law and the media industry are antiquated and outpaced by digitally dexterous individuals. The first is typically illustrated with accounts of how copyright is capriciously enforced with disproportionate penalties and how participants in digital culture are not always aware of using or republishing content illegally.[47] The second is tinted with the renegade romanticism of the "cool guys" outsmarting the stuffy copyright lawyers who are stuck in the twentieth century; in the eyes of said "cool guys," "copyright applies the brakes on the development of the knowledge society and creates a chasm of digital divide between producers and consumers."[48] Since both of these recurring tropes are legitimate but insufficient for sustaining a conversation about copyright, expertise and the digital commons, I acknowledge them here and proceed. As I noted in the introduction, productive knowledge—knowing and making in one rhetorical habit—has evolved historically in relation to continuously changing circumstances. Thus, in short, copyright was always complicated.

THE CREATIVE COMMONS AND THE GIFTING LOGOS

The Creative Commons (CC) was founded in 2001 by a group of open access enthusiasts lead by Lawrence Lessig, a professor of intellectual property law at Harvard's Berkman Center for Internet and Society.[49] According to his own account, Lessig was troubled by how copyright and the inventive practices and potential of the

World Wide Web were becoming incompatible; to him, the ownership presumption of copyright reflected the cultural habits of another time. As Lessig describes, lawmakers at the turn of the century were increasingly inclined to authorize the use of digital technologies whose explicit purpose was to block public access to copyrighted content.[50] On May 11, 2001, a daylong meeting of twenty-eight true believers resulted in an explicit goal: "To expand the shrinking public domain, to strengthen the social values of sharing, of openness and of advancing knowledge and individual creativity."[51] Thus, the CC organization began as a licensing agency. Shortly thereafter the organization launched the first version of the CC licenses. These were designed to mediate, on the one hand, the restrictions of copyright ("all rights reserved") and, on the other, the legally nebulous public domain ("no rights reserved"). They belong historically and ideologically to a cohort of initiatives, networks, and services intended to expand free and publicly available media content that includes the Wikimedia Commons, Jamendo, Pixabay, the Free Music Archive, and others.[52]

The purpose of this chapter is to examine how expertise is rhetorically constructed by the CC and the people who participate in it. Specifically, I demonstrate how the production and circulation of cultural stuff in the digital commons cohere through the gifting logos, through knowing-as-making-as-gifting. The practices facilitated by the CC, I argue, integrate simultaneously multiple rhetorical habits: the invention of cultural stuff like music, text, and images; the imbuing of the stuff with its inventors' lived experiences and interpretations thereof; and the presentation of the stuff as gifts. The gifting logos, as logos, is a language of making and knowing and gifting; a logic of making and knowing and gifting; and a critical concept that enables analysis of how making and knowing and gifting function as expertise in the digital commons. My intent is to explicate the qualities of the gifting logos. The preceding section established the historical, legal, and cultural significance of copyright. Against this foil, it is possible to analyze the gifting logos with reference to the CC, and not solely because the organization presents itself as a challenge to copyright. It is imperative, I submit, to understand how the infrastructure of the digital commons defines expertise in relation to traditional notions of knowledge, authority, and cultural value. In what follows I direct attention to how the gifting logos uses the CC licenses to impose order on the process of cultural invention; assigns value by individuating invention and/as gifting; administers the directionality of gifting with the terms of sharing and charity; manages its participants' intentionality; supports production en masse; and is kairotic, timing participants' rhetorical habits of making, knowing, and gifting in flux.

Tailored Licenses

The CC suite of licenses is an à la carte menu for providing access to cultural material. The licenses are configured into six combinations on a continuum from more to less control, imposed by the licensor on future users' activities. The CC explains the licenses as follows:

(1) The "Attribution" tag "lets others distribute, remix, tweak, and build upon your work, even commercially, as long as they credit you for the original creation."[53] This is the most permissive of the tags, "recommended for maximum dissemination and use of licensed materials."
(2) The "Attribution-ShareAlike" likewise requires users to credit the original producer of the content; in addition, it requires that users make their own productions, in which they use and adapt the original content, accessible to future users.[54]
(3) The "Attribution-NoDerivs" license retains the content intact, prohibiting derivative interpretations and adaptations. Users are allowed to recirculate the content, attributing credit to the original producer, without changing the content in any way.
(4) The "Attribution-NonCommercial" demands that credit be given to the original producer and that any use of the content, which includes derivative works, be distributed for noncommercial purposes only. Users who redistribute the content, either in its original form or in some new adaptation, may not do so for the purpose of profit. Furthermore, because this license does not impose the "ShareAlike" tag, subsequent uses can attach other licenses that are either more or less restrictive. Third-generation users may make their versions of the original available for commercial purposes.
(5) The "Attribution-NonCommercial-ShareAlike" license "lets others remix, tweak and build upon your work non-commercially as long as they credit you and license their new creations under the identical terms." It thus responds to the generational option of the license immediately preceding to move toward commercial interests.
(6) The "Attribution-NonCommercial-NoDerivs" license allows no uses other than redistribution, with credit given to the original creator. It is "the most restrictive of our six main licenses, only allowing others to download your works and share them with others as long as they credit you, but they can't change them in any way or use them commercially."[55]

In 2018, the CC reported that 1.1 billion works had been tagged with these licenses.

Understood as a grid or structure, the licenses' principal function is to impose order on the procedure by which authors, creators, and artists gift their stuff to the digital commons. The licenses dictate conditions of giving and receiving. Each tag is available for selection by the licensor such that she or he sets precisely the desired mechanisms of control. Indeed, the "disaggregated" configuration of the license tags, which lets individual licensors tailor their preferences for distribution, accounts to some extent for the CC's notoriety in open access circles.[56] Thus seen, the licenses themselves reflect a palpably Maussean aspect of the gifting logos.[57] To Marcel Mauss, gifting is intensely political insofar as it allows participants to dictate the actions of others. He demonstrates with the concept of "prestations" how gifts are given not simply between individuals, but as a form of control within social clusters. Rather than the simple expectation that one gift be reciprocated with another gift—two office workers at a holiday party exchange Starbucks gift cards—gifts are a means of choreographing social relations with respect to the future. They demand a specific course of action from recipients, who are in the giver's debt. Debt, Mauss explains, is part of a complex logic of multiple prestations. To the extent that givers determine the future of social relationships, gifts are a speculative investment.[58]

Attribution, Individuation, and Value

At the most basic level, or the most permissive end of the continuum, the CC licenses mark cultural content with the imprint of the individual creator. The "Attribution" tag, which the CC describes as its "most accommodating" option, is a mechanism of individuation. Attaching the "Attribution" tag establishes a relationship between the content and the creator that, insofar as it insists on recognition for an unspecified length of time, is reminiscent of the *droit moral* model of copyright.[59] "Attribution" is a technologically new version of the philosophically old notion that cultural "stuff" must be marked with the name of the person responsible for its inception.[60] As an illustration, imagine how a photo of a scenic vista or a majestic redwood tree captures the photographer's moment. A song harmonizes a musician's broken heart. A text narrates a privileged experience of trauma (assault, childbirth, illness and recovery). With the CC licensing of such cultural artifacts, the romanticism of the identifiable, originary creator is codified. In this instance, "codified" means both reified and literally "made into the code." The author myth endures as a photographer, musician, or writer places his or her "author-ity" into the digital code of the artifact. The act of licensing cultural artifacts says to those who download it: "Here is my gift to you! It contains what I know about the world. That is, it reflects my experience. And/But it is tagged with my name, my graph." The ambiguity of "and/but" in the last sentence is significant. In the gifting act, neither the gifted stuff nor the creator is unknown; the emphasis is on naming. (Pseudonyms are no less real than offline names in this case.) The giver who is named contributes to the commons with a gesture that braids together knowing, making, and gifting. The name is the structural baseline of what the licensor establishes as a participant in the commons. The gifting logos demands the individuation of a name.

The CC's individuation of creativity in the form of attribution and naming indicates how the gifting logos allocates value. That relative value corresponds to individual names is not necessarily a revelation or even a distinguishing feature of on- and offline engagements. A "good name" has always been valuable. Nevertheless, the relationship between the value of a name and the value of an artifact demands attention in the digital commons, especially to the extent that the two are mutually traceable. In gifting generally, value is staggeringly complicated. The value of a gift has little to do with the value of the object itself out of context, as anyone with children can attest. If I get the gift of a crumpled-up drawing from my son, its value is tremendous to me. To anyone else, it is worthless. This relationality and symbolic arbitrariness pertains to broader scales of gifting as well. A gift given at a particular moment or place, perhaps marking an occasion, may be valuable regardless of the object's inherent worth. In the Christian sacrament, bread and wine are valuable gifts not because of what they are, but as a function of what is invested in them. It must be noted, however, that to a hungry nonbeliever the elements may be considerably more valuable as bodily than as spiritual nourishment. Simply put, gifting always raises the question of value, and value is never simple. In the CC, makers and gifters collect social value within the commons as a function of the value of their gifts, their images, music, and so on. For this to be the case—in order for the gifting logos to function—content production has to be intelligibly individuated.[61] Content that is attributable to no one makes for a functionally weak gift. Here I must note that my intent is not to adjudicate whether the licensors that use the CC are truly altruistic or hungry for the self-affirmation that individual naming provides. Rather, my focus is on the rhetorical strategies by which they frame their habits of making and gifting and the consequences of the format (the licenses) in which they do. I am concerned therefore with how the ideals of gifted content and free access align rhetorically with a structure that enables individuation and control of gift recipients' future actions.

Theories of gifting, which account for the administration of value, tend to taxonomize different types of gifts, such as favors and sacrifices. To examine the value allocation of the CC licenses, I propose, it is prudent to think of such distinctions in terms of the grammatical subjunctive, the condition of what is possible but unrealized. In the most mundane circumstances, a favor means that when I do something for you (e.g., help you proofread a manuscript), I expect that in the future you will return the favor, either in kind (e.g., by helping me proofread my manuscript) or with something that you can do but I cannot (e.g., change the oil in my car). A sacrifice, likewise, presumes manipulation of a future scenario. I might sacrifice (etymologically "make holy") a chicken to the weather gods, imploring them to make my wedding day sunny. A sacrifice might also be an act of self-denial. If I let you have the last piece of pizza, it is a sacrifice on my part because the act forecloses the possibility of eating the last slice myself. This is a point upon which gifting theories, reinforced by mythic heroism or Christian theology, romanticize motives and consequences. Emphasizing that a sacrifice makes possible what would otherwise be impossible, gifting theorists tend to blur the issue of an expectation of return.

A sacrifice may be conceptually distinct from a favor, intelligible as an absolute gesture of grace, but the question of obligation is all but inevitable. In both genres of gifting action, a subjunctive potentiality is discernible.

By contrast, but in keeping with the grammatical metaphor, the gifting logos of the CC situates licensed content in the declarative mood only. The gifts tagged by their creator with one of the six licenses do not have a subjunctive, an alternate life in other circumstances. That they are given into the digital commons is their declarative condition. They are not sacrificial because the productive act in which they were generated and gifted to the commons does not foreclose other possibilities. There is no alternate reality in which the licensor herself ate the last slice of pizza. To be clear, this matter of value potentiality is widely disputed. At stake is the question of whether a gifted artifact could have had a life outside the digital commons, specifically what its value there might have been.[62] In the CC's own narrative, individual artists earn a reputation when they tag and gift their texts, music, or films. Making something freely available via the CC mechanism affords artists publicity and circulation, which in turn generates profit.[63] This recurring story is celebrated in multiple versions in the CC's report *The Power of Open*, a text that is explicitly intended to "inspir[e] you to examine and embrace the practice of open licensing so that your contributions to the global intellectual commons can provide their greatest benefit to all people."[64]

When licensors construct their music, texts, and images as gifts, the value of those gifts is managed in the declarative mood by the "Attribution" function. Regardless of whatever offline value the material might have, the declarative mood causes value to pool, or at least puddle, around the names of the gifters. Borrowing from social media, we might say that gifters' "accounts" or "profiles" are where value accumulates. If, as Lessig claims, the human agents at the periphery of the end-to-end commons network contribute value to an otherwise valueless, simple, or "stupid" structure, then the agents are at once the managers and the results of the gifting logos's value allocation.[65] In short, the gifting logos organizes value via individuation and naming. Thinking about the constructedness of gifts in the declarative rather than the subjunctive mood thus entails a move past the "What if?" question of offline value. Studying the digital commons, this move beyond the subjunctive mood operationalizes Heidegger's notion that gifts are an ontological given and, conversely, that the event of being is a giving-event.[66] In this case, the event of being a member of the digital commons and a participant in the CC project is a gifting event. Gifts in the digital commons *are*; that they *are* is organized by the logos, a praxis of distribution in a social network.

Gifting as Sharing, and Layers of the Logos

In the vocabulary of networked circulation, "*sharing*" is a predominant term. Historically "*sharing*" references the emergence of file-sharing in the 1980s and

1990s, particularly the development of compressed MP3 files that enabled the expedient sharing of music. In the more contemporary perspective of social media, sharing means recirculating content created by others in order to express a stance relative to the content or source; using a social media platform, a person might share an article, blog post, meme, or image with a network. For my purposes, the notion of sharing demands some conceptual orientation in relation to gifting, especially so that gifting theories may be made intelligible in a digital environment. In abstraction, sharing and gifting are distinguishable. One might venture to suggest that sharing is what you do when your central motive is to retain at least a piece of what is yours. I might share my pizza with you if I perceive that there will be enough for me as well. Gifting is what you do when your central motive is that others should retain what was never exclusively yours in the first place. I gift the things that I have not, possibly could not, fully appropriate. Friedrich Nietzsche's Zarathustra describes himself as burdened with wisdom the way a bee is burdened with honey, compelled to relieve himself by giving the burdensome substance away.[67]

Analyzing the CC, there are good reasons to stretch a definitive distinction between gifting and sharing. First, the two are used interchangeably by participants. The first paragraph of the 2015 *State of the Commons* announces, "Sharing is not just a self-less act. Sharing has concurrent and lasting benefits, multiplied for the *giver*, the receiver, and communities at large."[68] In this statement of purpose, sharing is not only caring but giving. The CC licenses are a "simple, standardized way to *give* the public permission to share and use your creative work." The gifted work is donated specifically so that it will continue to be shared and given. Second, the meanings of sharing that come together in discourses by and about the CC align instructively with the qualities of gifting noted in prominent gift theories. This alignment indicates that most of the important theoretical aspects of gifting are born out in the practices of CC licensing. Shared/given stuff circulates somewhere in between giver and receiver in a state of "being there." Shared content is in a Heideggerian sense a given. Or, as Marilee Mifsud notes, the cultural givens of *doxa* supply the shared social spaces of rhetorical invention.[69]

The gifting logos of the CC assigns its participants multiple and interchangeable roles as giver and receiver. As licensors' cultural contents are gifts to the digital commons, the licensors are the gifters. The CC asserts, "If you want to *give* people the right to share, use, and even build upon the work you've created, you should consider publishing it under a Creative Commons license."[70] Sofya Polyakov, one of the CC's success stories, "built a community of professional designers by helping them *give* away their designs."[71] Polyakov's testimony on the web page "Team Open," which narrates the progress of the CC, describes how the licenses enable gifting that ultimately draws business to professional designers.[72] Another featured story on the "Team Open" page is Khalid Albaih, a Sudanese political cartoonist who depicts the hardships of his home country. Albaih credits the CC with the large audience that his messages have reached; his story relies on the image of an artist giving his art to the world. When the artist gives his art, he gives his experience and knowledge of a particular place and its traumas. In other words, he gives his expertise contextualized rhetorically in relation to an event and an audience. Asserts Albaih:

> People should support Creative Commons if they care about what they're doing, and they want to get their work to as many people as possible; if they care about collaborating with people all over the world together and coming up with something beautiful ... this is what we're supposed to be doing—what the internet was made for.[73]

The CC explains that, with the "free, easy-to-use copyright licenses [creators get] a simple, standardized way to give the public permission to share and use [their] creative work."[74]

At the same time as individual licensors self-invent as gifters, the CC as a program is itself constructed via the gifting logos as a gift from Lessig to an unspecified, general recipient. The identity of this recipient varies: artists worldwide, the scientific community, participants in digital subcultures, or possibly humanity in its entirety. This gift, in turn, bestows power: the power to move beyond the constraints of copyright. The CC "gives you flexibility (for example, you can choose to allow only non-commercial uses) and protects the people who use your work, so they don't have to worry about copyright infringement, as long as they abide by the conditions you have specified."[75] Describing what it provides, the CC announces, "Our tools *give* everyone from individual creators to large companies and institutions a simple, standardized way to keep their copyright while allowing certain uses of their work—a 'some rights reserved' approach to copyright—which makes their creative, educational, and scientific content instantly more compatible with the full potential of the internet."[76] The CC, run by an international cadre of "volunteers"—the implications of this classification is that they give their time—is a gift of power. However cliché, it is the gift that keeps on giving.

That the CC license suite is a gift to the digital commons must be contextualized within Lessig's own jeremiadic account of post-1970s proprietary policymaking. His many essays and books, celebrating the brilliance of visionary coders and the architecture of end-to-end networks, describe how the wheels began to come off the free culture wagon when media empires began to lock up music, film, photography, and text.[77] This, Lessig explains, was a legal and corporate process of enclosure, bridging the twentieth and twenty-first centuries. The second part of his argument is that technology itself is effectively used to police copyright violations in a way that rivals the vigilance of the Stationers' Company.[78] As Lessig tells the story, the future looks dismal for the digital commons, indeed for the offline community as well. But the CC enters heroically with an elegant solution; a release valve to the constraints of copyright. But it's much bigger than that: Creative Commons has become a steward of our global Commons, a universe of openly-licensed content that has the power to spark everyday ideas and solve global challenges. We've unlocked the door to an alternate reality of free and open content, powered by millions of creators who share our values.[79]

Lessig's dystopic narrative is populated by givers and takers, recounting how Walt Disney took the Grimm brothers' folktales from the public domain and turned them into family films for profit.[80] The artists who license their works with the CC tags are, in Lessig's reading, givers. They replenish the resources by which they have been inspired. When the takers of the media world threaten to usurp all power, the CC intervenes. Just like any other gift, the exigency and timing of Lessig's gift to the world, the CC licenses, are critical to the gift's value. Lessig's gift comes in a time of need, as a strategy in a crisis and a remedy for an ailing (political) body.[81]

Intent, Transgression, and Choice

In the gifting logos, intent and agency are mutually implicative, subsumed and advertised under the notion of choice. The CC, explaining to prospective gifters what the conditions of donation are, repeatedly emphasizes choice: "Our free, easy-to-use copyright licenses provide a simple, standardized way to give the public permission to share and use your creative work—on conditions of your choice."[82] The interface explicitly titled "License Chooser" moves prospective content producers through a series of clicks that tailors a license according to the licensor's preferences.[83] Explaining the "License Design and Rationale," the CC states, "If a licensor decides to allow derivative works, she may also choose to require that anyone who uses the work—we call them licensees—to make that new work available under the same license terms."[84] Over a block graph visualizing the kinds of content that are most frequently tagged with a license, the CC reports, "More people are choosing to share with 'Free Culture' Licenses."[85] The *State of the Commons* asserts, "If we want to live in a digital world that is fair, diverse, vibrant, serendipitous, and safe for everyone, we will have to choose to make it that way." The implication is that gifting is a function of individuals' disposition. In other words, the gifting logos is contingent on intent. Some people surrender exclusive rights to their creation by choice. Unstated is that they are more generous than others, specifically those who do want to retain copyright. Copyright in this frame depends on individuals' ability to think of their materials as property-to-be-withheld or property-to-be-given. The gifts that constitute the CC are given deliberately and strategically.[86]

Within the gifting logos, the notion of choice may be contrasted with digital circulation practices that are seen as transgressive. For example, a copyright violation is often characterized (and treated legally) as theft. A copyright victim is deprived of the presumed value of the materials that legally belong to him or her.

No one would choose to be the victim of theft. Likewise, plagiarism, a practice of reproduction and redistribution facilitated by network technologies and often framed as an ethical infraction, posits a victim. A plagiarizer takes an original creator's work, digitally dis-integrates it, and presents it as his or her own. Cultural assumptions of an authentic relationship between the creator and the material are abused to accomplish the deception. She or he whose cultural stuff is plagiarized without consent is violated. The connection between creator and material is disturbed when, using technologies that are difficult to monitor, the material is stolen, perhaps especially so when the theft never becomes known to the creator. Participants in the digital commons are potential victims of a crime that may never come to light. The circumstances of their cultural stuff—the conditions of being for the stuff that conflates knowing, making, and gifting—are precarious. Indeed, although gifters of cultural stuff may choose the act of gifting, the consequences of their choice are uncertain.

Against this precarity, the gifting logos ostensibly imposes a mechanism of assurance. The gifter who operates within the gifting logos evades transgressive acts. Simply put, she or he who gives something away cannot be robbed of that thing any more than someone who makes fun of herself can be the butt of others' jokes. The potency is removed from the potential violation by the reordering of subject and object. Thus, the gifting logos authorizes plagiarism and copyright violations but retains order via the "Attribution" function. Expertise, to put it another way, entails a rhetorical effort to refuse infringement. What is marked with a name can be given away, but it cannot be entirely lost within the data of the digital commons. Consider an analog illustration. The 1960s activist Abbie Hoffman wrote a book about art, capitalism, and a countercultural movement against the state, whose title is a dare: *Steal This Book!*[87] With this title, Hoffman's rejection of art as property made him immune to theft. The title conscripted thieves as allies. The CC licensors, in a similar recasting of roles, mobilize the gifting logos to avert injury and make their own voices the center of future conversations. Thus, licensors' cultural stuff serves as the raw material from which more stuff might be made.[88] To texturize this illustration further in relation to the CC, consider the call to larceny and the gesture of gifting as acts of recruitment. Hoffman invites others to become conspirators in his movement against the commercialization of art.[89] The CC licensors make the recipients of their gifts co-creators of more digital stuff. The gifting logos recruits more producers and more gifters. It facilitates the process by which participants and materials in the digital commons multiply. And this recruitment is reliant on the ideal of choice.

Inheritance, Genes, and Copious Productivity

Complicating the gifting logos's discourse of choice is the recurring theme of inheritance, some of which implies intentional gifting (bequeathing) and some of which evokes gifted genetics. The CC's message that cultural stuff is inherited is productively ambiguous, relying on alternate metaphors that communicate what inheritance means. Describing the repository of licensed materials as "a treasure trove of content," many of the CC's promotional materials build on the notion of charity.[90] This charity, importantly, is generational; it is intended to "preserve our cultural heritage now and [for] generations to come."[91] The gifting logos here emerges as a dowry, a transgenerational chest (or treasure trove), wherein past generations' gifts await future generations' beneficiaries. A striking illustration of the inheritance discourse is the terminology of the licenses' three-layer design; the middle layer, the "human readable" version of the license, is called the "Commons Deed."[92]

The three layers of code that sustain the CC illustrate the language of inheritance and endowment. The first layer of each license is the legal code, "the kind of language and text formats that most lawyers know and love."[93] The second layer has "a format that normal people can read." This layer, the so-called Commons Deed, is "a handy reference for licensors and licensees, summarizing and expressing some of the most important terms and conditions." The third layer of the license is "machine readable." Simply put, it makes the various license configurations legible to the Web such that it can retrieve materials for those who search for them. For example, if I tag a photograph with the "Attribution-NonCommercial-ShareAlike" license, the CC machine sutures that information into the digital data bits that make up the photograph, making the photograph searchable in just that way.[94] The code layers, coordinating the capacities and interests of three different agents (more or less human), administer gifts with respect to future activity. They set the terms of how the inheritance may be used, both legally and mechanically. The machine-readable layer of the gifted material, which the human readable "Commons Deed" classifies as a gift, literally *makes* the digital stuff into stuff that governs its own future iterations. Tags become part of the stuff's digital makeup. Cultural artifacts' searchability, which the machine code constitutes, determines what will be found and how it will be used. Thinking of the layered license as a deed, it is important to note how the deed is laced with conditions of use; or, indeed, how the gift comes with strings attached.[95] The CC's "ShareAlike" tag reinforces this format, demanding that recipients of gifts package their own creations as gifts for others. Thus, the gifting logos depends on layers of code that dictate what humans as well as machines can know and make.

Alongside the language of inheritance whereby future generations benefit from licensors' generosity, inheritance in the CC also takes up its connotations with genes. In genetics, certain gifts (like musical ability or prominent noses) are inherited. Notably, their transmission is beyond the choice or intentional control of either the giver or recipient. That we are "hardwired" to gift our ideas and inventions, the CC asserts, is a "driving force for human evolution."[96] The gifting logos is genetic, which is to say it infiltrates genetic propagation. Let us for the sake of clarification consider a common metaphor for genetics: the pool. The familiar image of the gene pool is picked up in discourses about the CC's "global pool of content."[97] When it is, content blends with content, and the kinds of individuated contributions I discuss above become difficult to distinguish. An individual's gift is dropped into the pool, where it mixes with other gifts.[98] Gifter intentionality is complicated. The notion of individuated pieces of content is overlaid by the impossible prospect of separating individual droplets in a pool or identifying which drops were deposited by whom.[99] The gene pool does not submit to management or control in the same way that a treasure chest of jewels might. Nonetheless, the logos of gifts sets the conditions for both discourses. It constructs what is gifted as ambiguously contingent on either intentional generosity or an unintentional but coded design.

Whether by genetic multiplication or mounting treasure, the most prevalent theme of the CC gifting logos is *copia*, the abundance of digital stuff. When the organization showcases its impact and recruits prospective licensors and users, the premier accomplishment is mass. In multiple parts of the 2015 *State of the Commons*, in which detailed data is offered, a hyperlink moves the reader from the primary PDF to a massive html document with lists and tables quantifying impact. Inside the *State of the Commons* document a full-page graph shows an unequivocal rise in licensed materials between 2006 and 2016. From the left to the right, marking chronological progress, a shaded block rises exponentially. The caption reads, "Wow! Over 1 billion CC licensed works in the Commons in 2015." Another graphic represents one billion views with a single dot, then displays 136 dots to signify that "in 2015, CC licensed works were viewed online 136 billion times."[100] Yet another full-page display uses concentric and size-proportional circles to represent the types of content that are licensed: the largest circle represents 391 million images; the second largest, 46.9 million texts; the third in order, 18.4 million videos; the next in size, 4 million audio tracks. Another simpler design presents data regarding the "CC marked public domain, [which] has nearly doubled in size over the last 12 months." Visually and quantitatively, the message cultivated by the CC is that the "state" of the commons is copious. Its condition of being is most accurately understood as size, scope, and mass. The purpose of the *State of the Commons* document is to "report our best effort to measure the immeasurable scope of the Commons."

Engendering the production of copious digital stuff, the CC's invitation to prospective licensors is that if you gift your stuff to other people, they can use your stuff to make more stuff, and as more stuff is produced and more stuff is made accessible, the world will be better.[101] Cultural artifacts multiply both organically, as creators engage one another, and technically, as these engagements are facilitated by a layered network. This is a significant departure from the recurring claim in gifting studies that gifts that circulate within a community are marked by singularity. In these models, the recipient who serves temporarily as a steward of the gift enjoys its privilege only for so long as she or he possesses it. When that person passes the gift along to someone else in the community (or network), the gift's potency leaves her or him and moves on to the new beneficiary. By contrast, the gifting logos teleology is accomplished by accumulation; the logos itself (the structure, order, character, and language) of the gifting logos is cumulative and prolific.[102] It supplies those who participate in the massive production of digital stuff with a language to make sense of production itself as expertise. Put another way, expertise in the gifting logos is copious, consisting of a digital mass. The (re)production of digital stuff within the framework of the CC is an act of integration wherein knowing, making, and gifting are one rhetorical practice. Within the gifting logos, expertise is a rhetorical process that involves multiple actions: making digital stuff, capturing what the maker knows in that stuff, and gifting that stuff to the commons wherein it will multiply.

The *copia* of the gifting logos makes it possible to recognize digital commoners' immersive experience and to think of this experience in terms of the constant revisability of the content that surrounds them. In a networked context, cultural productions are both homochronic and homotopic, happening at the same time in the same place, with the same bits of data. Because this is so, because the gifters of the digital commons are reproducing cultural stuff in the same time and place, the gifts are always accessible. Expertise is not called upon in moments of demand, as is the case, for example, when experts are summoned to advise in the decision-making of a democratic public. Instead, expertise is omnipresent, or immanent. This immanence is beyond the gift theory precept that the gift and the giver perpetually retain a bond that allows the latter to manipulate a recipient's life, as Mauss argues. Constant accessibility means that the sacrificial element of gifting is, if not moot, then at least significantly altered. I argued previously that the notion of a gift as a sacrifice must be rethought in the digital commons, particularly in reference to its declarative rather than subjunctive mood. The digital commons gift has no condition of possibility elsewhere but is defined from the beginning as a given. Add to this that the digital commons gift is never sacrificed because of interoperability, which is the technical affordance that enables recipients of gifts to become producers of new stuff and givers of new gifts. The gifting logos of the digital commons (as opposed to Hyde's gifting culture or Mauss's gifting politic) accelerates the production of stuff and structurally hosts it so that expertise as such becomes homotopic and homochronic.

Kairos and Copyright Timing

The gifting logos of the digital commons is confounded on two fronts by the complications of time—one is about cultural expectation, the other is about legal agency. First, gifting as a social activity demands compliance with cultural expectations, or kairotic sensibility. Giving a gift requires an assessment of when to give, an analysis of the moment. It further requires a sense of how to await the recipient's response, as well as a sense of how long the wait might reasonably be. Bourdieu emphasizes how ambiguous the "lag time" of gifting is. He notes, "The period interposed which must be neither too short (as is clearly seen in gift exchange) nor too long (especially in the exchange of revenge-murders), is quite the opposite of the inert gap of time, the time-lag, which the objectivist model makes of it. Until he has given back, the receiver is 'obliged.'"[103] The duration of time punctuated by gifting action is never, in other words, inert. Bourdieu further characterizes the lag time as an important fiction that distinguishes separate acts of gifting from one another: "The interval that makes it possible to experience the objective gift exchange as a discontinuous series of free and generous acts is what makes gift exchange viable and acceptable by facilitating and favoring self-deception, a lie told to oneself, as the condition of the coexistence of recognition and misrecognition of the logic of the exchange."[104] The gifting logos demands such a manipulation of time as is necessary for each act of gifting to be recognized as reflecting the individual's choice. This demands perception of kairos. Without a sense of timing, the individual's intervention, wielding the cultural stuff of her or his expertise, cannot be intelligible as a gift.

In the CC, the ambiguity to which Bourdieu's gifting theory directs attention is magnified. Gift timing is fraught by the tension between instantaneity and perpetuity. A CC participant could access material (e.g., an image), adapt and revise it, and then publish the "new" material in the span of a few moments. Another participant could do the same with the "new" material within minutes. And so on. And yet the potential delay (of response, reception, and engagement from other digital commoners) is indefinite. The licensed material comes with a tag that, in stark contrast to offline gifts, bears not the recipient's name but the giver's. Compared to a birthday present, for example, the "Attribution" tag may be seen metaphorically as hanging from a silk ribbon just as one would expect on a regular gift. But the name on it is not the birthday celebrant's but the gift giver's. What, then, happens if the gift is never acknowledged? It would be strange to say the least if the recipient never opened the present. No doubt the lag time would disturb the relationship between the recipient and the giver. In the case of the CC licensor, the gift might or might not be received and opened—that is to say, accessed, used, revised, and recirculated—at some unspecified point in the future. The cultural material with which licensors enter into the digital commons is the kind of gift for which recipients must self-select. And until they do, time is indeterminate.

Second, the gifting logos's kairos must be thought of in reference to copyright, wherein time marks the duration of privilege. As noted previously, determining an appropriate period of time to be guaranteed by copyright is theoretically and legally fraught. For the moral rights adherents, the essential relationship that connects an author to a text is eternal, which might mean that copyrights ought to be extended in perpetuity. For the utilitarians, a cost/benefit calculus determines how long a period of economic reward must be to adequately incentivize the creation of content without extending privileges to one individual so far that the general public is negatively affected. In the case of the CC, the time covered by the licenses was a challenge from the start. A licensor who rescinds her or his gift to the commons might in fact retroactively make others' use of that content a copyright violation. Termination provisions, in other words, pose "an underappreciated risk" to the CC insofar as "all open-content licenses authorize otherwise unlawful conduct."[105] Because the prospect of revoked licenses, or licenses that suddenly lapse, presents such a challenge to the system of circulation (to the gifting logos), the CC encourages licensors not to think of their choices to tag content as temporary. To some critics, therefore, the licenses appear to impose an extreme version of the natural rights model, in which an author's rights to her or his materials are inviolable forever. The trouble is that copyright law itself flummoxes such "forever gifting." As Armstrong explains, time, specifically an individual's vantage point into the future, is a problem for the CC because copyright law "expressly makes the author's unilateral power to rescind the transfer irrevocable and nonwaivable."[106] More plainly put, a CC licensor cannot legally promise that she or he is never going to change her or his mind. The law insists that, should the licensor decide not to give away her or his expertise, her or his ownership of it is protected.[107]

That copyright law insists on individuals' perpetual right to rescind permissions—or, in the words of the gifting logos, to take back a gift—conflicts with the reality that ideas are irretrievable. Once one person has given another person an idea, that engagement between them cannot be undone. To be sure, copyright law may attempt to regulate the production of cultural stuff, to constrain what the idea recipient can do, particularly if the idea giver can prove some sort of creative originality. But the cultural influence that happens in the digital commons via gifted artifacts cannot be rescinded. Expertise in the commons cannot go back in the toothpaste tube, or, as it were, back in the gift bag. As Deazley notes, a problem with the "initial conceit of *use without permission* is that it fails to accommodate the fact that once a work has been published it necessarily enters a public arena; that is, it has ceased to exist within the individual realm of the author and instead has entered a public cultural space."[108] Even if the time span during which a CC licensor allows her or his material to be accessible in the commons is brief, it is longer than no-time. The exposure of the gifted material to the commons is a fact. Moreover, the multiple gifting sequences that follow initial exposure, consistent with the derivative structure of human ideas and of the CC licenses explicitly, are all but impossible to halt. There are, in short, no "take backs" in the gifting logos.

Given the way that time, especially the timing of gifts and permission, is an unknown variable for the CC, the cultural content of gifts is never at rest. Put another way, the gifting logos is in a constant state of flux. Following Heraclitus, this does not mean simply that things change, or that gifts evolve through multiple iterations of creativity, or even that the circumstances for cultural creativity change. Nor is the notion of Heraclitean flux captured by the image of a softly flowing river.[109] The indeterminacy of gifts imposes severe tensions on both the gifter, as previously noted in reference to acknowledgment, and the recipient. As the latter sits with the gift in hand, the knowledge that it could at any moment be ripped away affects any relationship that she or he might develop with it. For example, if I take a piece of music that someone has tagged with the "Attribution" license and adapt the notes into a jingle for a soft drink commercial, I have to confront in my mind the possibility that the original musician might change her or his mind and either revoke the license altogether or impose a "NonCommercial" restriction. As a recipient of gifted expertise, in this sense, I am at risk not only legally but constitutively as a participant of the networked logos. I am subject to its flux; what is more, my own expertise, the cultural artifacts that encapsulate what I know and what I make, are potentially disintegrable by the logos that fluctuates unpredictably. And so the flux is fueled by tension, or a fire as Heraclitus would have it. The gifting logos cannot be made still or fixed. On the contrary, the "in perpetuity" option to rescind codifies flux. To put a finer point on it, while there are no "take backs" of expertise, the *experience* of being "taken back from"—being confronted with the demand that you unmake what you have created, or at least hide it away—is an unavoidable condition of participation in the digital commons.

CONCLUSION

Participants in the CC are engaged in a rhetorical practice that allows them to make sense of and talk to each other about the digital stuff that they generate. This digital stuff (music, photographs, web designs, political advocacy materials, or a tutorial on how to start a landscaping business) encapsulates its makers' knowledge and know-how; it constitutes their experiences and interpretations thereof. This stuff, in other words, is expertise in the digital commons. The movement in the digital commons of this stuff is knowledge living its rhetorical life. In the digital commons, that life unfolds such that the processes of knowing and making are gifting processes. Put more directly, knowing, making, and gifting are not intelligible as a three-step sequence but must be seen as one rhetorical activity.

The gifting logos, qua logos, is both the rhetorical activity of expertise and the critical concept with which I analyze the activity. Orienting myself in relation to digital commoners, one might say that the gifting logos is their practice and my heuristic. This chapter has explicated the qualities and functions of that practice.

As I have demonstrated, the gifting logos enables and sustains both creativity and structure. The creativity is copious, geared toward the reproduction, proliferation, and circulation of stuff. The stuff is at once material and immaterial, which is to say it is made up of electronic bits as well as performative force. It gives rise to new iterations of itself, recruiting more producers of more digital stuff. Expertise that comes as a gift equips another expert in turn, whose artifacts move along to the next participant in the network. In the sheer momentum of this productivity, the gifting logos establishes order symbolically and technically. Order is imposed at the levels of social interaction and computer code as interventions and contributions are named, made traceable to a source; gifts from no one are nonsensical. Via individual attribution, the gifting logos allows givers to control their gifts, dictating the terms of future use. It allows them to manipulate time—the instantaneity and indefinite delay of the digital context—so as to manage the complications of appropriateness. Gifting procedures and timing are brought together by logos, which subsumes kairotic competence. Furthermore, the gifting logos solidifies givers' intentionality, ensuring that those who choose to give are protected from the kind of transgressions that digital technologies have made more likely and more severe. Givers are shielded from cultural theft and fortified by the perception of their own virtue. In one move, thus, the gifting logos makes social epistemology and cultural invention contingent on individual character. In contrast to this emphasis on choice, however, the gifting logos also embeds itself in notions of genetic propagation. It suggests that gifting is what gifted people do in order to usher forth human evolution. Just as Lewis Hyde and Mari Lee Mifsud play theoretically with the meanings of "gift" and "gifted" (as, for example, in the phrase "a gifted musician"), the gifting logos of the CC obliges creators of content to translate inherited abilities into chosen generosity. The gifting logos is an epistemic and inventive choreography of social and technical networks.

3

The Archival Commons

The digital commons convenes in the now. In the virtual spaces of a continuous present, the three components of the digital commons function interactively: the humans, the networks, and the cultural resources. In this convening present, the humans become at once producers and consumers of digital stuff, acting with the resources at their disposal. Through the networks of now, the digital commons emerges—appears, or eventuates. To reflect the Heideggerian perspective on the event of being, the digital commons "be's."[1] The event is a gifting event; in the gifting event of being present, the commoners produce culture through lived epistemic habits, making what they know into things like text, design, music, and code. But what about the past? And the future? A website has an average lifespan of one hundred days, after which the content migrates or disappears. This is more of a problem in some cases than in others. It is a problem, for example, for science and legal research, which depends on citation links' longevity. There is value in retaining such information via reliable links. But what about ephemeral knowledge of networked life? Is there a need to preserve, for example, the contents of a port authority "dot-gov" site that publicizes bus routes and timetables? Does posterity need a record of Pennsylvania's recycling pickup schedule? What about the minutes from a school board meeting? What about a WordPress blog in which a person chronicles his indigestion? Which pieces of digital data—the givens of the digital commons—must be preserved, by whom, and for what purpose? What will the digital commons need to know about itself in the future? What does the commons need to archive, and why? What is the archival expertise of the digital commons?

Archiving illustrates in intricate ways the rhetoric of expertise. Specifically, it is a catalogic form of expertise, a record that constitutes what it ostensibly records.

In an informal context, a family is defined by its scrapbooks, albums, and shoebox collections. It coheres as an identifiable unit insofar as the proofs of its history are curated. Treasured holiday ornaments and photographs are used to tell the stories that constitute knowledge of *us*. *We* are (because of) this knowledge. More formally, public archiving guarantees an authoritative acknowledgment of what is officially known. A public archive sustains the public, which could not function without the archive's records. Put another way, a public needs to be known by an archive. It needs archival knowing. For much of modern history, the charge to manage this kind of knowing has fallen to the archives of nations, keeping track of monarchs, states, and citizens. National archives institutionalize the link between knowledge and power, particularly as both require a rhetorical point of origin. Knowledge and power both function with increased strength when it is clear what their respective sources or groundings are. That the archive knows the public is to say that the archive curates expertise about the public's vitals: its numbers and statistics, its leaders and its enemies, its comings and goings, lean times and prosperous upswings.

The questions I pursue in this chapter are, What sort of knowing happens in an archive that is maintained not by a public but by a commons? What manner of archive does the commons make for itself, and how is the product of this effort made accessible? My study of expertise in the digital commons, that is, my explication of expertise as the gifting logos, turns in this chapter to knowing, making, and gifting as archival. I examine the prominent and widely used Internet Archive (IA), a digitized collection of collections of literature, music, photography, and film, as well as its most famous initiative, the Wayback Machine, a retrieval technology for past versions of 430 billion web pages. Exploring these archives, I analyze a cluster of discourses: (1) the extensive IA website, where I focus on interface structure, text and design, and especially the interactive features; (2) the IA blog, including the staff-authored content with reader commentary; and (3) popular press and media coverage containing interviews with IA founder Brewster Kahle.[2] In these discourses by and about the IA and the Wayback Machine, members of the digital commons construct archival expertise, which is to say that they generate a practice and theory of what it is to make and store knowledge. In so doing, they participate productively in the gifting logos, expressing its forms in their rhetorical habits.

I demonstrate in this chapter that via the gifting logos the integrated practices of making, knowing, and gifting become central to the digital commons' history. The invention of this history happens in the context of a palpable urgency, which recognizes the commons' ultimate limit and the disappearance of cultural inheritance. Making, knowing, and gifting are in this chapter curatorial: a continuous, collective epistemic effort directed toward the common self. The urgency rhetorically deploys the ideal of preservation that is familiar in archiving discourses, the constant threat of time. However, in a paradoxical tension with the urgent call for archival vigilance, the mode in which commoners access the stuff of the digital archive is a casual browsing.[3] In this chapter, the immersive *copia* of web-based production encounters what archival scholars have long described as an essential feature of the archive, excess. Further, the dialectic of the traditional archive's bureaucratic function and its alluring mystery encounter the digital archive's ambiguity of publicity and private intimacy. The historical orientation of traditional archiving encounters the presentism of the web. And the historiographical access methods that a traditional archive requires encounter the casual and aimless noctambulance to which a digital archive so well lends itself. With the gifting logos as the rendezvous point, the modern historian meets the networked flâneur.

The chapter begins with a conceptual introduction to the archive. In this section I engage particular precepts of archive studies and survey in brief the historical functions of archival institutions. This section, like the introduction in chapter 2 to copyright history and theory, is intended not to be exhaustive but to provide context for the analysis. My treatment of meta-analyses of archival scholarship and theory speaks primarily to scholars of rhetoric rather than, for example, curators or historians. This locates logos as central to the study of how expertise is produced by, and functions in, the archive.[4] In the analysis, I begin with the IA's inception and Brewster Kahle's launching of the Wayback Machine. Second, I note the rhetorical framing of Kahle's project as a gift to the commons and the rhetorical framing of the machine's gift to the commons as historical "stuff." Third, I consider how participants in the archival commons generate interpretations of function, that is, of the purpose of the IA and the Wayback Machine. Fourth, I analyze the significance of productive retrieval, specifically as a live event of making, knowing, and gifting. Fifth, I contrast the imaginary of the machine with the imaginary of the archive in terms of access to history. Sixth, I examine the archival model that emphasizes delivery over disposition, or selective structure. Here I discuss the practices of access required by *copia*, drawing on the nineteenth-century concept of flânerie. Seventh, I characterize the gifting logos with reference to time and a common experience of loss. Finally, I conclude with a return to logos itself as fundamentally archival.

ARCHIVAL KNOWING

Etymologically the archive is primordial, a commandment for commencement. As cognates like patri*arch*, *arche*type, and *arch*angel reveal, the archive is the principal and the principle, the first and the organizing condition. The *arkhē*, like the logos, determines from a source of power what is possible in realization and articulation. It is "the first law of what can be said, the system that governs the appearance of statements as unique events."[5] More simply put, the archive is an order-imposing, empowered place for common affairs. At its center is the archivist, the magistrate who oversees a community's valuable documents, curating the story that the documents tell when configured in patterns. The archivist is in a meaningful way at home in the archive. His or her inventive management of the archive's holdings reveals the community's need to be organized in a way that creates intelligibility both inward and outward. Archival administration is the making of stuff (usually documents, files, and records) that a society must do in order to function and endure. As noted previously, a public needs to be known by the archive in order to indeed be a public. The purpose of the archive is to reify the res publica. The question that this chapter poses is, What archival habits constitute the *res communis*?

Historically the public archive rose to prominence in lockstep with the late-eighteenth-century rise of the nation state. It was indeed specifically designed to manage records and curate artifacts that reflected the nation's grandeur. At this time, general interest in history informed, and was informed by, national publics' investment in their own history; history became a rhetorical resource for articulating national identity with reference to both origins and destinies. The National Archives in Paris were founded during the early stages of revolution in 1790.[6] A decree in 1794 determined not only that prerevolutionary documents seized by French revolutionaries would be kept in the archive, but also that extensive private records of aristocratic families would be moved to public administration. In London, the Public Records Office was established in 1838 as a result of the Public Records Office Act, which centralized management of court and government documents overseen by the Master of the Rolls, a civil justice appointment. The year before the Public Records Office Act, Queen Victoria assumed the British throne. Her reign, lasting until the turn of the century, was characterized by internal struggles over popular rule and international ventures for imperial dominance. In both France and Britain, national archiving must be contextualized with reference to certain historical events: public interest in historical authenticity, the formation of historiography as an academic discipline, the emergence of professions dependent on documentary authority (the birth of the bureaucrat), and the global spread of national imperialism.[7]

The archive is a perfect illustration of epistemic power. *Epistemic power*, for my purposes, is the political power wielded by those who are acknowledged as possessing knowledge, *and* the authoritative definition of privileged groups' experiences and interpretations *as* knowledge. An expert is powerful by virtue of a rhetorically constructed function. And epistemic power may be found in artifacts that a culture accepts as knowledge-stuff. A text is powerful to the extent that it is endowed with authority. To be sure, the cliché that knowledge is power is susceptible to the critique that having knowledge does not necessarily mean having power. It does not protect against exploitation or oppression. Truth has to be authenticated by something, and they who claim to have truth may still be vulnerable in real ways. Nevertheless, power in any political context articulates itself in knowledge practices. It demands the kind of management of self-knowledge that the archive provides. Power decides what knowledge is, and certainly what it is not. And power is practiced upon people in subordinate positions by various forms of epistemic violence. As Malea Powell describes in her study of public records of indigenous Americans, the "textification" of a people for whom text itself is foreign is a form of epistemic colonialism.[8] Archival records are paper knowledge, with power enfolded in the files. So, while knowledge is not always power, power always holds a stock of knowledge at its disposal.

Endeavoring to understand the significance of the archive, one is well served to attend to its two seemingly opposing qualities. On the one hand, as noted previously, the archive is a bureaucratic institution representing the public and the nation. It is by design official and perfunctory. Its authority and objective are inherent to organization and transparency. Characterized by Carolyn Steedman, the archive is "prosaic," "ordinary," and "unremarkable."[9] It is affiliated with other institutions of the state that, as Max Weber describes, must at all times focus on "purely objective considerations."[10] The bureaucracy registers only impersonal activities, which function as points of contact at which the governed may approach the power apparatus "in a precisely regulated manner."[11] The official who controls public documents controls the bureaucracy. She or he administers the archival files that contain traces that people leave as subjects to power, whether state, monarchic, or imperial. For instance, an archive of forensic reports contains information about "lives that never asked to be told in the way they were, but were one day obliged to do so."[12] An official archive of police investigations contains the stories of those who, in reference to the state via the law, were defined, indeed made knowable, as criminals, suspects, or witnesses. In order to function as an instrument of the bureaucratic public, the archive must be dusty dry and squeaky clean.

On the other hand, and despite the orderly character of the public archive, scholarly conversations about archival research usually reference an impenetrable mysticism, what Arlette Farge calls the "allure of the archives."[13] In descriptions of the archive's seductive draw, researchers cast themselves as intrepid explorers. Seduced by the unknown, they venture into the archive as though its back wall were something akin to the Narnia wardrobe. A secret, they imagine, lies somewhere in the hinter regions of the archive, beyond the official files. And only the truly worthy, those who are disciplined but also open to discovery, succeed in "*finding it* (whatever it is you're searching for)."[14] Their search "culminates in the rare, intriguing 'holy grail' find."[15] The mysticism that archival scholars embrace enables them to "help the dead, who do not know they are dead, finish their stories."[16] Doing this work, archival researchers must rely on knowledge practices that exceed the archive's structures. In meta-analyses of archival scholarship, mysticism is closely associated with the excess of the archive, its uncontrollability.[17] Excess is the archive's concept of "dis-tidiness." It indexes the existence of both the unknown/unknowable and the archived item that troubles all categories. David Gold writes, "Archival research [is] like putting together a jigsaw puzzle, except that you don't have the picture on the box for reference, there's more than one puzzle in the box, the picture keeps changing depending on how you fit the pieces together, and the pieces themselves change shape when your back is turned."[18] Much as the archive is an instrument of tidy governmentality, and transparency is an ideal of proceduralism, there is mystery in the archive. Somewhere amid the excess a discovery awaits.

Experiencing the allure of a secret, that thing that no one else knows, is what Jacques Derrida diagnoses as "archive fever."[19] To suffer from it is to imagine the archive as the site of truthful truth, the place in which satisfying answers to perennial questions like "Whence?" and "For what purpose?" might be discovered.[20] To Derrida, the "admirable historian" is driven by a "nostalgic desire for the archive, an irrepressible desire to return to the origin, a homesickness, a nostalgia for the return to the most archaic place of absolute commencement."[21] Archive fever is the cultural condition that posits the archive as a metaphor "capacious enough to encompass the whole of modern information technology, its storage, retrieval and communication."[22] In this diagnosis, everyone is a historian. Simply put, the archive, for Derrida, reflects logocentric cultures' feverish pursuit of the origins and bases of meaning, what Barbara Biesecker describes as "referential plenitude and the motif of truth."[23] As an institution, a big building filled with ostensibly true artifacts from a past that, as a correlate, must also be true, the archive teases us with the possibility of "being reunited with the lost past, and the fulfillment of our deepest desires for wholeness and completion."[24] Particularly instructive for my purposes in this chapter is how Derrida explains that the archive "produces as much as it records" and that "the archivist institutes the archive as it should be, that is to say, not only in exhibiting the document but in establishing it."[25] The search for true meaning and origins invents (makes) what it needs to find.

Archival expertise may be differentiated somewhat bluntly into two forms, substance and process. As a substance, expertise is the stuff of the archive, the material that gets collected, organized, and stored. An archive with letters written by soldiers in Vietnam contains expertise on the subjects of combat, fear, and suffering. Put simplistically, the archive stores information as a barrel stores fish. Information, which is integral to (though not synonymous with) knowledge and expertise, is retrieved on demand, as would be the case with the fish. In the archive, expertise as substance is traditionally contained in the form of text. As Gesa E. Kirsch and Liz Rohan emphasize in the introduction to their important anthology, however, an archive is not always a library-type collection of documents. A grandfather trunk or even a cemetery can be archival insofar as each contains the stuff of people's experiences, the materials of what they know about the world.[26] The substance of archival expertise may be material, textual, or indeed digital.

As a process, archival expertise is dual, entailing a mutually responsive relationship of supply and demand between archivists and researchers. For archivists, procedural expertise is the trained competence in how to catalog, describe, preserve, select, and display archival objects. These are processes not only of curation but also of screening, as Davis Houck demonstrates, describing his experiences with the accessible and at times inaccessible materials of presidential libraries.[27] The deep-seated investments and political ideologies of archivists necessarily shape how they practice their procedural expertise, spotlighting some things and leaving some things hidden in the back, uncataloged and inaccessible. Archiving procedures are acts of rhetorical invention, as Cara Finnegan reveals in her illuminating essay "What Is This a Picture Of?"[28] As archivists classify items one way or another, they produce the objects' identity in context. With respect to such principles as provenance or coherence among artifacts made by the same person, archivists establish a "chain of custody."[29] Archiving is the procedural expertise of archivists. Relying on certain principles of selectivity, cross-referencing, categorization, and closure, archivists are the expert keepers of things that, if not for their efforts, are "in danger of disappearing."[30]

For the interdisciplinary cohort of scholars working with archives, procedural expertise is a matter of research methodology. Seasoned scholars and novices alike return to the question of how to access an archive in an informed and coordinated way.[31] In these conversations, balance between rigor and sensitive attunement is central to researchers' prospects for success. Modeling rigor, Lynée Lewis Gaillet supplies a tutorial in archival research with a series of steps: *determine* the research question, *describe* the document, *categorize* the findings, *ascertain* the motives, and so on.[32] Tempering somewhat this rigor, meta-analyses of archival research encourage openness to "the unexpected find," which is most likely to happen when the researcher's diligence is aided by serendipity.[33] Kenneth Lindblom writes, "'Striking gold' in an archive is not only a matter of luckily finding a previously unknown text that one simply discovers like a chunk of shiny metal. It is a matter of having created the conditions in which one might find old straw out of which one might spin historical gold."[34] Creating such conditions requires tenacity and faith in the method. Influential scholars like Farge describe how impossible archival research may seem.[35] Powell, too, explains that access requires

> knowledge of a very specialized type: how to find and identify the documents within catalogs and holdings lists and finding guides, and to do so in such a way that your simple request would pass unimpeded through the system's many gatekeepers; how to fill out forms, pay for things, use the physical space of the archive—all of these an elaborate maze each time I visited someplace new, all designed to keep the knowledge safe, protected, away from the prying eyes of the uninitiated and the uninformed.[36]

In addition to the procedural expertise of the research methods required for archive access, access depends on the researcher's courage not to be deterred.[37]

Methods of access to the archive, despite historiographical ideals of scholarly disinterest, necessarily integrate the academic with the personal and idiosyncratic. As self-reflective archive scholars describe, lucky breaks and happenstances often lead to rewarding scholarly projects. In this sense, it is not only the process of curating an archive that is productive. Rather, the entire process by which the curated materials are accessed and interpreted is creative, including the aspects of the process that are personal. Those who retrieve archival artifacts make history with those artifacts. This reality puts pressure on Diana Taylor's distinction between the archive, which fixes the artifacts of the past in their original form, and the repertoire, in which participants interact directly with the objects and rituals that contain historical knowledge.[38] The implications of the distinction for Taylor pertain to epistemology and performativity. Challenging the dominance of the archive as a keeper of cultural knowledge, she explains how repertoires transmit knowledge and experience in live and embodied actions.[39] Taylor's definition of the repertoire, however, depends on an understanding of the archive as stagnant rather than, as I explore in the analysis section, a generative and live event involving networked participants.

Regarding methods of access, it is worthwhile to consider here the dialectic of the public and the private (personal) as a perpendicular axis to the aforementioned dialectic of the public (official) and the mystical. This is not to say that the mystical allure of the archive coincides with what happens in private. Rather, the publicness of the archive must be understood in relation to the unknown secret that the bureaucracy belies *and* in relation to the personal and intimate, which the bureaucracy dismisses. So, while the archive curates the affairs of *the public* (as in, for example, the national public), its collections may be accessible publicly *and*, in a sense, intimately. The archive may be accessed *in public* and *as a home*. The researcher who has developed a method of access feels at home among the artifacts. The archive's intimidating scope does not impede his or her process.[40] The aesthetics and official trappings of bureaucracy subside, and the forms of the home emerge. Steedman characterizes the archive's domesticity with reference to Gaston Bachelard's description of intimate space.[41] To Bachelard, "all really inhabited space bears the essence of the notion of home," and a home provides the intimacy of reflection.[42] Those of us who know the pleasure of exploring our grandparents' cellars, attics, and armoires know the feeling exactly: the thrill of the hunt and the safety of a loving home, all at once. The archive may be thought of as a home, filled with memories. It *houses*, or domesticates, the artifacts of the past. In such a space, playful manipulation of those artifacts is contained. At stake is how far the manipulation may go. I know for certain that at my grandmother's house moving an antique teacup from one place to another—from its proper place to a wrong place—was forbidden. Likewise, I recognize that moving files in a national archive is against the rules. What, then, of the digital archive, wherein artifacts that have been moved by a visitor can be returned instantly to their tentatively proper place by a code? What if every visitor had this prerogative?

The term "*digital archive*" tends to refer generally to one of two things: it contains either digitized versions of texts, images, or recordings that originated in analog form or artifacts that were "born digital." Both kinds of digital archives intensify the complexity of certain aspects of traditional archiving, particularly delivery and access. And in the present moment, even brick-and-mortar archives are rarely offline entirely. However, archives' use of digital technologies and the web varies. At one end are archives that have digitized most of their holdings and made them searchable by anyone with internet access. At the other end are archives that publish a website with little more than open hours, location, and a curator's contact information.[43] In between the extremes are archives that publicize descriptive directories of their collections but not the content itself; translated to an analog library model, these in-between archives provide digital access to their catalog. They allow researchers to prepare for a visit to a physical archive. Commenting on this function, Ramsey claims that "the digital archive can never be anything but a supplement to the traditional archive."[44] The merit of this assertion depends on one's definition of both an archive and a supplement. If a traditional public archive gives to the public what the public needs—a sense of itself and its history—the digital archive affords the digital commons a similar but more networked epistemic reflection. As I explain in the following section, the digital archive draws participants into the self-making, self-articulating practice of the gifting logos.

THE WAYBACK MACHINE AND THE GIFTING LOGOS

In 1996, computer engineer Brewster Kahle started collecting "snapshots" of individual web pages using a technology that he and his colleague Bruce Gilliat created to track and predict user patterns on the World Wide Web.[45] In the same year, Kahle founded the IA, a California-based nonprofit organization. Three years later he sold the tracking technology to Amazon.com and began expanding the IA to include multiple collections of digitized books, films, photographs, and radio and television programs. In 2001 the IA launched the Wayback Machine, providing free access to the ten billion web pages gathered primarily as "data donations."[46] The name "Wayback Machine" became colloquially interchangeable with the IA itself.[47] For twenty years the machine amassed web materials from virtual spider bots that crawled the web and captured momentary versions of individual websites. In September 2018 the IA contained over thirty petabytes of content, including four million audio files, four million videos and images, eleven million books and texts, and a hundred thousand software items.[48] The Wayback Machine itself makes available more than 338 billion web captures.[49] It is an archive of the digital commons and a project of expertise.

A visit to the IA home page (archive.org) begins simply with six categories represented in the top left-hand corner with small pictorial icons: a computer screen representing web materials, an open book representing text, a snippet of film representing video, a loudspeaker representing audio, a floppy disc representing software, and two overlaid photographs representing image. In their design, shape, and size, the icons match the company logo that appears elsewhere on the screen, a stylized basilica in black and white. The six categorical icons appear again at the center of the home page, there in color and with the added categories of television and concerts. At the center top of the IA home page is the whimsical logo of the Wayback Machine, accompanied by a text field, beckoning visitors to search the internet. If a visit to the IA site may be thought of as a sequential activity, the process is to this point elementary. What the archive contains is made to seem simply available, a given mass of accessible information.

In pursuit of its motto, "Universal Access to All Knowledge," the IA is a massive collection of collections. It is affiliated with such notable institutions as the Prelinger Archive of films, Project Gutenberg, and the Biodiversity Heritage Library. The digitized materials of the IA are presented in a nested fashion. Under the heading "image" a visitor finds both a single picture from an individual musician's album cover and an entire collection titled the "Cover Art Archive." The video category contains the "television news archive," a collection of "feature films," "news and public affairs" (containing over three hundred thousand items), and a ten-minute video from 1953 on the importance of posture. The audio label opens to a set of collections including "Old Time Radio," "Cairo Public Radio," and "WUVT-FM," a "freeform broadcast radio station located in Blacksburg, Virginia, serving Blacksburg and Montgomery County, Virginia." The smaller collections contain individual items, such as episodes of the radio drama "*Yours Truly, Johnny Dollar*" included in the collection "Old Time Radio." The classification system of the holdings is cross-referenced, which makes topical navigation feasible. The nested content, however, makes an overall grasp of the organizational hierarchy elusive. The home page is at once enticing and overwhelming. The impression of what the archive holds is crafted less for instruction than display; the archive tells the visitor "Look how much we have! You can have it all!" rather than "Let me show you how to find what you are looking for." The gift of the archival expertise is a resounding "Tada!" rather than a methodical tutorial.

The Genius's Gift and the Gift of Stuff

In chronicles about the Internet Archive, Kahle figures as an eccentric visionary whose magnanimity facilitated his transition from entrepreneurship to philanthropy. His story is familiar in the world of technology start-ups: Having made a quick fortune in the 1990s, he directed his energies toward the greater good.⁵⁰ The gifting *logos* as embodied by Kahle is, put simply, that technical knowledge (of computer science, programming, and data management) produces a thing (a machine) that Kahle gives to the commons. "It is not about driving slick cars," Kahle claims. "It's about using this technology for the betterment of education and people. I'll take that any day over random stock option grants."⁵¹ When asked whether the IA would consider moving its storage to a cloud model, a blogging staff member emphasizes the long-term perspective required for public service: "Because we are charged with the permanent preservation of data, we are also cautious about entering into any arrangement where a change of funding (or of service provider governance) might result in accounts being summarily closed and data being destroyed."⁵² The emphasis on preservation in the staffers' response indicates that the stuff of Kahle's genius must be curated as a public trust. In a 2009 *Washington Post* article in which Kahle compares his digitizing initiative to the Google Book delivery system, he presents the IA as infinitely nobler: "Broad access is the greatest promise of our digital age. Giving control over such access to one company, no matter how clever or popular, is a danger to principles we hold dear: free speech, open access to knowledge and universal education. [...] We are very close to having universal access to all knowledge. Let's not stumble now."⁵³ Knowledge and education, Kahle suggests, must be given to everyone.

Parsed more finely, the gifting logos organizes not only Kahle's gift to the commons in the form of a machine but also the machine's gift to the commons in the form of the past, or the stuff of the past. The stuff of the past contains within it the knowledge of those who produced the stuff *and* the potential for the knowledge that present-day interpreters might make as a result of interpretation. The Wayback Machine "offer[s] permanent access for researchers, historians, scholars, people with disabilities, and the general public" to digital collections and archived web material.⁵⁴ Popular commentaries elaborate: "The purpose of the Wayback Machine is to copy and store the Internet [...] so any curious browser can use the data for historical research or to study the evolution of the Web."⁵⁵ In discourses by and about the Wayback Machine, the machine delivers digital materials that were invented in the past. An engagement with those materials, just as with materials in traditional archives, potentially renders knowledge about the context in which they were originally produced. The materials themselves, nevertheless, exist in the present, stored on San Francisco hard drives, as do the insights that an interpreter might produce about them. Put another way, the knowing that is made of and about the retrieved web documents is a hermeneutic making that tasks the present-day retrievers, not the original web designers from, say, 1997. The latters' epistemic task is already completed, and its results are imprinted in the web materials that they have left behind. The Wayback Machine hands over the stuff of the past that it has made by capturing a live event, a web artifact, when it was taking place. And as it does, more stuff is made in the recipients' processes of knowing.

The term "*stuff*," referencing one part of the triadic aggregate of the digital commons (the humans, the resources, and the network), continues in this chapter to be useful for my analysis. Regarding archival expertise, moreover, it is especially significant that scholars recognize archives of stuff as comparable to archives of documents for the purposes of historiography. Simply put, it is instructive to imagine the digital bits that constitute an archive like Kahle's alongside the dusty heirlooms that may be found in a trunk or a basement. Kahle claims, "The problem with the internet is not that there's too much information out there, it's that there's not enough good stuff. We are looking to radically increase the amount of material on the web."[56] Notably, the content of the IA is almost always referenced in terms of its byte size, or quantity for processing. When asked in 2002 by an interviewer, "How much stuff do you have here?," Kahle replied, "In the Wayback Machine, currently there are 10 billion Web pages, collected over five years. That amounts to 100 terabytes, which is 100 million megabytes. [...] It's the largest database ever built."[57] Another commentator puts it rather unceremoniously: "The Internet Archive is just a library. It just happens to be a library that mostly is composed of bits."[58] Bits, or stuff, fill the archive of the digital commons. The bits are measured and managed en masse. An IA staff blogger, describing the process of storing web captures on computer hard drives, boasts, "We can do fun stats. We now know [that] the web weighs 26,500 pounds, the average web page weighs 80 micrograms, and 160 joules per query."[59] The IA delivers (gives) a product (stored cultural knowledge made into digital stuff) by the pound.

One of Kahle's anecdotes about the origins of the IA reveals how archiving the digital commons, not unlike the fifteenth-century Venetian commercial privileges for use of the screw press (to print text and to make olive oil), is fundamentally about making stuff.[60] He recalls:

> I was standing there, looking at this machine that was the size of five or six Coke machines, and there was an 'aha moment' that said, "'You can do everything.'" [...] Every two months, the Wayback Machine downloads and stores every Web page it can put its virtual hands on—that is, every public Web page on every public Web site.[61]

The machine in Kahle's story is a hard drive storage container, comparable to a soft drink dispenser. He envisions how such a machine manages soda just as a digital archive might manage artifacts. That the artifacts are capsules of experience and interpretation (indeed, of knowing) is elided in the juxtaposition. Within the gifting logos, the knowing and making that happen archivally—the cultural artifacts that reify knowledge and are stored in an archive—result first and foremost in stuff. To this point, the digital archive of the commons is similar to a brick-and-mortar archive. Stuff is not unique to the digital commons. What is significant in terms of the qualities and functions of expertise is the ubiquitous emphasis on quantification, standardized in the byte format of data.

In discourses about the IA and the Wayback Machine, the reproductivity of the gifting logos is a source of great pride. The staff emphasizes that it is a good thing that the gifting logos is so prolifically productive. Those who access the IA and comment on its blog frequently announce that they, too, want to participate in expanding the archive. One commentator writes, "I have 65–70 academic technology books to donate. How do I go about this?"[62] The IA's blogger responds, "We appreciate donations. You can bring them or send them to Internet Archive, 300 Funston, San Francisco, CA 94118." The spirit of donation upon which the language of the blog is predicated facilitates quantitative increase. Under the "About" section of the IA blog, a commentator named Berry Kessinger extends the following offer:

> I have recorded & restored thousands of 78s from the 1920s & early 1930[s], mostly the mainstream jazz of that era. Most are from 78 collections I have bought & sold, and others are from files shared with me by others. I have spent thousands of hours on this over the past 5 years. I have more than 4,000 songs on more than 150 CDs, and an alphabetized catelog [sic] (by artist). I would be happy to share them with you, if you are interested.[63]

The offer receives the following reply: "To Berry Kessinger; yes, PLEASE post your collection! I am not affiliated in any way with internet archive, but I think the uploading process is fairly straight forward. There are instructions somewhere on the site. Sounds like you have some real classics and it's very kind of you to be willing to share them." In this exchange, Kessinger becomes a philanthropic jazz archivist. The gifting logos constructs him vis-à-vis his collection of stuff as an expert. Moreover, his collection becomes proof of jazz music's past such that it may be donated to the commons. Berry and his new friend convene on the node of the collection, mutually intelligible via the logos.

What Is It All For? And How Far Away Is History?

When analyzing the IA, the question of purpose is almost irresistible. The sheer quantity of stuff, much of which would be excluded from a traditional archive for lack of enduring value, presses one to ask, What is all this for? Who is going to use what parts of the massive collections, and why? What is the point? And yet, as urgent and tempting as this line of thought appears to be, it is misleading. Most responses would lead to half-satisfying insights regarding the cultural rather than individual search for origins and truths. And one is reminded of Derrida's diagnosis of our feverish impulse to seek possession of the past. According to Steedman:

> To want to go to the Archive may be a specialist and minority desire (only a Historian's desire after all), but it is emblematic of a modern way of being in the world

nevertheless, expressive of the more general fever to know and to have the past. Wanting the past may be attributed to certain turns of thought by which individual narratives of growth and development (particularly narratives of childhood) have become components of what we understand a modern self to be.[64]

The question, "What's the point?" prompts little more than a premature conclusion. To manage the temptation to ask, I propose that we must first pause upon the insight that the IA is indeed there, that its integration of what is known, what is made, and what is gifted is a practice of the digital commons. Only after this first realization are we ready to investigate the documented uses of the IA and the Wayback Machine.

In terms of the predominant uses of materials in the IA and especially the Wayback Machine, an ambivalence is discernible. On the one hand, digital archiving promises to serve the same romanticized functions as a traditional archive; on the other hand, most news stories about the Wayback Machine's utility are about forensic evidence. Importantly, both motifs rely on the notion of a gift from the machine to the commons. The romanticism of the IA is notable, for example, in frequent references to the ancient Library at Alexandria, after which the Amazon Alexa retrieval technology was named, and which is quite evidently a guiding light in Kahle's vision. In interviews, Kahle frequently mentions the Alexandrian collection as a yardstick for his own success. He describes enthusiastically how the Greek and Egyptian collectors sought to gather one copy of every book in existence, housing all literary items of value to humanity in one place.[65] With twenty-first-century technology, the IA can pursue the great Hellenic ideal of preservation with the added layer of storage redundancy. Indeed, a collaboration between the IA and the modern-day New Library at Alexandria enables duplication of content to minimize the risk of loss.[66] In the event that the California archive burns to the ground, the machines in Alexandria ensure that the data remains. In short, the relationship between the IA and the Library at Alexandria is characterized by both nostalgia and technological proceduralism as risk management.

Emphasizing preservation as the archive's principal function, Kahle and his colleagues describe how the task that they have undertaken not only serves the greater good, but does so while extending their gift into the future. Kahle explains:

> A professor at UC Berkeley said that students use the Web as the resource of first resort, which is a huge change. But that's a little dangerous if the Web doesn't have the good stuff on it, and many people complain it doesn't. Instead of trying to whip students to go back to the physical library, let's put the good stuff on the Net. [. . .] Students [are] using not the best we have to offer and that is a tragedy. We are the establishment. We should be making tools that allow children and students to have access to it all. And we're letting them down so far.[67]

In this account, the IA's objective is to continue the noble tradition of an "open society," which "public and philanthropic enterprises have supported [. . .] through the ages."[68] In the story of this open society as told by Kahle, future generations' welfare depends on archival expertise. The quality of expertise must be carefully safeguarded. It must be managed rightly by those who can fend off technology's threats while placing knowledge on technologically sound pathways to the commons. The IA's generational preservation, which echoes that of brick-and-mortar archives, enforces the perennial hope that archived material will make the past meaningful for the future.

Beyond the romance of preservation, the Wayback Machine regularly serves a forensic function, as previously noted. Media coverage of the technology reports that in a series of cases involving intellectual property, legal researchers generated incriminating evidence by retrieving past versions of web pages. For example, instances of "cyber-squatting"—sly entrepreneurs who buy a domain name associated with a major brand in order to sell it to its rightful owner—have been prosecuted using evidence from the Wayback Machine. The machine contains what in court has been received as objective proof of a moment when criminal activity left a trace. When computer manufacturer Dell sued the group responsible for the website DellComputersSuck.com, its legal team relied on archived pages captured from the delinquent site. After being contacted by the Dell corporation's attorneys, the accused party quickly attempted to convert the website into a discussion group, removing the original content. To make the case that it ought to be allowed to seize the domain name, Dell argued that the brand had been used "in bad faith," a claim that was supported by evidence from the WayBack Machine.[69] In a more conspiratorial case following the crash of Malaysian Airlines flight MH17, the Wayback Machine logged a social media post by Serbian separatist Igor Girkin (known as Strelkov) on the Russian site VKontakte. The post, which said simply, "We just downed a plane," was quickly removed, only to be rediscovered in a snapshot archived in the Wayback Machine. From there it was analyzed by the United Nations Security Council. The IA announced its heroic contribution to the forensic discovery with the Facebook post: "Here's why we exist."[70]

In legal contexts, the Wayback Machine's gift of archival expertise is a material truth. It is interpreted and framed as such by those involved with the IA, as well as by those involved with law enforcement offline. The machine delivers key materials that confirm that in a past moment an event happened. Of this event, textual traces exist. The gifting logos makes evidence, specifically the objects of evidence, or evidence that is objective. Worth noting in discourses about this evidence and its retrieval is the subtext of a triumphant "Gotcha!" With this revelatory function, the downfall of criminals is their own folly. Those who assume that the digital activities of the past are lost in some ethereal cyberspace are justly punished when their wicked deeds inevitably come to light. Someone is watching. More to the point, someone is archiving; someone *knows*. That knowledge is retrievable, which is to say *givable*, as a result of what the Wayback Machine *makes*. The machine gives evidence to the court, and to the commons it gives the satisfaction of knowing that even digital things eventually come to light.

Serving not only lawyers but also data scientists, the Wayback Machine supplies web researchers with a large-scale information source.[71] The IA staff enthusiastically explains: "Historians, sociologists, and journalists could use Internet libraries to hold up a mirror to society. For example, they might ask when different ethnic groups or special interests or certain businesses became a presence on the Internet."[72] Polishing this mirror, the IA suggests, web scholars access the Wayback Machine to collect and study data on topics that in the present moment are culturally and politically managed primarily online. Research that uses the Wayback Machine, in other words, could analyze, for example, how race and class have figured in online news coverage between 2000 and 2016; how climate change has been discussed by ordinary citizens in online forums over the past two decades; or the chronological evolution and economic significance of so-called "mom blogs." A web scholar interested in the relationship between graphic design and online commerce might trace the layouts of major shopping sites (eBay, Amazon, Zappos) over time. This tracing of what is ostensibly gone is possible via the materials of the Wayback Machine. In the aforementioned instances the Wayback Machine delivers the past. Worth noting, however, is that the past in these cases is not too far removed. The machine is not traveling far or, indeed, "way back." What, one wonders, is the difference then between a digital archive and a data set when it comes to expertise?

In common usage, a distinction between an archive and a data set may do little more than orient various sciences to one another. A historian studying suffragist activity in the nineteenth century might seek out an archive from the League of Women Voters; the archive would contain pamphlets, posters, recruitment lists, meeting minutes, and so on. A scientist researching voter registration campaigns during the 2012 and 2016 presidential elections would develop a data set. Given the importance of web-based communication during those elections, however, the data set would be faulty if it contained only materials from traditional media. The political scientist would be remiss not to examine activities and materials online. And for this she or he would need an archive, specifically a web archive. To this point, the terms "*archive*" and "*data set*" match a scholar's designated time frame. What makes the distinction chafe, and what supplies a rhetorical opportunity for the IA and Wayback Machine to play with the ambiguity of function, is captured by the notion of "web historian." The Wayback Machine *archive* gives researchers concerned with the *recent* past a *data set*. In a traditional sense, however, history isn't history until it is experienced as remote. And how remote is 1996, the year when Kahle's bots began collecting snapshots? What sense does it make, then, to address users of the Wayback Machine as "time travelers," as Kahle does? Does the machine in fact "*give* the general public easy and meaningful access to our collective *history*"?[73]

Resources for responding to these questions may be found in the combination of common sense and presentism that characterizes expertise in the digital commons. As I noted in the introduction, the digital commons convenes in the now. Websites such as wallstreetjournal.com and realsimple.com engage readers by delivering expertise in the present. The information of the former is time sensitive because it is news, and the instructions of the latter (including how to decorate cookies) do not need a past. Once the cookies are done, the information is useless. The *Wall Street Journal*, of course, has a history, and its history is enmeshed with the history of the nation. For this reason, a hard copy of the newspaper is filed daily, cataloged, and preserved by professional librarians in brick-and-mortar libraries. The prospect of applying the same archival process to the newspaper's website is complicated by a number of factors (the compression of information, the continuous change of content, the translation of content between online and offline versions, etc.).[74] In the midst of this, the Wayback Machine presents itself as a response to the pervasive cultural attitude that habits and texts in the digital commons do not have enduring value and do not merit preservation. The machine insists on archiving content that by most standards is ephemeral or even trivial, including and especially from the early years of the World Wide Web. The IA steps in, activates rhetorically the mythos of historiography and preservation, and defines digital stuff as amounting not only to data sets, but to an archive. The gifting *logos* makes into history that which happened only recently, pressing into its bits certain value. It places knowing into a diachronology, a sense-making structure oriented toward time.

The purpose of cultural preservation on the one hand, and the purposes of forensic and social sciences on the other, share a commitment to truth. In reference to each, expertise as a gifting logos delivers what may be known as true. The legal researcher who discovers evidence of web-based infractions presents them to a judge or jury, saying, "This is proof that the accused committed a crime. This is what really happened!" Expertise becomes the bureaucracy's currency of authenticated fact. And in an alignment of motives, the same approach to authenticity is reflected in comments about the Wayback Machine's historical significance, made by those who speak more about enduring cultural value than about sufficient evidence. Those who truly believe in the importance of preservation treat the historical artifacts of the web as they would the relics of any other civilization. They say to the commons, "This is what the site really looked like on this date. This is what really happened!" As an archive, the machine provides access to what the web "really was" in its promising infancy.[75] Thus, there is allure to an archival search for authentic history, even if the history is not so far away. Expertise is the logos through which the past is given to those who seek truth. For the paralegals who focus on evidence and for the romantics who focus on cultural preservation, the Wayback Machine *makes* the past real. It *gives* knowledge of human activity to the present.

Copia: Productive Retrieval

Just as the teleology of the Creative Commons in chapter 2 is motivated by copious productivity, measured and displayed in graphs, so too is the IA's emphasis on *copia*, the abundant production and accumulation of cultural material. With this emphasis, the logos of expertise—that is, the language, habit, and sense of how knowing lives productively—is massive. Aggregating en masse, it measures itself in quantity: "Founded in 1996, the Internet Archive has an historical web collection (the Wayback Machine) of over 150 billion web pages, about 240,000 movies, over 500,000 audio items (including over 70,000 live concerts), over 1,800,000 texts, 1600 education items, and over 30,000 software items. And we're growing bigger every day!"[76] Quantifiable growth is here an indicator of progress, frequently presented with comparative figures. Kahle remarks in interviews that the IA's holdings are several times larger than the twenty million books in the Library of Congress.[77] In such comparisons, the IA and the Wayback Machine are great because they are massive. The logos attaches expertise to *copia*. And the exuberance that permeates the status of aggregating mass is seemingly contagious.[78]

The reproductive functions of the Wayback Machine and its participants' excitement over cumulative mass function as a kind of recruitment call. The IA issues a call to the digital commons for participants in the making of archival expertise. The IA and the Wayback Machine present their audience with multiple ways of contributing to the enterprise. For example, one of the Wayback Machine's most popular features is the "Save Page Now" function, which allows the instant creation of a permanent URL, stored in the Wayback Machine.[79] The person who saves the page becomes in effect a temporary IA staff member, directing the technology's capture of web materials toward a specific site in a specific moment. With this directive, a web page is permanently stored, and more material for the Wayback Machine is generated. The archival action reflects a value judgment on the part of the person making the directive. Something that he or she knows about the world leads him or her to make of the page a permanent, curated artifact. In the moment when he or she chooses to "Save Page Now," expertise of assessment is gifted to the IA. The person who creates a new record in the Wayback Machine is contributing free labor to the archival commons.[80]

Another participatory feature that facilitates the growth of the IA is the Archive-It initiative. Launched in 2006, the purpose of Archive-It is to supply basic tools of digital archiving to individuals and groups whose collections operate individually and as part of the IA's collections. In this way, "the Internet Archive hopes to democratize knowledge by *giving* global communities the ability to save, manage and share their cultural treasures for free."[81] "Democratized knowledge," or the expertise produced in the digital commons, is thus an effect of commoners' use of the IA's tools for archiving. These tools assume by design and distribution that the expertise of the commons is a cultural treasure. The Archive-It technology was "developed in response to the needs of libraries, archives, historical societies, museums, and other organizations who sought to use the same powerful technology behind the Wayback Machine to curate their own web archives."[82] In many cases, users of the Archive-It technology have specialized knowledge of curatorial procedures and experience with archiving in a traditional context. They are archivists in a different sense than the staff of the IA, giving their expertise to their own projects directly and to the IA indirectly.

Via the Archive-It initiative, the archival commons multiply (in members as well as in content) almost organically. As a writer for the *Guardian* notes, the IA functions less as a library and more "like the Svalbard Global Seed Vault, an underground Arctic cavern built to shelter backup copies of the world's food-crop seeds."[83] With seeds, crops multiply, thereby fending off starvation and depletion of resources. To participate in the IA's initiatives is to sow the seeds of cultural survival so as to contribute to the archival commons. In this way, Archive-It is not only a mechanism for recruitment or a product of free labor; it is an infrastructural induction of digital commoners into the gifting logos. Thinking of it and the Creative Commons licenses together—which is both conceptually sound and a legal reality in many cases—as infrastructure reveals how the commoners are brought into contact with each other through production and, indeed, the gift of stuff. The stuff circulates for continuous regeneration (the CC) and is stored and curated as the commons' knowledge of itself (the IA).

In the archival commons, retrieval of expertise is a live event, a productive being-with the commons. That the retrieval is both live and productive makes Taylor's distinction between the archive and the repertoire instructive, particularly in reference to acts of gifting. As noted previously, Taylor argues that while an archive separates documents from their creator, a repertoire does not, relying instead on live epistemic performances. In Taylor's account, documents in an archive can be accessed (for example by a researcher) independently of the context in which they originated. The knowledge contained within the document outlives the knower in time and space. It is fixed beyond the reach of present-day hands. A repertoire, by contrast, "requires presence: people participate in the production and reproduction of knowledge by 'being there,' being a part of the transmission. As opposed to the supposedly stable objects in the archive, the actions that are the repertoire do not remain the same."[84] In a repertoire, embodied subjects engage in action directed toward a topic or a material; the repertoire is a form of knowing and transmission during which participants learn from each other and derive agency by manipulating the material at the center of the practice. Taylor's reading of the functions of an archive disallows this agency.

To be sure, it would be a stretch to map Taylor's distinction between the archive and the repertoire onto my own analysis with too much force, despite her multiple references to digital culture and its implications for digital archiving.[85] Nevertheless, her illuminating point is the emphasis on liveness and the productive agency of the repertoire's participants. For insofar as participants in the digital commons are present to each other through the network and act directly with the cultural stuff that the archive provides (in this case the IA and the Wayback Machine), theirs is a kind of agency that visitors to a traditional archive may not experience. The documents curated in a brick-and-mortar archive may not be susceptible to change, which is central to Taylor's understanding of the repertoire. But the materials in a digital archive exist in a form of constant manipulation. Digital configurations change continuously. Thus, to understand the productive dynamics of retrieval in the digital archive, we might think of how Taylor's repertoire centers on epistemic habits rather than epistemic materials. Digital stuff, as noted before, is usefully conceived as blurring the line between stuff and habit. Connected by the gifting logos, those who participate in the repertoire of the digital, archival commons practice productive retrieval.

An Archive or a Machine?

The functional synonymity of the names Internet Archive and the Wayback Machine may be instructively considered with reference to the concepts of *archive* and *machine* respectively. As an archive, the IA/Wayback Machine requires attentiveness to the issues raised in the "Archival Knowing" section of this chapter. It is imbricated in myths like the search for origins, a coherent narrative for an imagined community, a civic teleology, and a dialectical tension between the bureaucracy of files and the mysticism of buried treasure. On the other hand, as first and foremost a machine, the IA/Wayback Machine activates a different set of myths. It joins the ranks of other technological inventions that in their own times were enveloped with excitement, optimism, even thrilling uncertainty, or what Leo Marx calls the electrical sublime.[86] As with other sublime experiences, positive amazement is mixed with a sense that one is not entirely in control. In every historical moment, new technologies, particularly communication technologies, have been tagged by enthusiasts with the hope that improvements in the mechanics of human interaction would eliminate misunderstandings and lead to genuine engagement. The continuous dream is always, "This new machine will turn out to be the solution to our problems, delivering us into a better future!"[87] This attitude is always on a loop, celebrating the newest technology with which old shortcomings might be remedied.[88] As a machine, the IA/Wayback Machine is invested with force and utility. It serves its users, even though its force may at times exceed their control and expectations.

Reflecting this electrical sublime, vivid reports by journalists and industry leaders ascribe to the IA machine an almost animate force.[89] In the reports, the machine empowers users to wield its potential, but as with other sublime phenomena, excess itself exceeds the wielding.[90] The machine threatens to thwart human control, even as it was built to serve human masters. Describing her visit to the IA's California headquarters and conversations with Kahle, the *New Yorker*'s Jill Lepore tells the familiar story of Kahle as a mad scientist. One can almost hear Colin Clive demonically shouting, "It's alive! It's alive!" as Lepore writes:

> Three towers of computers stand within each niche, and ten computers are stacked in each tower: black, rectangular, and humming. There are towers like this all over the building; these are only six of them. [. . .] Up close, they're noisy. It's mainly fans, cooling the machines. At first, the noise was a problem: a library is supposed to be quiet. Kahle had soundproofing built into the walls. Each unit has a yellow and a green light, glowing steadily: power indicators. Then, there are blue lights, flickering. [. . .] He smiles as he watches. "They're glowing books!" He waves his arms. "They glow when they're being read!" The machine hums and is muffled. It is sacred and profane. It is eradicable and unbearable. And it glows, against the dark.[91]

When the emphasis is on the machine rather than the archive, the IA/Wayback Machine comes alive. It is aglow with mysterious and only partially realized potential. It illuminates the dark dystopia in which, "without cultural artifacts, civilization has no memory and no mechanism to learn from its successes and failures."[92] In the glow of the machine, humans are safe from a future of ignorance.

The name Wayback Machine, an homage to the cartoon *Rocky and Bullwinkle*, makes reference to time travel, specifically the technology that would enable it. In the children's television program, the character Dr. Knowitall invents a transportation machine (the WABAC) that reveals "the real side of what we thought was history."[93] And indeed the fantasy of time travel reverberates in commentaries by the IA's staff. An IA blog post from 2010 addresses an audience of "fellow time travelers," announcing, "For those who have yet to travel back in time, the Internet Archive Wayback Machine allows you to browse through over 150 billion web pages archived from 1996 to a few months ago."[94] Users agree that the Wayback Machine allows "a seeker of information" to "go way back, to the dawn of the World Wide Web."[95] A reporter notes, "Clicking on an old site is like time travel. I visited a December 1996 issue of Web Review (webreview.com) and found a cover story on 'Christmas Cookies' [. . .] and an article dismissing privacy concerns about the new-fangled Web technology."[96] The Wayback Machine is constructed in these reports as a machine rather than an archive, specifically a machine that transports its users to another time.[97]

As with most time travel fantasies, the appeal of the trip is to reach and (re)experience origins of some kind. Describing the Wayback Machine's function, commentaries that praise Kahle's gift to the commons are nostalgic: "The year is 1996. The Web is a strange and wonderful place, full of promise and potential. The buzzword of the day is dot.com. Most of us have never even heard of a dot. bomb. Oh, those were the days."[98] A writer from *Newsweek* magazine narrates, "Once upon a time on the web, novelty abounded. [. . .] Now you can relive those unjaded days and browse the entire history of the amazing World Wide Web."[99] In these accounts, the Wayback Machine moves wistful travelers to a time and place that was "quaint and refreshingly simple."[100] It belongs in a genre of time travel stories that rather formulaically move a contemporary protagonist into the past so that he or she may, through a series of complications, fix what is wrong with the present. Put another way, time travel stories center on a hero's discovery of the solution to present-day troubles. The past is the hero's resource. The implication of the nostalgia is that, if we could access a bygone time, we might restore the web's potential. This, of course, is Kahle's ambition and his project's gift to the commons. He gives the gift of time travel so that the commons might set itself right.

Although the notion of a time travel machine is intelligible in digital culture insofar as it conflates time and space—in digital networks, out of sight and in the past are both descriptions of the inaccessible—it is clunky. Such a machine seems cartoonesque and conjures the image of nineteenth-century transportation mechanics and the aesthetics of the "Age of Steam."[101] This aesthetic is implied both by the way in which the Wayback Machine itself is animated (as just described) and in how the project is oriented toward larger cultural structures, such as exploration and, indeed, archiving. In a telling analogy, the dean of libraries at the University of Michigan equates "what the archive does for the internet with what the British Museum did for the British empire."[102] This comparison is instructive, perhaps not despite but because of its implications. The dean's remarks bespeak an empire that travels the world in a machine (a boat or a plane), conquering cultures and collecting artifacts. The British Empire took thousands of cultural artifacts from their creators and placed them in the British Museum to glorify Britain. In the museum, the artifacts were preserved for posterity; the conquerors and/as curators positioned themselves as rescuing culture from the more "primitive" contexts in which the artifacts would surely be ruined. It would be strange to take Dean Courant's analogy to its logical extension and claim that the Wayback Machine steals cultural artifacts from their creators. Nevertheless, the gifting logos of archival curation imposes a certain order. It frames how the things that are made (cultural artifacts), which contain what is known (the experiences and interpretations of particular agents in particular places), are made accessible as a gift. When the gifter constructs the material as a gift (the content of the British Museum or the holdings of web materials in the IA), this gesture not only invents the material in a certain way but obligates the commoners, to whom the gift is imparted, to orient themselves toward the material accordingly. Specifically, what is given to them cannot be conceived of as theirs already. The stuff that the machine took and then gave has been altered, and its relationship to creators has been transposed.

As I have explained, the Wayback Machine may be read as at once an archive and a machine, specifically a machine of productive retrieval and transportation in time/space. Therefore, notwithstanding the *Rocky and Bullwinkle* reference, I propose that another pop culture story better illustrates the gifting logos of the Wayback Machine: *Monsters Inc.*, an animated film about a company town in which the central industry is a "scare factory." From the factory floor, monsters enter the bedrooms of little children and frighten them to produce hair-raising shrieks. The children's screams are collected in tanks that supply the town of Monstropolis with something reminiscent of nuclear power. The relevant aspect of the film is the method by which the monsters enter the children's rooms: the scare factory has a storage facility full of bedroom doors, each one suspended from a conveyor belt. A single door is retrieved on demand, and by walking through it, a monster is transported through the liminal boundary. In the case of the Wayback Machine, the gifting logos, particularly the notion of productive retrieval, may be understood via *Monsters Inc.* as a making of doors. Put simply, the answer to the question, "What does the Wayback Machine *make*?" is "Doors!"[103] Its gift is the encounter, and the encounter must be built. While the analogy is not perfect, the insight of door making is worth what may seem like a silly detour. The Wayback Machine does not travel back in time, nor does it transport anyone anywhere. Rather, it supplies on-demand access points that were made, or captured, a priori.[104] The notion of discovering the past, a leading motif in IA discourses, bridges the lore of archives and machines.

Archival Delivery and Disposition

In terms of the pentadic rhetorical canon (invention, arrangement, style, memory, and delivery), the IA overwhelmingly prioritizes delivery over arrangement. Delivery is itself the majority of the IA's archival practice. Here we must think of delivery both as in "delivering a speech" and as in "delivering a pizza," because the issue is one of performance as well as supply.[105] As the visitor to the IA site develops an impression of the archival model, that impression is principally of mass storage (as opposed to disposition or selectivity). As one user notes, "I love the Internet Archive! It is a wonderful resource [...]. However, at times I find it a bit chaotic. It is hard to find the really good stuff among all the noise."[106] The IA, proverbially put, delivers. In part, the emphasis on delivery rather than arrangement (or selective ordering) is connected to digital archives' relative freedom from physical containment. In a brick-and-mortar archive, space and the resources to manage materials are finite. There is only so much room in a building, and there are only so many archivists to curate. In creating the order of a coherent message, selections must be made, and selections necessarily depend on judgments, which in turn depend on assessments of value, prudence, audience, and so forth.[107] The IA, although constrained by the space and resources required for hard drive storage, is significantly less limited by the size of its holdings physically. It has the capacity to deliver content to visitors faster and in larger quantities than a traditional archive.[108] For digital commons utopianists, this means a democratization of the archive whereby nothing is excluded. No elitist curator with horn-rimmed glasses gets to separate the wheat from the chaff. For the skeptics, it means that the archival commons become a storehouse of chaff, the junk stuff that no one threw away. Regardless of one's assessment of the digital archive's prerogative to forego exclusion, rapid and copious delivery creates certain complexities of order and access.

Coping with the potentially overwhelming excess of the archive, the IA site relies on a system by which visitors select categories, collections, and individual items with icons, thumbnail images, and hyperlinks. As noted in my discussion of the icons, the system begins with the basics but gives advanced users the option of more complicated search methods. From a programming perspective, a digital archive is necessarily underwritten by algorithmic order; an IA staff member might say that what seems like a data dump, or delivery of material in bulk, is in fact just as indexed, cataloged, and organized as any traditional archival system. In digital archives, order is mathematical.[109] That there is an archival code refutes the indictment against the IA that materials are delivered without meaningful order. Simply put, an IA programmer might insist that there can be order even when almost nothing is excluded. In the archival commons, inclusion and access are integral to the gifting logos, setting the terms of the rhetorical management of expertise.

For instance, discourses about access to the IA and the Wayback Machine's materials return again and again to the issue of a full-text keyword search function. Both regular and novice users on the blog repeatedly ask the IA staff when the entire collection will be made more easily searchable. Simply put, users express a desire to employ the IA and the Wayback Machine as they would a search engine like Google.[110] When "to Google" is used as a predicate, it references an information retrieval process that requires some, but not significantly specialized, competence. Google does not require that a seeker of information specify anything other than a topic found inside the digital text. By contrast, searching the Wayback Machine, like searching a traditional archive, requires that users specify metadata, or information *about* the archived item, rather than its internal content. A staff member explains: "Site Search for the Wayback Machine will help you find the homepages of sites, based on words people have used to describe those sites, as opposed to words that appear on pages from sites."[111] This means not only that access to the Wayback Machine's content requires procedural expertise (comparable to the kind a traditional researcher needs to use an archive's catalog), but also that structure within the machine is generated by the user. In the process of indexical retrieval, users invent order among the items delivered by the machine. The machine is responsible for delivery, while users are responsible for disposition or, in the terminology of archiving, provenance.[112]

That the structure of the IA is topical rather than analytical, in keeping with the emphasis on delivery rather than disposition, demands attention to the difference between order and access. Specifically, the distinction is between order and access as epistemic processes, organizing what is known and accessing what is known. For orientation, let us assume that a person delivering a speech needs analytical knowledge, while a person delivering a pizza needs topical knowledge; a traditional archivist curates an archive with analytical knowledge and a digital archivist manages a digital archive with topical knowledge. To be clear, there is nothing inherently deficient about pizza or a digital archive. Topical knowledge is invaluable to the digital commons, both infrastructurally and archivally. Indeed, the code that supports the IA embeds order, topically organizing massive amounts of material. But even with the code, which is perhaps intelligible only to some, access to the materials is hardly simple. It is difficult for a member of the digital commons to get a *sense* of the archive, establishing how its projects fit together and how relevant information might be located. As scholars note regarding brick-and-mortar archives, access is complicated. It requires resources, skill, and persistence. You have to know whom to speak with, how to ask the right questions, and where to hang your raincoat so as not to unnerve the archivists. You have to know that records of records are not the same thing as the records themselves; discovering an index of correspondence does not mean that you will be able to read the letters themselves. Archival research in the traditional sense is done within a tension between the ideal of transparent access—inspired by the modern idea that a people must have access to its history—and the notion of finding something hidden, what Lewis Gaillet calls the "holy grail moment."[113] Structure may be put in place to facilitate access, but access in a full sense depends on more than order.

The trouble with massive delivery and deep access is rhetorically significant considering the language (or logos) of the given. When the IA gives the commons what appears like a world of culture, the giving buckles under its own mass. Mari Lee Mifsud theorizes that the gift, or that which functions as a given, must be *haplous*, self-evident, requiring no explanation. The knowledge and expertise that are transmitted generationally (in her case the Greeks' wisdom passed down in Homeric nuggets) are *haplous*.[114] They are culturally assumed premises: the given. "Simple," of course, is here both a misnomer and an overstatement. The simplicity of the IA motto, "Universal Access to All Knowledge," is presented as a self-evident good, which obscures how not-simple the processes of delivery and access are. Mifsud explains that a gift is *haplous* when it speaks for itself. The *given* is that which is *taken* for granted, circulating in the commons for everyone to access. Access, nevertheless, is more demanding as a habit than Kahle and his staff acknowledge. It reveals how expertise as a logos is layered; access to one kind of knowing always requires another kind. The members of the digital commons, as the IA discussion forums reveal, actively search for the right access point into the archive. They do so against the pressure of quantity and in a coordinated effort to maintain the logos of the gift. That the IA is a gift to the commons is a myth that requires maintenance, especially regarding access. Or, to deploy the explicit terminology of gifting, knowing how to receive requires as much symbolic competence as knowing how to give.

That the IA/Wayback Machine's gifting logos is directed more toward copious delivery than disposition, and that targeted access is difficult, create an environment conducive to archival flânerie, or a kind of ludic, inventive posture. The figure of the flâneur, animated by Charles Baudelaire's *poesis* and theorized by Walter Benjamin, is a carefree ambulant of the modern metropolis. He—or she, a flâneuse—wanders the crowded streets, "botanizing the asphalt" and sampling cultural habits and artifacts.[115] Without serious commitment, the flâneur moves through multiple ambiences, playfully constructing a lifestyle and/as a distraction, a remedy for boredom. The flâneur invents himself and his own story in a nonpermanent fashion from the cultural resources that he passes randomly.[116] He is aware of the dark edges of modern life and knows that the arcade's industrial luxury is a simulation or a façade. Coping with this awareness, the flâneur busies himself with stuff while pretending not to care too much. He protests the accelerated (re)production of contemporary popular culture with his "ostentatious nonchalance."[117]

The archive of the digital commons supplies commoners with the experience of flânerie. It offers a "sheer postmodern tourist archeology."[118] In this space, the flâneur discovers that the Wayback Machine "was designed as a gee-wiz interface to show people some of what the archive contains and hint at its possibilities, to catch interest."[119] What the flâneur encounters is "a browsing interface, a wow-isn't-this-cool interface."[120] As Kahle puts it, "It is fun to surf the past."[121] Historical research, he implies, does not have to be all that serious as long as the constructs of "expertise" and "method" are negotiable. Beyond the machine's affordances for entertainment, "it's come in handy for real-life purposes as well."[122] Touristic flânerie in the environment of web history is, in recurring commentaries, distinct from "real life." Flânerie through the past, the practice of browsing aimlessly through archived web captures, is an "unreal" or imaginary form of travel. In the street the flâneur meanders without an intended destination. In the digital archive he rides the time travel machine without the constraints of preset search tags. In a dual sense, then, the flâneur has all the time in the world.

When access to a digital archive is characterized as flânerie, it is possible to understand the gifting logos as amenable to impermanence. In a sense, knowing, making, and gifting are integrated even in the most traditional archive; traditional archives in the procedures of curation make knowledge of the past and give the public access to it. But in the digital archive, this process is continuous, reversible, playful, and networked. The productive practices of the digital archive, in other words, happen all the time, involving not just curators and researchers but any of the digital network's nodes and participants. For them, the repercussions of experimentation are mild. Theoretically, flânerie is a process of continuous self-fashioning onto the Teflon-like surface of an inessential self. The flâneur can change his mind at any time and reject the selections he has made. The subjectivity that he creates with a configuration of cultural artifacts is meant to be temporary. In the digital archive, a visitor is allowed to manipulate the collections directly because they are pliable and can always be restored. The retriever of data sits at home, removed from the digital archive's materials.[123] She is not accountable for them because her impact on them in the practice of access is limited. If she downloads fragments from several different collections in the IA and the Wayback Machine and makes them into something new, she is not spoiling the collections for anyone else.[124] Ramsey notes that this "lends to the collections a sense of informality as some of the strictures of researching within the archive are voided."[125] The consequences of productive access are negligible because an individual data retriever's impact on the data is reversible, and because the assumption is that flânerie by definition is not quite serious.

Loss, Time, and the Disappearance of Digital Stuff

In contrast to the attitude of the flâneur, who has all the time in the world, much discourse about the IA and the Wayback Machine bespeaks an awareness of loss and the urgent need to stop it. The archival project of the digital commons is to prevent the kind of loss that seems both inevitable and unmanageable. As an IA blogger notes, "The Internet is quite fleeting. [...] So if you want to have culture you can count on, you need to be able to refer to things."[126] The IA's self-definitional texts describe how it "is working to prevent the Internet—a new medium with major historical significance—and other 'born-digital' materials from disappearing into the past."[127] A blog text about memes, which the author defines as "successful transmission of culture," claims that "when you lose culture, you lose context and meaning to the words and thoughts that came before. The Wayback machine will be a part of ensuring they stick around for a long time to come."[128] In an interview with the *Los Angeles Times*, Kahle claims, "What happens to libraries is that they burn. And they get burned by governments. The Library of Congress was burned once; it was burned by the British. So let's design for it."[129] In these accounts, the IA gives to the commons the world's literary heritage in order to prevent the loss thereof; by the same token, its machine ensures that the cultural artifacts of the web do not "disappear into the past."

Popular press coverage echoes the idea that the IA/Wayback Machine's central function is preservation, specifically against imminent loss. A web journalist writes, "Whole chapters of our history which may only be documented on the Internet, may be lost."[130] Another agrees, "Wayback grabs [...] pieces of history before they disappear and puts them into a virtual Internet museum for historians, academics, and nostalgics to browse."[131] Here, the machine's archival work is done against the backdrop of the human and digital apocalypse. History is ending, but certain materials are "up for grabs." Such interpretations of the Wayback Machine's function are permeated by the notion that Kahle and his team in the early days of the web understood something that everyone else missed. Because they did, they began curating materials that the rest of us thought were valueless: "Information is fleeting. [...] Thankfully, someone is keeping track."[132] An essay in the *Economist* recounts how the original 1994 web version of the magazine was lost and then recovered, thanks to the Wayback Machine. The author writes, "Little thought has been given to recording information for posterity. The rapid turnover of content on the web has made total loss the norm."[133] With a muted sense of "Oops!" he quips, "So much for the idea that the internet never forgets. It does." The consensus in popular analyses of the Wayback Machine's service to the commons, its gift, is that archiving digital artifacts prevents loss of them and what they represent.

The ubiquitous language of the Wayback Machine's web page "snapshots" is indicative of its rhetorical reliance on urgency. Captured by a technology on the move (through the network), the snapshots are transported to the central machine, the archive. In its analog context, a snapshot by definition is a photograph taken in a hurried moment, a quick click based on a "snap" judgment. Such a photo depicts what someone wants to remember and fears forgetting, hurrying to preserve it before the moment passes. Hikers posing in front of the Grand Canyon must move along the trail. A hummingbird lingers in the air for mere seconds. Acute awareness of the quickly fleeting experience of seeing these events necessitates the production of a photographic snapshot. Because the moment is captured in a rush, the judgment itself to produce an artifact is not based on in-depth reflection. The tourist who takes a snapshot of the Eiffel Tower may not stop to think that she is reproducing a photo of which there already are millions of copies. A person who takes a snapshot of a tasty meal may not stop to ask whether the subject merits permanent evidence. In this sense, the snapshot metaphor is in keeping with the IA's orientation toward inclusivity over exclusivity, as previously discussed. A snapshot turns a quickly fleeting moment into archival material, making it knowable even as it fades. Only in this form can the moment be given to anyone, ever.

The urgency of the Wayback Machine's efforts is constructed specifically in relation to its restorative function. The machine fixes what is broken in the web, specifically "link rot," the common term for a hyperlink that no longer leads to the information intended. Link rot happens when web content is relocated or removed. Attempts to retrieve the content are met with the dreaded "404 message": "file not found." In response, the Wayback Machine establishes links to archived content. It produces material to cover a gap in what may be known. Its expertise is the making of material in the face of a disintegrating network; what *was* known is about to disappear, but the Wayback Machine makes a record of it. In some cases, IA explains, this is a productive practice of translation: "Internet libraries can change the content of the Internet from ephemera to enduring artifacts of our political and cultural lives."[134] Link rot is a sign of digital material's mortality, a condition that appears to transfer symbolically onto its human creators. A woman who lost a web project collaborator asks the IA staff for help: "Thanks for all you do but I would like to find out how I can access—successfully—a site which used to belong to my friend who died suddenly without leaving instructions for us Moderators to do something with the site afterwards. [. . .] Please help us, this really is a question of life and death."[135] The commentator's plea is a demand that the IA place its gift, its saved and curated material, in between her and a friend's death.

The kairos of the IA's gifting logos, the time sensibility of its rhetorical expertise, makes the future dependent on the continuous production of digital stuff, ensuring against disintegration. Kahle envisions his undertaking as part of a history of knowledge production that is tied to cultural being: "Knowledge lives in lots of different forms over time. [. . .] First it was in people's memories, then it was in manuscripts, then printed books, then microfilm, CD-ROMS, now on the digital internet. Each one of these generations is very important."[136] Elsewhere he claims, "I am not interested in building an empire. Our idea is to build the future."[137] Again, the Wayback Machine is Kahle's gift to the commons; the machine's gift is the past, or more accurately a door to the past. If, per Heidegger, being is a gifting event, then the gift as an event forecloses the imminent nonbeing of digital data. Preservation of data in the archival commons is a gift against data loss. Data must be thought of here as the material of what is known—data is what is made with what is known. It is the product of epistemic making. If being is a gifting event, then nonbeing is the risk or precarity that always threatens the gift. In the gifting logos, thus, the epistemic habits of the digital commons are productive because, as such, they keep nonbeing at bay.

CONCLUSION

In this chapter I have explicated the functions and characteristics of the gifting logos as expertise in the digital archival commons. As in chapter 2, I focused on the structure and significance of productive habits, the teleology of *copia*, and attunement to time. Perhaps the most prevalent among the functions I identify, whether the emphasis is on the construct of "archive" or "machine"—and the IA/

Wayback Machine deploys its dual character strategically—is delivery. Delivery, and its partner concept of access, are the ideals of the gifting logos in an archival context. In a basic sense, a traditional archive delivers artifacts to researchers and visitors; a machine, specifically a time travel machine, delivers an intrepid explorer to a distant destination. Whereto, then, does the Wayback Machine transport travelers?

My analysis suggests that the machine moves its users away from our present troubles and into a space where we become flâneurs. It supplies access to the past, delivering it to us—or us to it—in a way that does not demand analytical order, or what I refer to as rhetorical disposition. Unlike historiography in the brick-and-mortar archive, which relies ultimately on rigorous methodology, flânerie in the digital archive requires perusal. It must, because perusal is a reasonable and manageable response to *copia*. What we digital commoners are encouraged to do as we are confronted with massive amounts of stuff is browse. When the flâneur encounters the knowing, making, and gifting that constitute archival expertise, the machine says, "Here are the artifacts of your past. I have been collecting them and keeping them safe. Do with them what you will." The flâneur, who must never care too much, appreciates the opportunity to manipulate history just as he is accustomed to playfully manipulating other cultural artifacts. In the arcade as in the archive, he appreciates a gift with no strings attached.

Clashing with the nonchalance of the flâneur is the digital archive's unmistakable urgency. As I demonstrate in the analysis, Brewster Kahle and his team understand their project as preservative. The IA/Wayback Machine, to them, curates digitized objects and web documents in order to save them from being lost. In this account, history is a knowing and making that forecloses disappearance. The data retrieval that the machine performs is a productive knowing that keeps oblivion and obsolescence at bay. The Wayback Machine produces proof of life, or proof that the digital commons has in toto generated something beyond utilitarian exchanges. (Recall my introductory mention of bus routes and school board meetings.) As I explain in this chapter, the presentism of the web requires that we, for the sake of peace of mind, take stock, assuring ourselves that the technologies that we rely on every day are more than advanced vacuum cleaners. A vacuum cleaner has no past; the floors always get dusty again. And a continuously updated website is continuously disappearing. But the archive/machine contains snapshot proof that the web has a past, and that with it the digital commons has produced something cultural. It replaces lost time with preserved stuff.

In what is perhaps the most beautiful reading of Heraclitus's logos, Heidegger proposes that we seek a definition of the term by considering how "to lay" (*legein* in Greek) comes to mean "saying and talking."[138] Approaching this matter, which "probably decides many things," he demonstrates that to lay things down is to arrange them in proximity and relation to each other. To lay down is not to toss willy-nilly, just as saying something is not the same as making noise. Rather, "to lay is to gather." As he then notes that "gathering is more than amassing," he turns attention to the laying procedure as curatorial: "To gathering belongs a collecting which brings under shelter." Further, the act of placing something in shelter demands a selection, "arranging everything involved in the bringing together, the bringing under shelter."[139] Thus, against the simple convention of understanding logos as word, Heidegger translates the Heraclitean logos as "the Laying that gathers," to which he attributes a "revealing-concealing character."[140] And with this reading of Heraclitus, he locates logos as essentially archival, the principle of archiving and the principal gesture that selects and arranges archived objects. Steedman picks this up when she describes the archive as "wanting things that are put together, collected, collated, named in lists and indices; a place where a whole world, a social order, may be imagined."[141] This is the archival function of the gifting logos as expertise; the Laying that gathers is wrapped up rhetorically as a gift and bestowed upon the digital commons.

4

The Popular Commons

Compared to the quotidian life of the commons, the appeal of pirate lore is the *un*common. It is the call of the sea, enticing us to believe that somewhere out there an uncommon life awaits those who are bold enough to seek it. To be a pirate in the narration of Robert Louis Stevenson or the action adventures of Johnny Depp as Captain Jack Sparrow is to shirk the drudgery of terra firma. And if the prospect of a "pirate's life for me" is sufficiently compelling, the commoner sets sail for the open ocean, challenging the authorities that dictate propriety. A pirate takes up arms against a sea of injustices, or least against the social norms that constrain his or her adventures. He or she seeks an alternative future when the old ways of life on land have become inadequate. Piracy is thus an irresistible rejection of established power. It is a regime of violently self-interested but possibly egalitarian governance. This brazen rejection is what connects the robberies of the Caribbean in the late seventeenth century with the unauthorized literary culture of the Western frontier in the mid-nineteenth century and the open access movements of the late twentieth century.[1] Piracy as an idea provides commoners with the audacious prospect of an indeterminate future. It says, "Whatever you get your hands on rightfully belongs to you. All treasure to the commons!"

During the 2006 parliamentary election in Sweden, piracy turned into a political movement. In early January, the not-yet-official Pirate Party, led by Rick Falkvinge, launched a small website outlining a series of six campaign strategies, the first of which was to collect two thousand supporter signatures to qualify for candidacy in the election. The Swedish financial newspaper *Dagens Industri* published a story about the party, which was picked up in the days following by other Swedish and international media outlets. In its first week the Pirate Party collected five thousand signatures, and the website received millions of hits. A few months later, the party drew another wave of media attention when the Swedish police raided the facilities of The Pirate Bay, an online index of peer-to-peer file-sharing. The police seized multiple internet servers belonging to The Pirate Bay and to the Pirate Bureau (Piratbyrån), the anticopyright organization that founded The Pirate Bay in 2003. And although The Pirate Bay did not itself host or distribute proprietary content, but rather functioned as a search engine for so-called BitTorrent files, the organization was charged with multiple copyright violations. The charges outraged the Swedish public, whose subsequent commentary focused on the entertainment industry's influence over police interventions. As the news media reported on the story, the Pirate Party's membership doubled in three days. Mass demonstrations were held in major cities around the country. Nine months after its founding, the Pirate Party received nearly thirty-five thousand votes in the Swedish national election, becoming the largest party without representation in Riksdagen, the parliament.[2]

Between 2006 and 2009 the Swedish Pirate Party grew slowly but steadily, keeping its advocacy focused on the issues of the initial campaign. When the trial of The Pirate Bay concluded on April 17, 2009, and the website founders were sentenced to heavy fines and a year in prison, the Pirate Party harnessed the public's interest in intellectual property rights and the prospect of an open access society. Thousands of new members registered within hours of the verdict. It was no surprise, then, that in the June election for the European Parliament, the Pirate Party received over 7 percent of the Swedish vote, earning one seat for candidate Christian Engström.[3] This upswing did not carry into the national election of 2010, however, when the party once again missed the 4 percent mark for a parliamentary seat. Seemingly undeterred, the party presently persists in an international network of pirate politicians.

This chapter is a study of a political organization, born of the digital commons, and more significant a study of the political entailments of the gifting logos. The driving question, simply put, is, What are the politics of expertise in the digital commons? The Pirate Party illustrates the development of a grassroots party out of an informal online community primarily concerned with file sharing. As a movement, the Pirate Party connects commitment to digital stuff—here, as in previous chapters, stuff like music, imagery, and software plays an important role—with an articulation of a program for the common good. Such an articulation is definitive of political discourse. For my study of this articulation in the digital commons, Sweden offers an especially instructive case because of the deep-seated tradition of *Allemansrätten*, which literally translates to "all men's right" or "every man's right," or more idiomatically, "the right of common access." *Allemansrätten* is sanctioned by Sweden's constitution, requiring that "everyone shall have access to nature," regardless of private property boundaries.[4] In effect, *Allemansrätten* is a habituated custom of free movement and recreational activity; any activity that causes no harm to the ecosystems of land and shoreline is a common right. For the Pirate Party, the idea of access to nature translates rhetorically to a claim about access to culture. Its "Program of Principles" demands an "*Allemansrätt* for knowledge and culture, [which would] benefit society's development as a whole."[5] To be sure, the Pirate Party in Sweden is not the first to link natural and cultural commons for the purpose of advocacy. Scholars and activists alike have turned to the intersection of ecological and cultural ideals of what belongs to all. Quite significantly, however, a rhetorical gesture toward an *Allemansrätt* to culture has special resonance with a Swedish audience. Access, and the shared ownership of resources in which all have an interest, imply legal and ethical duties that Swedes generally accept.

The purpose of this chapter is to examine a political organization that made open access a central issue in a national election and, in so doing, explicate the political significance of the gifting logos. When studying the politics of the gifting logos—that is, studying how the integrated rhetorical acts of making, knowing, and gifting have political impact—it is initially instructive to split the notion of a "given" into two meanings and to draw on a classical understanding of rhetorical tropes. Most basically, a political given is the civic equivalent of business as usual. As noted in previous chapters, a cultural given is that which is beyond question, requiring no explanation. Similarly, the political circumstances that dictate ordinary life are "a given" to the extent that they are taken for granted. To say that politics is a "given" is to note that certain procedures and hierarchies endure generationally. Those who are charged with maintaining the procedures pass the task on to their successors. The political given stabilizes potential instability, ensuring continuity. Against this continuity of the given, those who are exploited by the dominant regime may resist. When Benjamin Arditi characterizes emancipatory agitation as dependent on the disruption of "the given," he is describing a condition and set of institutions as prior to politics.[6] To Jacques Rancière, "Political intervals are created by dividing a condition from itself"; in this condition, identities are defined "in a set place in a given world."[7] In short, the given world is the politics of the status quo. When Rancière distinguishes between the status quo, which he names the "politics of policing," and the politics that ruptures the given order, he instructively demonstrates the important link between the given and the *arche*, an institution of origin.[8]

A second meaning of "the given" in a political context is the act of "giving sense"; we typically refer to this as *making* sense. This is an interpretative gesture wherein the gift contains the substance of what may be known. This meaning of the political *given* is the focus of the chapter. By definition, certain critical events are marked by fearful confusion, or unknowing. They are moments of uncertainty and instability in which an individual agent or movement offers (gives) a concept (or a cluster of concepts unified as a platform) so as to establish social order. The giving here is made of tentative intelligibility. A gap has appeared in the social structure, and an action or utterance puts in place a construct that fills the gap. The construct patches a hole of uncertainty in the political fabric. Imagine a subversive guerrilla group that stages a coup, burns a government building to the ground, and then steps up to the smoldering podium, announcing, "This is who we are, this is what's best for everyone, and here's what's going to happen now!" In this event, the construct that is given responds to the absence of constructs that was caused by the disruption. Politics, then, is a giving of a construct. This giving presumes that a construct was made, and in the process of making, knowing and interpretation were to some degree solidified. Knowing, making, and giving are integrated as a political act. Most important, the construct contains a notion of the common good. It identifies a path toward life and happiness charted by the giver of the construct.

Both of these ideas—the given as status quo and the given as a construct delivered in a crisis—are relevant for investigating the politics of the gifting logos. The reason it is prudent for my purposes to approach them as a dialectic is that they depend on one another. The tension between them sustains them. Any status quo that keeps the life of the commons stable and its institutions intact eventually gets disturbed by political activity. Disorientation ensues. A crisis prompts questions of identity and purpose. Purpose is about judgment of value. "Who are we?" the commoners wonder. "What is good for us? What must we do to ensure order and prosperity?" In the exigence of this ambiguity, a construct is given by a person or group with a political agenda. The construct names the group or movement, the people whom the group hopes to lead and represent, and a program for realizing the common good.

It is imperative in this book, which draws on the gifting logos to study expertise, to examine how the political impact of the given relates to what may be known in and about the digital commons. For the opposite of "the given" is not "the taken" but the strange. Both of the aforementioned versions of how the given relates to political structures are based on what is commonly *known* and how interventions are *made*. Whether the given is the status quo or a particular construct, it is predicated on how things are interpreted and understood. That is, it is implicated with expertise in situated moments. And expertise integrates, as I argue, knowing and the production of stuff, including political stuff like a policy or a party platform. To analyze the given, the familiar, and the strange, it is helpful to turn to rhetorical tropes. Tropes, as commonplaces, simultaneously comprise the given wisdom of a community and the ways in which the assumptions (the taken for granteds) of that wisdom are twisted so as to generate new perspectives, arguments, and insights. The reader might imagine the Talking Heads singing "Same as it ever was," mashed up with the Byrds' "Turn Turn Turn." Tropes are stable and predictable, yet profoundly responsive to rhetorical manipulation. This is why they are so potent. In Aristotle's typology of the *koinoi topoi*, tropes come together in a system of *doxa*, a cultural given from which arguments may be generated. Within that familiar system, however, tropes are constantly employed for persuasion in a way that entails strategic disturbance. The person who uses a trope to make an argument relies on the tension between what is well known by the audience and what is not yet known, or even what is potentially shocking. A number of examples from political discourse may be invoked here. The disturbance of a trope makes (invents) new knowledge. Tropes are the disruption of the given through which new interpretations and knowledge are invented.

This third case study of the gifting logos as expertise builds on the previous two, and differs somewhat from them. In chapter 2, expertise is circulated and regulated via the infrastructure of the Creative Commons licenses. In chapter 3, expertise is archived and accessed via the Wayback Machine and the Internet Archive. In the present chapter, expertise functions as a political program wherein the Pirate Party literally *makes* itself *known* to the commons, presenting itself to the Swedish electorate. The rhetorical practices by which it does so are the object of my analysis. I am concerned with how the party invents a political construct that is, in a word, givable. Noting that an instability of tropes, an instability of what is familiar, generates an exigence for interpretation, I ask, What does the Pirate Party tell its audience about itself, about what its politics are, and about how a healthy polity functions? What is the character of the political construct that the Pirate Party gives to the commons, wherein its plan for the 'political destiny of the commons are contained? What, according to the Pirate Party's platform, is the common good? In this chapter the question of expertise in the digital commons is not only, What is entailed in the knowing and making of something?, but also, What is entailed in the making of an interpretive construct about the common good in a political context?

My analysis in this chapter covers several sets of the Pirate Party's public messages, including (1) the party "manifestos" (*valmanifest*) from the 2006 and 2010 Swedish general elections; (2) online articles and web content wherein party representatives comment on intellectual property controversies, important events like the raid on The Pirate Bay, and political victories like the 2009 European Parliament election; and (3) the party's "Program of Principles," articulated initially in January 2006 and updated in June 2009, April 2010, and April 2017. In both national election campaigns, the party organized its manifesto into distinct parts referred to as *sjökort*, which means sea-card, or a nautical map used for navigation. Keeping with the marine metaphor, each page of the map is imprinted with a compass watermark. The 2006 manifesto contains three maps in one fifteen-page document: one is for personal privacy (*skyddat privatliv*), one is for copyright and culture (*upphovsrätt och kultur*), and one is for patents and knowledge (*patent och kunskap*). In the 2010 campaign, which followed the upswing of securing representation in the European Parliament, each of the three maps is its own ten-page document: knowledge (*kunskap*), culture (*kultur*), and integrity (*integritet*). Through these texts I trace the Pirate Party's rhetorical efforts to introduce its political agenda, define its exigence, and designate a future of prosperity for the commons.

In order to contextualize the political discourses of the Pirate Party, I approach it as a populist movement. Two features of the party justify this approach. First, the Pirate Party presents itself and its agenda as antagonistic to "the establishment," a term that it attaches to both the Swedish government and the international entertainment media industry. Second, the Pirate Party is populist in its media aesthetic, which carries an irreverent and somewhat "folksy" tone, particularly in critiques of the aforementioned establishments. Given the scope of my book, it is important to note that populism is not the only conceivable political orientation for the digital commons, nor even for the commons more generally. Furthermore, the gifting logos is in theory ideologically agnostic. As a rhetoric of expertise, it may be deployed by advocates for any ideology. Neither the digital commons nor the gifting logos is populist by necessity or definition. Yet as a function of certain historical, economic, and technological circumstances, populism has gained momentum in the digital commons in the early twenty-first century; the gifting logos is both a rhetorical resource in that momentum and an analytical means of studying its impact. As the next section reflects, I approach the Pirate Party as populist less with reference to the organization's time and place and more for its rhetorical character. The goal of the introduction I offer in the following pages is not to retheorize populism through a digital lens. Instead, my intent is to survey in brief the features of populist rhetoric in a way that highlights issues of recurring significance.

DIGITAL POPULISM: A RHETORICAL APPROACH

As noted in most treatments of populism, the term is difficult to define. The questions "What does it seek?," "How does it work?," "Where does it happen?," and "Who carries its banners?" lead to such different case studies that a general theory is elusive. The difficulty arises from historical variation and the tension between descriptive and prescriptive definitions. Definitions by content, which attempt to establish that certain political movements are populist because they advocate for "the people," are hamstrung by the challenge of demonstrating how populists' advocacy for "the people" is distinct from nonpopulists' advocacy for "the people." The distinction is fraught because a great deal of political advocacy contains a promise to serve the people's interests. Further, if populism emerges only under certain circumstances in time and place, such as in an agrarian society, then it may be difficult to locate in western European and North American politics at present. If only those political movements that explicitly self-identify as populist may be legitimately classified as such, then the analytical utility of the term may be undermined (excluding, for example, the study of US neoconservativism). If populism is defined empirically with reference to the characteristics of particular groups, then the possibility of new populist forms is undercut, along with the prospect of analyzing those forms.

Taking a rhetorical approach to populism, this chapter posits that populists may be identified as such when they wield populist discourses. These constitutive and instrumental practices exceed any particular ideology or party. First, populist rhetoric is characterized by antagonism between the powerful who exploit and the powerless who are exploited. As populist agitators intensify this antagonism, their various grievances and objectives congeal, forming a subjectifying agenda, or what Ernesto Laclau calls an "equivalential chain of unsatisfied demands."[9] I return to Laclau later in this section. Second, and as part of the congealing process, populist rhetoric is organized around the articulation of a political identity. This identity, which forms in tandem with the congealed cluster of unmet demands, has a sense of purpose drawn from a mythical origin and a sense of destiny for the future. Third, populist rhetoric reflects a theory of representation that sustains its political agenda; in this context, representation is a dual term. It refers both to a representative system of government and to a language through which the identity and objectives of a people may be conveyed, or indeed represented. I discuss each of these aspects of rhetorical populism in the following subsections.

A Rhetoric of Antagonism

Populist movements gain momentum from the rhetorical practices of antagonism, the maintenance of an oppositional tension. This tension endows the project of populism with purpose, organizing problems and strategies along a frontier. Historically, the battle line separates (and connects) a noble peasantry and a rising capitalist industry. In imperial Russia and nineteenth-century US agrarian territories, perhaps the two most commonly referenced examples of populism, antagonism arose in response to the experience of exploitative infringement.[10] Both movements were inspired by the idea that small-scale farmers were called to the grand destiny of defending their way of life, in which "one is in touch with the underworld of dead ancestors, the actual maternal earth, and all is under the divine sky."[11] In so doing, according to the populist myth, the virtuous people would seize its own political agency, wresting power from the hands of the oppressor. Political efficacy within the framework of populism, in other words, is measured by the people's destined struggle against whatever is understood as not-the-people. This antagonism posits that the goodness of the people must face off with the evil of an elite, the specific constitution of which varies. The discourse of populism needs a villain, just as a story about pirates needs the British Navy and the East India Trading Company.

Populist antagonism emerges when a sufficient portion of the governed believe that governing institutions have become inadequate or corrupt. General frustration and a hostile disenchantment with politicians and political parties spread. These experiences are intensified by the perception that the existing political and social order is imploding. A vocal segment of the population begins to argue publicly that the political process itself excludes the people, that a party structure determines ideology rather than facilitates pluralism, and that the incompetence of political leaders is matched by their malevolence toward constituents.[12] In such circumstances, populist movements oppose dominant parties, not primarily by critiquing specific policies but by accusing politicians of failing to represent the *volonté générale*, the general will of the people.[13] Such accusations rely on the *volonté générale* as a trope, the turning of which plays on what is thoroughly familiar—the general will sounds quite close to something like common sense—and what lies beyond the knowledge or insight of politicians. For while the failure of representation is frustrating, it is not as severe in populist discourses as the more fundamental failure on the part of political leaders to *understand* the general will. In the Rousseauian tradition, the will of the people is sacred, and anyone who wields power must be keenly attuned to it. Without this attunement, accountability falters. The inability of the elite to respect the general will is a symptom of moral oblivion, a detachment from the basic virtues of the simple people.

Populist discourses that identify political party structures as opposed to the interests and character of the people similarly denounce other institutions. They insist that the people are constrained not only by the ineptitude of politicians but also by administrative and corporate bureaucracies. In the network of established powers, the good people are trapped. Their capacity to flourish independently and realize their full potential is stunted.[14] Without politicians, bureaucrats, and big business, so goes the populist argument, the people's will would prevail.[15] It would serve as a corrective to special interests. On this point, the moralism of a simple people that elites cannot understand coincides with the ideal of small-scale producerism, especially insofar as intermediary institutions constrain the free flow of creativity that produces authentic and useful things. The producerist ideal distinguishes those who make things from those who do not and ascribes to the former superior morality. In the history of populist discourse, the makers are farmers and craftsmen, laboring with their hands to produce wealth in tangible form.[16] They sustain life on the farm and in the workshop, resisting urban and industrial forces. The nonmakers are the useless and virtueless agents of institutions that suppress the people.

For my purposes, the endurance of the producerist ideal within populist discourses is notable in a postindustrial context. Twenty-first-century digital populists like the Pirate Party are quite obviously different from nineteenth-century farmers and craftsmen. They are in general educated urbanists, neither simple in lifestyle nor especially grounded in a rural setting. Yet as I demonstrate in this chapter, their scornful rejection of political and bureaucratic establishments echoes that of their rhetorical counterparts from another era. Their language sketches an image of the small-scale digital artisan, virtuous as a function of productivity, plucking away in humble quarters. In this transhistorical image, the kerosene lamplight glows as gently over hands on a keyboard as it once did over hands on a wooden workbench. It keeps the artisan in the comforting knowledge not only that he or she is laboring to make something authentic, but that doing so is an act of defiance.[17] In the producerist ethic, to make something authentic is a political activity; in the making itself, precious experience and knowledge are wrought. The next section of the chapter indicates that, just as the cottage industry of the nineteenth century was characterized by populists as courageously defying a growing mass industry, so do twenty-first-century digital populists imply that their small but mighty inventions struggle against movie studios and record labels.[18] In the political program of digital populists, the people's productivity must be brought into the sphere of policy-making. There it must be articulated by a nonpolitician, an outsider who understands the value of the people's experience and creativity.[19]

Despite the resentment that infuses populist antagonism, optimism endures. It thrives on populists' fundamental conviction that although politicians and bureaucrats are incompetent, even potentially "demonic," the people will eventually prevail.[20] They will shirk the artifice of conventional leadership, topple the institutions of the elite, and set up a new political order. This is an order that "existed in the past and which the errors and misdeeds of the political class, trade unions, public bureaucrats, big business and high finance have disrupted."[21] In the new (yet traditionalist) order, those who govern will be incorporated with the governed. What Richard Hofstadter calls an "effective assault" on the enemy will, according to populist teleology, usher in a political form in which the people's will and best interests are served by representatives who understand them.[22] This righteous reckoning is meant to be; nevertheless, it must be hard won. Populist rhetoric thus circulates a "politics of faith," wherein the primary objective of all organized efforts is the improvement of the human condition.[23] In this effort, nothing must be held back, and a "lack of enthusiasm will be considered a crime, to be prevented by education and to be punished as treason."[24] As Margaret Canovan writes, populist politics "has the revivalist flavor of a movement, powered by the enthusiasm that draws normally unpolitical people into the political arena."[25] As a faithful political program, populism demands intense loyalty. Populist rhetoric is designed to convince adversaries and allies alike that its politics serve the common good and, moreover, that a better world is not only possible but inevitable.

Articulation of the People

One of the most important functions of populist rhetoric is to articulate "the people," to *make* the people socially and politically intelligible. This entails a pseudo-mythic presentation through symbols of what the people are like. In keeping with the antagonism outlined in the preceding subsection, symbols of the people's character and purpose function dichotomously, distinguishing the people from various villains: politicians, bureaucrats, corporate stooges, and "foreign financiers."[26] Regardless of the right- or left-leaning ideology of the populists who invoke it, the myth of the people tends to highlight essential goodness. "The people" are inherently virtuous, possess a transcendent knowledge of the world they inhabit, live in harmony with that world, and endure through the superficial flux of what comes and goes. Populist discourses couple this virtue with systemic victimization, implying an innocent people afflicted by powerful leaders' misdeeds and confined by circumstances beyond their control.[27] The people are caught in a predicament, an unnatural condition of unrealized potential. Religious imagery is common in representations of the people, as it accounts for the past and the future of a utopian origin and an ordained destiny.[28] In accordance with a divine plan, the people persist and prosper despite their enemies.

Populist discourses articulate the people by associating the mythic place of the past with a promised land of the future, which may be either a return or a new Edenic discovery. Having defeated their enemies, the people establish an organic community (gemeinschaft) beyond formal society and its problems.[29] For my purposes, this emphasis on an alternative space wherein the people's sovereignty is realized connects the rhetorics of digital populism with more traditional forms. Historically, the people's place and populism's origin are, as most commentaries note, a farm. Farmers organized politically in the nineteenth century against the impact of industrialization. More than just a plot of land, then, the people's place in the populist imaginary is a community of farmers living *with* land that is alive. The aliveness of the land is the responsibility of those who cultivate it. The community is, as Hofstadter notes, ecumenical, admitting and making room for newcomers, as long as they adhere to certain norms.[30] The members of the community are embedded in a network with one another and the land through which they produce things. This is the constitution of life, according to traditional populism. Likewise, in the digital context populist idealism invents a space that must be actively maintained. The space is open, or accessible, and transcends the limits of modernity such as national borders and political institutions. Underdogs and iconoclasts are free to assume leadership roles in an ebb and flow that is determined by the community. And just as the idea of the farm is more than a literal farm, digital populism's ideal place is less a place than a site. A network of virtual sites, like the farmland network, connects people in ways that facilitate productivity. The people's ingenuity thrives without rigid and clueless bosses, administrators, or politicians. Thus, digital populists articulate "the people" as a community with reference to an idealized space.

The notion that populist discourses articulate the people must be understood as distinct from the institution and idea of representation. Articulation in a political context, as Ernesto Laclau explains, entails a particular kind of rhetorical invention, a "social productivity of a name."[31] To simplify Laclau's theory: it is not the case that a group of individuals convenes around a set of problems or action items upon which they agree, and that this group then is called populist by others or even by its members. Instead, what precedes the recognizable group is "an equivalential chain of unsatisfied demands."[32] A relation is established among claims to various unmet needs (for clean water, reliable infrastructure, safe neighborhoods, social services and public education, etc.); that relation congeals into a "stable system of signification."[33] The needs come first, and the political group and its recognition of itself as such come second. The system of signification, which may for illustration be thought of as a political program, generates a popular identity, which is more than the sum total of the needs and demands.[34] Based on the earlier explanation of tropes as inventing new insights from familiar resources, we might say that the stable system of signification has fixed certain meanings for political ends and in so doing has articulated a position. Rather famously, Laclau conflates populism with politics by definition: "If populism consists in postulating a radical alternative within the communitarian space, a choice at the crossroads on which the future of a *given* society hinges, does not populism become synonymous with politics? The answer can only be affirmative."[35]

Laclau's approach to political articulation, and to populism in particular, is instructive in this chapter as he emphasizes the gift of a name. In Laclau's work, naming is a rhetorical act of giving wherein what is given is actionable intelligibility. He demonstrates that the makeup of "the people" depends on both antagonism (against whatever elites are identified as not-the-people) and equivalence (among needs and demands). This makeup is not only a process of invention but also a giving. If political terms are empty until they are filled by "a particular set of circumstances in history" then, "the construction of 'the people' will be the attempt to *give* a name to that absent fullness."[36] In the tumult of conflicting demands that characterizes any polis, those who name a set of unified demands name an agenda; those who name an agenda name a party. The naming action, which entails sensemaking of the tumult and incorporation of the agents involved, is inventive. It interpretatively stabilizes chaos, and produces a program for what comes next. Thus, giving a name to a political platform is an epistemic and inaugural activity. Francisco Panizza writes, disentangling populism from any left- or right-wing ideology, that antagonism is "a mode of identification in which the relation between its form (the people as signifier) and its content (the people as signified) is *given* by the very process of naming—that is, of establishing who the enemies of the people (and therefore the people itself) are."[37] Where Laclau explains how the articulation of "the people" is the gift of a name that proceeds from concatenated demands, I submit that the gifting logos's political implications for the digital commons become evident.

With some adaptation of Laclau's theory, it is instructive to think of populist discourses as at once prescriptive and descriptive of the people—that is, of the political agents that populist agitators strive to mobilize. Populist discourses function at once constitutively and representatively. While this is hardly a revelation in the context of political language, nor does it distinguish populists from other political groups, the duality is significant in my analysis of the gifting logos's political impact. Political discourses operate in a fecund terrain between, on one side, descriptions of what the people are like and what they want, and on the other side, prescriptions of what "the people" ought to be like and what future they ought to pursue. The descriptive aspect is proof that a political candidate understands the people. The prescriptive aspect indicates that an "imperfection marked by urgency" exists, and that something could be other than what it is.[38] In this indeterminate space, a political program is rhetorically invented and submitted to an audience. This rhetorical invention is conducted through the gifting logos, fusing knowing, making, and giving. Digital populists (such as the Pirate Party) ascend a literal or figurative podium, hoist their party program, and say to voters, "Here is the construct we have created to give to you. It captures who we think you are, and what we believe is sound policy for the common good. Pending your approval, we are ready to assume power as your representatives."

Representation: Governing Symbols

Representative government is based on the idea that elected spokespersons bring forth the voice of the people, specifically the people who chose them. This arrangement assumes that elected representatives understand those on whose behalf they speak, are capable of giving voice to others' preferences, and are intent on voicing those preferences with as much fidelity as possible. In other words, representation is partly about ability and partly about an ethical contract. Populist discourses make representation an issue in the antagonism they generate against established political powers. They reject politicians and political parties partly on the grounds that they cannot and do not speak for the people. Moreover, populists argue, representation cannot function as long as the people have limited access to their representatives. At the same time, populists use representation as an argument for populist leaders. The leaders purportedly can and do speak for the people because they are consubstantial with them.[39] They represent the people in institutions of government without actually becoming absorbed or corrupted by those institutions. The authenticity with which they speak for the people is resistant to governmental proceduralism. As Arditi explains, "Populists distrust representation as a corruption of the general will and see themselves less as representatives than as simple placeholders or spokespeople for the 'common man.'"[40] Populist leaders claim to serve representative functions as personified symbols of a collective experience.

The question of whether a political representative can speak on others' behalf may be extended to a question of symbolic representation generally. There, in the realm of signification, the question is not whether politicians can be trusted to represent the people's will, but whether a sign can be trusted to correspond to a referent. And thus the populist skepticism toward elected representatives provides a political reason to be concerned with signification. If the symbol system that governing elites rely on to make "the people" intelligible actually misrepresents the people's experience—and populists argue that it always does—representation is troubled in multiple ways.[41] Even if the symbol system is made by the people themselves, it is limited. This is an epistemic matter insofar as naming something reflects an attempt at knowing it. Symbols enact judgments of interpretation. A politician cannot have a notion of his or her constituents and their world without making certain interpretive efforts. These efforts make a thing, a construct of "the voters" or "the citizens" or "the people." Further, signification is not only an epistemic matter but relatedly a matter of control, which again marks the realm of the political. In constructing a symbol that validates certain experiences while eliminating others, the symbol maker exercises power. As I explain in chapter 3 with reference to archival expertise, institutional knowledge is authoritative. Representation, in short, imposes definitive and existential limits on what is represented.

Although the connection between deconstructive language philosophy and the erosion of representative government in the late twentieth century is interesting and important, it is not of primary concern here. Rather, my focus is on instability and uncertainty as such, specifically when these conditions are strategically engendered by political power seekers. The "crisis of representation" in which Panizza locates the emergence of populism is about a pervasive loss of confidence.[42] He demonstrates how populist discourses become viable during "changes at the level of the economy, culture and society, such as processes of urbanization and economic modernisation, shifts in the demographic balance between social classes, and between regional and ethnic groups, as well as, more recently, globalization."[43] The digital populists that I analyze in this chapter ascended politically amid the changes that Panizza lists. Their persuasion depended on widespread uncertainty not only about representative government but also about symbols and meaning fundamentally. Economic and cultural uncertainty provided them with an opportunity to run for elected office, but more important, they circulated political discourses that defined the terms of a particular condition. Their emergence illustrates how the gifting logos exerts political influence by creating and supplying—making and giving—a bit of knowability when such a thing is in short supply. When the structures that had long been taken for granted became unstable, the gifting logos intervened, giving a construct of the common good. It offered a (party) platform to stand on, a political remedy for ambiguity. As I note in the introduction, the opposite of the given is not "the taken" but "the strange." In the early 2000s, Sweden's political moment was culturally strange.

Swedish Populism and Party Politics

For decades after the Second World War, Sweden was a steady-as-she-goes social democratic welfare state. During the upheaval of the 1970s and 1980s, and as a result of constitutional reform in the early 1970s, new political groups formed, disrupting the party blocs of the Swedish parliament.[44] These "challenger parties" aggressively opposed traditional government and the bureaucratic state.[45] They were openly critical, drawing momentum from a surge of public disenchantment. In the 1991 national election, the Social Democratic Party lost its sixty-year dominance, receiving only 38 percent of the popular vote. In its place, a coalition of four centrist and bourgeoise parties formed: the Moderate Party, the Center Party, the Liberal People's Party, and the Christian Democratic Society Party. The coalition drained support from the social democratic base.[46] As Dennis Westlind writes, "The dealignment of working class voters from their traditional party combined with instability and change within the other traditional parties led to a 'window of opportunity' for new parties."[47] Still, the coalition fell four seats short of the parliamentary majority, making it reliant on the recently formed and rather unorthodox New Democracy (Ny Demokrati), Sweden's first right-wing populist party. In a context of uncertainty, as Arditi explains, voters responded to "charismatic leaders who present[ed] themselves as self-styled saviors."[48]

The public discourse of New Democracy must be mentioned in this chapter because it contextualizes, even portends, the eventual emergence of digital populists like the Pirate Party. From its inception as an unlikely candidate for parliament, New Democracy's media strategy focused on a few tactics: enthusiastic support for market deregulation and carnivalesque antagonism toward the political establishment.[49] This was perhaps the first time that the Swedish electorate saw an irreverently critical minority party levy a serious challenge against the familiar political order. Throughout the 1990s and early 2000s, various peripheral challenger parties arose, including the neo-Nazi and neofascist Sweden Democrats, which doubled its share of the electoral vote between 2002 and 2006.[50] But the early 1990s populist discourses of New Democracy were, compared to the Sweden Democrats, less hostile than impertinent and less belligerent than silly.[51] They provided an alternative not only in content (a new political candidate) but in form, embracing the appeal of spectacle. Westlind summarizes New Democracy's syllogistic advocacy for political representation:

"[T]he current political system is boring. People want fun, New Democracy is fun, therefore New Democracy represents the people."[52] New Democracy parodied and ridiculed politicians and bureaucrats, accusing them of obstructing the people's freedom. In effect, the party ridiculed voters who would consent to what it denounced as antiquated welfare paternalism.

The feature of New Democracy's antagonism that most directly foreshadows the Pirate Party is the emphasis on outsidership. New Democracy was originally spearheaded by an odd couple that shrewdly branded itself as an internal clash: "the duke and the butler" (*greven och betjänten*).[53] Ian Wachtmeister was a prominent businessman with aristocratic heritage; Bert Karlsson, who owned a middle-class amusement facility, was known for his vulgar appearance and comportment. For these charismatic figures, distancing the party from conventional politics was a matter of media comedy. They advertised themselves to the electorate as different from the dysfunctional leadership of stale politicians. That they had little experience with either politics or government reinforced the argument they performed, that the political system was defunct.[54] Gianfranco Pasquino explains, "Populist leaders promise that they will get rid of traditional politics as soon as possible, although they do not explain which kind of new politics they will construct, other than to say that the leader will be fully accessible to the people."[55] Wachtmeister and Karlsson enacted a conspicuous contrast to Swedish politics as usual. Under their leadership New Democracy succeeded for a few years in convincing many that "the duke and the butler" would provide better political representation than experienced politicians.

Populism, as Peter Worsley argues, may be more appropriately characterized as a dimension of political culture than as a particular party or group.[56] This is an instructive posture to assume in examining how and at what moments the digital commons engenders a political movement. Populism may be seen as a political dimension of the digital commons. It is a useful term with which to study what happens when members of the digital commons act rhetorically on their political imagination and do so both on- and offline. The Pirate Party, although it failed as a candidate for the Swedish parliament in 2006 and again in 2010, persists. Its platform, its construct of the common good, resonates with the commoners for whom it is designed. For many, it makes sense, which is to say it has epistemic validity and political potency in the everyday life of the digital commoners. As the party learned several times over, a national parliamentary election may or may not register this resonance in terms of votes. Regardless, the Pirate Party at its peak in 2009 was Sweden's third largest party by membership. Beyond Sweden, around thirty Pirate Parties have formed internationally, coordinated by Pirate Party International. In the textual analysis that follows, my focus is less on the Pirate Party's electoral success than on its rhetorical inventions. The questions driving my inquiry are, How does the Pirate Party articulate itself, its politics, and its vision of a healthy polity? With what words and images does it offer the commons a political destiny?

PIRATE POLITICS AND THE GIFTING LOGOS

The Pirate Party's rhetorical priority as a newcomer in 2006 was to define its central cause as a legitimate political issue. The party had to demonstrate publicly that its agenda was distinguishable from The Pirate Bay, the Pirate Bureau, and other online file-sharing communities. To establish political legitimacy, the party needed to publicly define file sharing as relevant beyond free music downloads—indeed, as a matter of popular freedom from regulatory overreach. Following the Pirate Bay police raid, parliamentary candidate Mika Sjöman announced, "The police pulled the plug not only on the servers that distribute completely legal so-called torrent-files, but also on the political organization the Pirate Bureau, which is independent of The Pirate Bay, a political organization that is trying to affect how the established parties address these issues in the election of 2006."[57] The suppressed premise of Sjöman's claim is that a political issue was literally taken offline and policed out of public debate. He accuses an established authority of interfering with a surging political agenda. In the same article, Sjöman places file sharing at the center of a historic moment: "With the possibilities of file-sharing, we have today a fantastic chance to give everyone social citizenship, that is, general access to a modern version of a public library."[58] The 2006 election manifesto echoes his assessment: "File-sharing is something positive for society and for citizens. [...] Today the Internet serves the same function as the public libraries did a hundred years ago."[59] To facilitate file sharing, according to Sjöman, is to extend universal social citizenship. From the outset, file sharing rhetorically becomes the Pirate Party's entry into the Swedish government.

To frame file sharing in terms of information access, Sjöman and his party continually reference the public library, an institution with a meaningful history. Specifically, they emphasize how libraries provide free access to culture, serving the common good. Sjöman explains, "We pirates are a movement with an ideology. [...] Our ideology in the file-sharing issue, I submit, ought to be compared with why there is public education and public libraries."[60] In this remark, the function that the concept of the library serves is to overlay the past and the present. In the present, Sjöman notes, libraries and file-sharing technology both provide access to content. Beyond this, in a historical perspective, libraries are a populist tradition in Sweden, established around the same time as public education. It is notable that in the quotations cited here and elsewhere, the party uses the term *folkbibliotek*, which means the people's library, rather than the more common *bibliotek*, or simply library. Sjöman states, "The foundational value [is] that all citizens shall have free access to culture. That is just as important for Sweden's development today as [it was] about a hundred years ago when the people's libraries [*folkbiblioteken*] were created."[61] The library is the rhetorical weight that anchors the Pirate Party's ideology in history, gives credence to its populism, and legitimizes its agenda in the present, suggesting that providing access has outgrown brick-and-mortar delivery systems. It is the file-sharing movement's turn to serve the people, Sjöman contends.

That the Pirate Party makes access a central motif in its campaign is less remarkable than the rhetorical resources at its disposal for doing so. Access is what the party demands as it seeks legitimate status in political debates and representation in the national government. And access to digitized content is what it promises to provide. What rhetorically distinguishes the Swedish Pirate Party from the open access movement internationally is the potency of the connection it establishes between access to culture and access to nature. In Sweden, as noted previously, the notion that free access is good for the commons is widely accepted and enforced legally by *Allemansrätten*, the right of common access. Appealing to this shared custom, the Pirate Party's 2006 "Program of Principles" states, "We demand a publicly-grounded intellectual property right that will enrich individuals' lives, enable a healthy corporate climate, create a general access right [*Allemansrätt*] for knowledge and culture, and thus benefit the development of society as a whole."[62] The same document asserts, "Intellectual property rights are a way to legislate material qualities for immaterial values. Ideas, knowledge and information are by nature non-exclusive, their common value is that they can be shared and spread."[63] With these demands, the Pirate Party places itself on the side of populist advocacy. It speaks for the people's rights. No meaningful distinction is evident between rights to land and rights to culture; stuff is stuff. And idealized spaces to which access is promised are comparable, whether the networks are geographic or virtual. Moreover, the campaign uses an organic language of physical terrains, climate, and health wherein access is not only desirable but natural.[64]

The Rhetorical Exigence of a Copyright Crisis

As I have explained, populist rhetoric is effective when an antiestablishment critique validates widespread disenchantment with existing institutions (governmental, administrative, bureaucratic). The first decade of the 2000s, characterized by rapid technological developments and international tumult, presented such a circumstance. In this opportune moment, the Pirate Party defined its terms of political contestation. It emerged with the rhetorical sovereignty to name a crisis and offer a solution. In this rhetorical act, the party introduced itself to the digital commons and to the Swedish voting public with a concept that it claimed had lost its functional definition: copyright. The 2006 "Program of Principles" announces, "Today's copyright law is imbalanced. A society in which culture and knowledge are free and accessible to all on equal terms benefits the whole society. We claim that a widespread and systematic abuse of today's copyright law actively counteracts these purposes by limiting both the supply of culture and access to culture."[65] In relation to a conceptual and legal imbalance, the Pirate Party presents itself as the agent that can and will establish balance. If copyright has lost the definition it was once intended to have and "needs to be returned to its origin," then the Pirate Party's political agenda is a rhetorical task.[66] Where there is ambiguity, the party offers clarity of purpose.

In its rhetorical task of definition, the party contextualizes copyright in an urgent crisis. It suggests that an immediate choice must be made to determine the future of copyright law, and the consequences could be dire. The 2006 election manifesto reads, "Technical developments have put Sweden and Europe at a fork in the road. New technology offers fantastic possibilities to spread culture and knowledge all over the world at almost no cost. But it also makes it possible to build a surveillance society the likes of which has never been seen."[67] Consistent with the political campaign genre, the dichotomy of utopia and dystopia is stark. The candidate is on the right side of a struggle against a dismal future. Says the Pirate Party, "We are on our way toward a society in which everyone is under surveillance 24 hours a day."[68] The same looming crisis appears in 2010, when the time frame has shifted to the present tense: "We find ourselves in a control-society where practically everyone is registered and monitored."[69] The Hobbesian notion of a control society—or perhaps a more contemporary connection may be drawn to the Netflix drama series *Black Mirror*—connects authoritative institutions and governmental oversight on the node of technology, specifically technology that internetworks *and* monitors cultural habits.[70] In this way, the technologies that facilitate cultural productivity, or, by contrast, allow copyright holders to usurp power, reflect the political choices of those who elect leadership. After the 2009 European Parliament victory, party founder and chair Rickard Falkvinge spoke explicitly about two alternative futures, urging prompt action: "The conflict is [...] going to grow all over the world until we either have a repressive information society in which you aren't allowed to have your own opinions, or the information technology ends up in the hands of citizens."[71] Falkvinge commented similarly after the Pirate Bay trial: "We have a revolution right now, right in front of our eyes, that's bringing culture and knowledge to the public to a greater extent than when libraries were first instituted."[72] The act of definition creates a political urgency wherein the Pirate Party's intervention is necessary.

Despite the crisis, the Pirate Party's full-throated endorsement of information technologies and the networked culture that they facilitate characterizes technology as an absolute good. Indeed, the party's unbridled enthusiasm appears to detach information technologies from their economic and political contexts. Somewhat awkwardly paraphrased, the fundamental assumption of the Pirate Party's value system on this issue is that the existence of something proves the goodness of that thing. Moreover, the goodness of the thing, in this case information technologies, means that its future expansion is a foregone conclusion. The 2010 Pirate Party election manifesto states, "Thanks to the new technology, we find ourselves in the information society. It is important that we seize its fantastic opportunities, both on a personal and societal level."[73] Elsewhere the document similarly states, "Thanks to new technology, today everyone can share in an almost unending cultural treasure."[74] In the 2017 "Program of Principles," the fervor has increased:

> We live in a unique time in human history. Never before have so many [people] had the ability to communicate so easily with each other. Never before have so many had access to so much knowledge. Never before has the spread of information contributed to so many technical, cultural, and economic advancements so quickly; and opened new conditions and opportunities for participation and democracy.[75]

According to the Pirate Party, the *emergence* of the information society evinces its value and merit.[76] That more of the same will appear in the future is even better.[77] As a political party, the Pirates announce their intention to pursue the common good by accelerating the technocultural developments of the present.

Political discourses about an immanent choice tend to combine rhetorical sensemaking with agenda setting. For example, when Falkvinge uses the word "*revolution*" he offers his audience a sense of what is and what could be. The latter, he implies, could eventuate in one of two ways, and a prudent decision must be made to ensure the people's prosperity and freedom. This is Falkvinge's rhetorical act: as he effectively articulates "revolution" by particularizing it in time and place, pitting state control against what belongs in "the citizens' hands," he invents the political program of digital populism. The Pirate Party becomes a viable representative not only for those who care about the free flow of digital content, but more generally for those who care about the people's sovereignty. The party distinguishes itself on this point from other political groups. More traditionalist politicians, Falkvinge suggests, either fail to appreciate the crisis at hand or remain entrenched in their support for old establishments, including those affiliated with the copyright industry. As Sjöman writes in an essay titled "Basic Course in Pirate Ideology": "Many of us young [people] now feel that we are about to lose a large part of our digital culture-life. And in *our* life, that matters."[78] The urgency of potential loss is palpable, as is the implication that the crisis matters more to some than to others. The party thus places its agenda along a generational fault line.

The Rhetorical Antagonisms of Digital Populism

The Pirate Party's discourses reflect a generational antagonism that is both progressivist and nostalgic. It separates the young from the old, explicitly rejecting the latter's capacity to manage technocultural innovations. The former, according to the Pirate Party, are better (smarter, more attuned, more amenable to participatory cultural production) because they are young, just as new technologies are better because they are new. Change is coming, the party promises, whether we choose to embrace it or fail even to recognize it. Change brings better technologies; better technologies are better because they make more stuff and provide increased access to it. Commenting on the copyright lobby's financial impact on the Pirate Bay trial, Falkvinge states, "We have geezers from an old industry that progress is running away from, spending their last coins trying to stop the technological development."[79] To Falkvinge, the older generation in which many of his parliamentary opponents belong is an obstacle to the common good and an ideal political future. In the same comment, he refers to those who advocated for the Pirate Bay's conviction as "dinosaurs," implicating a species whose inability to adapt led to its demise. Progress is rapidly running away, and "geezers" cannot keep up any more than the dinosaurs could outrun a meteor.

One of the most colorful illustrations of the Pirate Party's generational antagonism is the comment section of the aforementioned "Basic Course in Pirate Ideology." The article originated as a response to criticism from Swedish journalist Liza Marklund regarding open access trends. In the excerpts below, Sjöman's supporters trace the technological progress that renders the Pirate Party's agenda an outcome of history itself:

> Liza, you should listen to your children. You are crabby and backward [striving], just like the dinosaurs.... I mean the media moguls.[80]

> I read her op-ed and it gave a bad taste of old and petrified thinking.[81]

> A tip—Listen to your children instead of forbidding them. It might be the case that they understand something that you don't understand. [...] Times change. Don't fear change just because you have not yet understood, or wanted to understand the benefits. The fear you exhibit results only, as your children so wisely put it, in backward-striving.[82]

> It's probably true that steam engine makers had trouble when the combustion engine was introduced but where would we be today if it had been restricted by legislation?[83]

> Of course people who have supported themselves with a traditional system get angry when they can't do it anymore. Spinners were angry when spinning wheels were invented in the 1800s. A new invention makes some people superfluous.[84]

In these comments, old machines have outlived their utility and are continually replaced by new technologies. This, in the Pirate Party's interpretation of progress, is the logic beneath political decision-making. That which is new must be good for the commons and must not be hindered. On the contrary, choices must be made to increase new technology. "Angry spinners" obstruct and "steam engine makers" are the enemies of the common good.

The Pirate Party's comparison of those who resisted change historically and those who do so now is obviously metaphorical. Critics of the party are neither dinosaurs nor steam engineers. The point, however, is to persuade potential party supporters and new members that dinosaurs and steam engineers are bad. They are, in the commentators' rhetorical frame, rejectable subjectivities. They became extinct because they stood in the way of progress. Against this opposition, a cluster of unmet demands and discontents gives rise to a common subjectivity, and the subjectivity is running forward to meet the future with open arms.[85] As one commentator suggests explicitly, the movement's purpose may best be understood through the eyes of children. In their innocent joy, children are eager for the future. Not only are they deft at using new technologies—there is an implied image here of a child teaching her grandmother how to use a smartphone—they are not so cynical as to resist change. With this image of a promising future for those who pursue it as children do, the Pirate Party's populism aligns skepticism toward machines (particularly industrial machines) with the common good of a simple and virtuous people. A potential paradox thus emerges in the genre of rhetorical populism, wherein the people's innocence and technological savvy overlap. The machines that the Pirate Party dismisses represent an era of mass industrialization. This raises the question of what technologies the virtuous people will use in the future.

Populist antagonism, as previously noted, cuts in multiple directions simultaneously. In the Pirate Party's drama of dinosaurs and steam engineers who resist change, another enemy is the culture industry and its corporate structure. The charge against this industry, whom the Pirate Party portrays as internationally conspiratorial, is that it has long enjoyed overreaching copyrights. It profits from legal precepts held over from another era, hoarding cultural artifacts beyond the people's reach. According to the 2010 "Program of Principles":

> Millions of classical works, songs, films and art are held hostage in the media corporations' vaults, not in high enough demand by their focus groups to be profitable but potentially too lucrative to be set free. We want to make all of these works free and accessible to all, before the celluloid of the films is ruined by [the tooth of] time.[86]

In this narrative, a treasure is being kept from the people, who have a rightful claim to it.[87] Retrieving it requires nothing less than the bold resolve of pirates. Sjöman likewise criticizes an "indefensible control by media corporations over our culture" in a statement about government regulation. He claims, "File-sharing has in a short time limited the top lists of what is popular [generated by] media corporations. That scares them."[88] Or, as a commentator notes, "The only ones who won't be happy are the fat record company bosses who lose billions in a market that's no longer theirs."[89] The Pirate Party's antagonism targets the media industry's authority to dictate the terms of cultural circulation. This authority makes the industry a political opponent. Thus, the subjectivity of the party and its followers is articulated antagonistically.

The criticism that the Pirate Party directs toward international entertainment media focuses specifically on the industry's toxic artifice. Industry as such is unnatural, the party accuses, destroying the fecundity of creative practice. According to the 2010 election manifesto, the "ever stricter exercise of an antiquated copyright [law] doesn't only create integrity problems, but also problems for culture. [In this way] the copyright industry and the laws that it proposes and endorses contribute to the *stunting* of cultural growth."[90] In the excerpt, the Swedish word for "stunting" suggests a brutal severing of organic material. The word is most often used in the context of genital mutilation. The implication is that natural regenerativity is violently curtailed by copyright. In the 2017 "Program of Principles," another image of copyright's destructive impact on the natural state of being comes from the idea of spatial movement in nature. It extends what is natural in terms of culture from productivity to wandering: "The copyright industry systematically opposes all efforts to pace new trails through the cultural landscape."[91] The English idiom *"trailblazing"* is here a close approximation, but nevertheless misleading. *"Blaze"* is itself industrial, the work of a deforestation machine. What I translate as *"pace"* is a word for walking on foot. And the word for *"trail"* is one that would only appear in a forest. "Stig" is inconceivable in a city. To wit, wandering on a trail is what *Allemansrätten* ensures. The purpose of wandering is to explore. Copyright prevents commoners' natural right to experience a cultural landscape. The unnaturalness of it against the presumption of *Allemansrätten* legitimizes the Pirate Party's political agenda.

By establishing a rhetorical antagonism against corporate media, the Pirate Party associates itself with the cultural creativity of the people. Taking this position, the party proposes not only that everyone should have access to everything, but that anyone can make anything. The rights of artists are necessarily the rights of all, because in "participation culture," anyone can make stuff:

> Participation culture shall be promoted. The boundaries between creator and audience have been erased. Today we all create culture by writing a blog, commenting on someone else's blog, uploading films to YouTube, etc. This presents new demands on how we define the concept of culture. Participation culture today is often treated step-motherly as a second-class culture. The Pirate Party believes that participation culture instead should be held up as exemplary.[92]

Notwithstanding the muddled metaphor of a stepmother and a class distinction, the clear claim is that the people's creativity is devalued by the copyright establishment, comprised of lawmakers and media moguls. In this claim, the assignment of value is, as ever, a political matter of privilege. As the manifesto announces, "The Internet means that we are no longer relegated to the cultural canon prescribed from above."⁹³ The positive valence of this remark is self-evident inside the rhetorical frame of digital populism. The Pirate Party envisions a people who have the right to and inherent capacity for cultural production. That it is technologically possible for people to make stuff means that the stuff they make is good and that their right to make it is inalienable, goes the party line.

The affirmation of the people's creative pluralism troubles the traditional division of high and low culture. The party draws a rhetorical distinction between industrial media productions and the value of authentic artistry, specifically emphasizing the benefits of diversity. File sharing thus becomes a populist project serving the people and fending off cultural homogeneity:

> Unfortunately, much of [the] cultural [repository], just like knowledge, has historically been a privilege for the few. The technological developments of the past few years, however, create vast opportunities for more [people] to experience, practice, and [financially] support themselves through culture. Never before have young Swedes had so many different genres of music in their collections. Never has it been so easy to find random film titles.⁹⁴

The Pirate Party identifies as its constituents those who prefer unique and idiosyncratic cultural artifacts and the artists who make them. Repurposing the Frankfurt School's indictment of the culture industry, the party denounces mass-produced culture as inauthentic while also implying that those who manufacture and sell it are complicit in maintaining the high/low class hierarchy. What makes the adaptation of the Frankfurt School argument rhetorically possible is an indeterminate antiestablishment posture. The party positions itself against the culture industry *and* against traditions of taste; it aligns itself with artists and artistry, unifying the people's potential to make and consume stuff. This alignment allows the Pirate Party to animate populism with piracy and art as one. In so doing, the party creates a concept of the common good in which boldly defying norms and laws is not only political but ethical and existential. To accept the concept they offer is to find meaning in the prospect of becoming a pirate, an artist, or ideally both.

To its list of opponents, the Pirate Party adds, as populist movements must, established politicians and parties. Institutions of government are to blame for the people's problems and limitations, the party contends. Upping the ante on this rhetorical antagonism, the 2006 election manifesto differentiates between itself and other party candidates along the lines of good and evil. It is clear that the choice of leaders happens in a moment when any decision carries severe consequences: "Terrorists can attack the open society, but only governments can abolish it."⁹⁵ The same document connects information technologies to the ineptitude of established politicians: "Much of the poor legislation that's passed passes mostly because the established parties do not understand the internet and the new technology. They haven't fully considered the consequences of building a control society in order to preserve the old [institutions], instead of seizing the opportunities of the new era."[96] Ignorance makes politicians pitiable, the manifesto implies, necessitating political leadership that seizes opportunities for the people. Important to note here is not just the accusation of incompetence, which is thoroughly familiar in political discourse. What campaign would not accuse its opponents of being incompetent? Notably, the Pirate Party denounces its opponents on epistemic grounds. It claims that established politicians do not *know* enough about technology or digital culture. They do not *understand* the people in the present moment, nor can they envision the future. Unlike them, the Pirate Party "gets it." It understands the people, embraces popular preferences for digital culture, and has the foresight to advance a leadership plan. This is the gifting logos's political articulation. A concept of the commons is made, containing an interpretation of the people and their shared desires. The concept dictates what is good for the commons. And it is given to the commons as a platform that may be voted upon as a covenant for the common good.

Popular Rights to Privacy and Integrity

During its first year, the Pirate Party's advocacy was dominated by the idea that "democracy presumes a strong protection for personal integrity."[97] Indeed, the campaign documents from 2006 devote more attention to privacy than either copyright or patents. For the purpose of policy-making, the campaign organizes privacy into three categories: data storage, personal surveillance, and what might be translated from Swedish as "message freedom" (*meddelarfriheten*) or "letter secrecy" (*brevhemligheten*). Although all three are brought together under the theme of file sharing, the stakes for message freedom are especially high. The concept illustrates why privacy is a political action item for the Pirate Party: "[The legal policy of] letter secrecy shall be elevated to a general communication secrecy. Thus it shall become unlawful to tap/listen to others' phone calls, read others' email, SMS [text messages] or other messages, just as it is today unlawful to read someone else's letters, regardless of the technology or its administration."[98] In this excerpt from the "Program of Principles," an individual protection is transposed from analog to digital communication. Just as opening an envelope with another person's name on it is intuitively and legally impermissible, so should it be with electronic communication. The Pirate Party presents itself as a guardian of the people's right to communicate privately. The intimacy that a letter transports from sender to receiver is inscribed onto the Pirate Party's political program. The party becomes an advocate for something as precious as a personal connection. If the people cannot depend on the assumption of privacy, this changes who they are by making porous the membrane between the individual and the commons. As the notion of what is "personal" is compromised, an urgent need arises for a party that articulates a popular identity wherein privacy is valued.

In the Pirate Party's second national election campaign, the political message contextualizes personal privacy in relation to other individual rights. Privacy becomes a political value that extends beyond an individual's data storage. The threat of an invasion of privacy is presented not as a possibility that someone would find out what kind of music a person keeps on file, but rather as the possibility that any and all information is unsecured. Worth noting is that the campaign texts treat privacy and integrity as interchangeable goods. According to the 2010 "Program of Principles": "Protection for individual privacy [private life] is encoded in Sweden's constitution. From this fundamental right flow other important human rights such as freedom of expression and opinion, freedom of information, the right to culture and the right to personal growth."[99] Framed in this way, privacy is the original premise for individual expression and personal development. That the category is *human* rights suggests that privacy in a digital context, rather than being a matter of firewalls and wiretapping, is existential. Without a guarantee that private life remains secluded, the full potential of that life cannot be realized. A human *is* her or his information, the Pirate Party suggests. A statement following the 2009 European Parliamentary election raises the stakes by shifting from the individual's development to society as a whole: "In order for a society to grow culturally and technologically, citizens must have a guaranteed right to privacy."[100] The same statement associates privacy with citizens' rights to control personal information, whether the information is "dry" (such as a home address) or contains "facts from private life such as food habits." Insecurity regarding individual privacy is a threat to the common good.

The political significance of privacy in the rhetorical frame of the Pirate Party is dependent on a continuous evaluation of digital stuff. Simply put, data is stuff; data has value; value is political. This calculus is complicated by how the value of digital stuff is contingent not only on various markets but also on the ambiguous relationship between stuff and producers of stuff. The term *"personal data,"* for example, has a range of potential meanings. This merits special commentary as I turn toward the chapter conclusion on the politics of the gifting logos. In a database, personal data may refer to aggregated metrics about a person: height, weight, age, diseases, medications, and so on. The value of privacy in this example is obviously high. On social media platforms, personal data is collected in the form of user habits; user information about habits is profitable, for instance, in targeted advertising. A person who orders hiking gear online is likely to receive promotional messages about travel, treks, and of course more gear. From another perspective, personal data may be thought of as the content that a person produces in a digital network. It means less digital action than digital invention, if such a distinction may be tentatively posited. With reference to chapters 2 and 3, this is the "stuff" that circulates through the Creative Commons licenses and is curated by the Internet Archive. Whether or not it has monetary value, its meaning and value for its producer determine her or his preference to disseminate the data or keep it private. An important boundary may be drawn here between privacy and publicity in the digital commons. To offer an obvious example: an artist may be either eager or reluctant to give others access to a private collection of erotic films or a set of autobiographical writings on substance abuse. The stuff that the artist has made, as I demonstrate in chapter 2, accumulates around her or his node in the network, constituting her or him at that node as a productive agent. Her or his personal data is personal in the sense that it digitally *makes* her or his person. For the Pirate Party, then, personal data is integral to the articulation of the common good, albeit ambiguously so. In part, personal data is a function of productive (inter)activity. Societies advance culturally and technologically, the party claims, when people's creativity is unrestrained. This creativity is at once personal and common. It can be unrestrained only when creators are guaranteed that personal data, which is to say "stuff" in multiple senses, is protected; this includes digital records, actions, and inventions.

By explicitly valuing privacy, the Pirate Party rhetorically negotiates a prevalent dialectical tension of modern political discourse: the common good and the rights of the individual. From within this tension, the party offers a political program that includes access to a networked infrastructure, cultural circulation, interactive cultural productivity, and a deregulation of copyright. At the same time, the party emphasizes that none of these developments or objectives may be allowed to compromise individual integrity. The network must exist, in other words, but the individual must be protected by a kind of insular secrecy. This insularity is the individual's right. The Pirate Party's politics finds itself in a Frostian predicament wherein, divided by a fence, networked neighbors are at once contiguous and isolated, sharing neither good will nor pine cones or apples. As Frost writes, "We keep the wall between us as we go." Networked connectivity is what brings culture to the many screens of the people, and this is a good thing according to the Pirate Party. Connectivity assures the people's prosperity and engagement with one another. Nevertheless, the party that idealizes the World Wide Web finds itself challenged by scale. Populism has a rhetorical need for the notion of a gemeinschaft; in this social form, where everybody knows your name, privacy is impossible.[101] At the same time, however, global publicity is also incompatible with the gemeinschaft ideal. The common good cannot be achieved if everybody on the planet knows your name, your address, your medical history, and your music preferences. The rhetorical mechanism with which the Pirate Party manages these complexities is its anti-state antagonism. This antagonism defines privacy threats specifically in terms of government overreach and surveillance. If these impositions are removed, the gemeinschaft of the digital commons will form organically. Natural pathways will be drawn through the cultural landscape, and access to them will be granted to all. In this iteration of the gemeinschaft, commoners need not fear invasions of privacy. For the Pirate Party, serving the people means giving them access to all things, while promising that access to them will be limited.

CONCLUSION

In its first year as a political organization, the party that emerged out of an online file-sharing group focused on the ideal of common access. Indeed, in the preceding excerpts it is clear that the Pirate Party has consistently directed much of its antagonistic rhetoric toward various authorities who keep cultural resources away from people. Without specifying exactly what the commons must have access to, the Pirate Party's early message was singular: "The only thing we are interested in is facilitating an open society and democracy, that the march toward a control-society is stopped, and that culture and knowledge are set free."[102] This focus defined the party's political program against the agenda of other parties: "We are the only party that will never compromise away the free and open society in favor of any other issue. [. . .] In Swedish politics, we are alone in this."[103] With the rhetorical center of gravity on access, the Pirate Party articulated a political agenda; it made and presented a political plan. That is, seen through the lens of the gifting logos, the party made itself intelligible to the commons. It gave itself politically to the commons. It offered a concept of the common good, incorporating a sense of the people and a prescription for governance. In so doing, it made the people knowable by offering them an interpretation that was acceptable. In terms of the populist politics of epistemic rhetoric, the Pirate Party invented itself as a leader that understands the people and recognizes what is best for the future.

Four years after its initial launch, the party's advocacy effectively interlaced universal internet coverage with two recurring motifs of populist discourse: access and representation. "We submit," the party announced, "that the right to broadband is as obvious as the right to running water, electricity, and plumbing. A person shouldn't be discriminated against and excluded from modern society just because they live in a certain place in the country."[104] In the 2010 election, the Pirate Party conjured an imagine of a poor soul isolated in the Swedish wilderness without modern conveniences and abandoned by all, including and especially the political establishment. This lonely creature remained disconnected, unable to communicate with the outside world. Speaking for this voiceless victim of state-sponsored discrimination, the Pirate Party demonstrated its commitment not only to broadband for every man, but also to political representation for the everyman, the figure of the *Jedermann*. In populism, both access and representation reflect how the people must be oriented in relation to those who govern, ensuring an ethical political order. To the extent that the people have access to politicians, the former are empowered to hold the latter accountable. The representative relationship, as noted earlier in the chapter, is what enables politicians to speak for the people. Representation requires attunement and understanding, and access serves as a corrective when either attunement or understanding falters. The Pirate Party's campaign aligns the reach of representation for those who have no voice—indeed, they hardly have running water—with the reach of a broadband network. The party represents the best interests of the people, however remote they may be. Thus, digital populism rhetorically conflates access to political representatives, a process in which the governed reach out to those who govern, with access to cultural content.

Delivering a political concept, the Pirate Party's digital populism is an enactment of the access ideals that resonate in chapters 2 and 3. In chapter 2 I explicate how Lawrence Lessig and his team present the Creative Commons licenses as a way for creators (musicians, photographers, software coders) to provide access to their materials under specifically dictated conditions. The suite of licenses manages access and order via individuated attribution. In chapter 3 I demonstrate how the same ideal of access appears in the discourses of the Internet Archive and the Wayback Machine. The Internet Archive catalogs and delivers digitized versions of millions of cultural artifacts; moreover, it offers free access to archiving technology so that new archives can be continuously created. The Wayback Machine gives access to the inaccessible, transporting time travelers to websites of the past. What enables this time travel in reality is a retrieval technology for archived snapshots, or page captures. In both chapters, access is political. It is a value-laden means to an end, as well as an end in itself. Access is what people deserve and what will ultimately lead them to self-realization. As stated in the 2017 Pirate Party "Program of Principles":

> Technological developments have led to an equalizing of access to knowledge. [...] Millions of children and young [people], who previously didn't have the opportunity for an education, now have access to the collected knowledge of all of humanity. [Even] if no other education is available, they have the opportunity to educate themselves. The revolution of information technology and free access to knowledge and culture thus gives many people new opportunities to take control over their lives on their own.[105]

In this chain of association, the Pirate Party explicitly connects access with self-determination. Access to stuff (indeed, "all of humanity's knowledge") is a contact process wherein the people of the commons convene, and the distinction between artist and audience, or maker and taker, is fluid. Those who make this process possible—Lessig, Kahle, and the Pirate Party—claim to be serving the common good.

This chapter situates the Pirate Party within the framework of a dialectic, of two interdependent meanings of a political "given." The first meaning posits the given as the status quo. The given political order is an inherited set of institutions and procedures. When this inheritance is disrupted, which happens intermittently as a result of infinitely complex historical developments, a need arises for clarification, definition, and order. In other words, an exigence arises for a politically invested epistemic intervention. Responding to this exigence, a rhetorical agent (in this case the Pirate Party) emerges, inventing or indeed articulating itself through an agenda, a chain of subjectifying demands. The agent steps onto the scene of the commons with a concept, which contains an analysis of the state of affairs, an interpretation of the people and its destiny, and a vision for future possibilities. This is the second meaning of the political given, that the rhetorical agent gives the concept to the commons, presenting it for consideration. The classical theory of rhetorical tropes, as I explain in the introduction, illuminates how both senses of the given depend on tension between what is familiar and unfamiliar. Tropes are familiar, indeed commonplace. They organize what is commonly known into abstractions. They allow those who are connected by the same repository of cultural assumptions to communicate. Importantly, however, tropes are available for rhetorical manipulation, turning toward what is unfamiliar and strange. When widely shared assumptions change, tropes adapt. Conversely, when tropes are turned, widely held assumptions change and new perspectives are created. For the purposes of the Pirate Party, discourses about what is ambiguous in the present moment (such as copyright and cultural distribution) and discourses about what ought to be accomplished in the future (such as technological infrastructure) operate in a dialectic of what is known and what is unknown.

In this chapter I use digital populism as a frame of reference for studying the political implications of the gifting logos. I analyze the campaign discourses of a group of file-sharing "pirates" in order to assess the politics of expertise in the digital commons. To end this chapter and turn toward the conclusion of the book, I want to emphasize that the issue of the gifting logos's politics cannot be fully framed by anything smaller than logos itself. What this means is that while the three rhetorical practices integrated in the gifting logos (knowing, making, gifting) entail political activity in various particular ways, logos is political in a profound sense. That gifting as a habit is political is evident in Marcel Mauss's ethnographies. That knowledge is political is evident in chapter 3, in which I discuss the power that an archive wields in relation to that which is archived. That the making of stuff is political is evident in most theories of production, whether industrial or pre/postindustrial. Beyond these practices, what must be noted is that, as Rancière writes, "Before the *logos* that deals with the useful and the harmful, there is the *logos* that bestows the right to order."[106] A premise of democracy is that in situated deliberations over what is useful and harmful, or right and wrong, political agents compete. The winner gets to govern. But prior to this argumentation is an imposition of a condition upon the deliberants. And the condition ascribes rhetorical agency. The imposition—it may be called "bestowing," via Rancière or "gifting" as in this book—contains from the outset certain arrangements of power.

To put the matter bluntly, it would be silly to write a book that presents a concept like the gifting logos, end the book with a chapter on the concept's political implications, and then fail to finally acknowledge that logos was political to begin with. To illustrate why "*disagreement*" is a pivotal term of politics, Rancière explains, "Before the gauging of interests and entitlements to this or that share, the dispute concerns the existence of parties as parties and the existence of a relationship that constitutes them as such. The double sense of *logos*, as speech and as account, is the space where this conflict is played out."[107] In Rancière's terms, my textual reading of the Pirate Party attends to particular speech, while my analysis of how the gifting logos functions politically attends to logos as an account. I have focused my inquiry in this book on expertise, using the gifting logos to investigate how digital epistemic material is invented and circulated in networks. This chapter must end with an explicit recognition that logos is political not primarily because it is about authoritative epistemology but because logos fills the relational space between humans. Rancière is right that logos precedes and exceeds arguments over who gets what. And yet those arguments always and by necessity follow from the relation once it is established. We humans know no other way. If the first order of the order is to invent interlocutors, the second is to speak.

5

The Gifting Logos

Both the concept and practices of the digital commons tend to bring out extremes. Extremes characterize what we believe about the digital commons and how we behave within its aggregate. Utopianists believe that communication technologies are the solution to the world's problems and the path to a better future. To some degree they may be right. There is no shortage of possibilities in a global network. In my assessment, a hopeful attitude toward the digital commons isn't foolish. Tragedy is neither inevitable nor total, and we commoners do indeed accomplish remarkable things. We may have access to something that approaches what Elinor Ostrom called "polycentricity." However, and as studies of, for example, social media indicate, global networks also facilitate the worst impulses of humankind on a massive scale. A critical point of view of how the digital commons has operated thus far is imperative. Technophilia and its enactments, the fervent busyness of the "wifi life," must not prevent us from recognizing that the platforms that facilitate concerted efforts to combat disease, poverty, climate change, and so on also permit violence on multiple scales. Yet luddite cynicism is just as clumsy with its conspiracy theories and rants. What I have aimed to show in this book is how we might understand the complexity of the digital commons with reference to other forms, both cultural and natural. Through three case studies, I have presented the gifting logos as both a practice of the commons and a lens for the study thereof. My intent in this final chapter is to explicate five characteristics and functions of the gifting logos. These are drawn from insights that may be traced through the case studies, connecting digital infrastructure, digital archiving, and digital populism. It goes without saying that the five variously intersect and reinforce one another.

1. The gifting logos assumes participants' awareness in order to function.

In the gifting logos, the overlaying of knowing and gifting places significant emphasis on awareness and its counterpart in rhetorical theory: intent. If gifts are messages, as I claim in the introduction, then their viability as such depend on the message sender's awareness (of the activity) and the message recipient's confidence in the sender's awareness. To be sure, plenty of messages are communicated accidentally, and interpretations are made without being verified. Still, successful gifting happens when the giver is aware that she or he is giving a gift, and the beneficiary assumes that the action was intentional. "*Successful*," in keeping with a commons ideology, means the health and sustainability of the relationship and the network. We might even go so far as to say that a gift is intelligible as such when it is given on purpose. From the point of view of the logos, the question is, What does an intentional giver expect in terms of outcome? And to what extent does this expectation correspond to the giver's motive? Both questions target a rhetorical action and its origin. Both inquire about how rhetorical agents intervene in particular situations so as to exert influence over others. If the giver anticipates obligation and gratitude, the gift may be a mechanism for setting the mood of the community (the commons) overall. This mood has significant consequences if it shapes how future inventions in the commons are generated. For example, someone who believes that Brewster Kahle created the Internet Archive to preserve cultural artifacts for future generations may be compelled not only to participate in digital archiving, but indeed to think of the archiving of information in digital form as a priority. If so, the gifting logos establishes an orientation toward the curation of what is known and made, specifically made in the form of accessible content.

For the Creative Commons (CC) licenses, licensor intent determines how certain tags moderate access and the rights of possession. Before selecting a tag configuration, prospective licensors are reassured that they may choose precisely how they wish to give their content away and how the content may be used. "We are not the enemy of proprietorship," Lawrence Lessig and his people imply.[1] To paraphrase their pitch: "The gift is your choice! If you choose to give of the material that you have made, its value will increase, as will the value of what you make 'IRL,' in real life." This is the widely advertised story of brilliant but struggling artists who, after circulating content via the CC infrastructure, gain fame and fortune. They choose to give and in so doing become part of an imagined future in which cultural artifacts are made freely available to the commons. Thus, they choose the future conditions of the commons by dictating the conditions of their licenses. With the CC, it is instructive to connect intent, which is central to the functioning of a gift, with control, which, as noted in chapter 2, marks a creator's right to dictate a creation's public existence. Copyright (and its legal enforcement) from the beginning has been about material proprietorship and the notion that an essential imprint of a creator remains in the substance of the creation, even after the creator publicizes it. If this mobile imprint and its recalcitrance through circulation are placed in the context of gifting, as Mauss does with the concept of prestations, matters of ownership and control become matters of rhetorical intent.

In chapter 4, the locus of awareness within the gifting logos has shifted but remains significant. As my analysis of the Pirate Party's discourses indicates, the party places the onus of electing competent leaders on Swedish voters. Voters choose politicians who make a persuasive case for their superiority over other candidates. The choice, the practice of intentional action, has thus shifted from the giver of a rhetorical gift to the recipient, specifically the recipient of a political campaign. The recipient must choose the gift (of a policy program) actively, and in the context of other alternatives. In this instance, the gift is an articulation of the people and the people's best interests. It congeals, Laclau would say, as a chain of equivalential demands that, because they are unsatisfied, prompt a political strategy. The Pirate Party makes sense of the exigence in which it rose to prominence, which is to say that it produces and offers an interpretation of Sweden in a particular time and place. This time and place, according to the party, demands a decision about whether to embrace the information technologies of the future or to fossilize. The virtues of emergent technologies in this vision of the networked society are self-evident, according to the party's message. That the technologies exist indicates their goodness and inevitable increase in scope. What the voters are asked to do is choose "the path of openness."[2] Those who do, in the Pirate Party's assessment, are self-selecting as recipients of the party's gift via their intent. Intent in the role of recipient separates the cool kids who "get it" (i.e., those who embrace digital networks and the implied techno-future thereof) from the dinosaurs and steam engineers who do not.

To say that the gifting logos assumes intent on the part of participants is not necessarily to say that the complexity of rhetorical agency has been resolved, or that in the digital commons the relationship between intent and expertise has been made simple because of the gifting aspect. Rather, the point is that invitational and hortatory iterations of the gifting logos repeatedly emphasize intent and choice as points of entry into the networks. And not only as points of entry, but as ways of maintaining the integrity of one's own node with respect to future precarity. In this way, the productive interactions of the digital commoners are predicated on the idea that their fully conscious decisions lead to a future for the digital commons that is consistent with individual choices, and that those choices may be secured and fixed in digital form (or, indeed, the binary code of a "vote or no vote"). Equally important is the idea that certain dystopic futures may be foreclosed by making the right choice at the right time, for example, in an election and/or with a contribution to digital archiving.

In gifting theory, participant intent may be more or less definitive, depending on where the theorist places the focal point (for example, whether there is a superordinate being or social form that is served by instances of gifting). And in this theoretical conversation about gifting intent, there is a place for happenstance. If I leave my packed lunch at the bus stop by accident, a hungry person who finds it may perceive it as a gift. Rhetorically speaking, however, the packed lunch cannot be understood as a gift. Furthermore, unpredictability foils the plans of rhetors and gifters alike. Even when I foolishly believe that I am in control of what I communicate to others, my intent may not govern the outcome. For example, if I give a friend a book with the best of intentions for her reading pleasure, it may turn out that she already owns a copy. Notwithstanding these gifting "infelicities," as J. L. Austin might say, the gifting logos's promise is that the individual choice of those who make stuff will not be lost in the tumult and speed of digital networks.[3] Even as invention becomes networked and difficult to pinpoint, the individual node at which expertise integrates knowing with making and gifting remains traceable.

One of the recurring and elusive subjects of this book is original creativity, specifically how creators are connected to what they create—if they are indeed connected in an enduring sense,—and how expertise connects knowers and makers to the thing that they make. In dealing with this subject, the gifting logos's assumption of intentionality points to rhetorical agents' motive. When I take a picture of my feet halfway buried in a sandy beach, I am painfully aware of how trite my artistry is. I am making a copy of a copy. I may earnestly be attempting to capture my personal experience of finitude against grandeur or rootedness in the ebb and flow of the tide. Regardless, I cannot even for myself identify the aspects of the photo that belong to me uniquely. Anyone could confront me with the possibility that I stole the idea, just as anyone could steal the idea of "Feet in Sand" from me. Nevertheless, I may feel compelled to use the image as a means of unburdening myself. As Nietzsche says, I may be selfishly driven by a desire to let gifts flow out of me as from a well, endowing my eyes with a "goldlike gleam" of self-satisfaction.[4] So, if I *make* the idea of my experience—whatever I was experiencing while watching the waves roll in—into the digital bits of a jpeg, and I deposit the bits into the commons network as a *gift*, marked with my signum, it exists as a product of me. Paradoxically, it is when I give something away that I am able to constitute myself in the network as its point of origin. When I lean on individual intent, the gifting logos affords me a privileged relationship to my creation and its impact in a way that traditional copyright, confounded by networked productivity, cannot.

2. The gifting logos derives rhetorical potency from tensions between artifice and nature.

To understand this feature of the gifting logos and its implications for the rhetoric of expertise, it is helpful to think of the idea of what is natural and the idea of what is artificial as being held together (and apart) by an electric charge. The charge is what supplies the gifting logos with rhetorical power. It is not that the two concepts are independent, nor is it the case that a higher order resolution of the tension is possible in a Hegelian sense. Rather, the rhetorical potential of the tension depends on how well it is wielded in a persuasive effort. In chapter 2, for example, I demonstrate that the CC's discourses of inheritance, in which something of value passes from one generation to the next, refer intermittently to genetic transmission and to charitable donations. One is organic and the other is not, but in both meanings, the idea of a gift comes across with considerable momentum. Making the case for the genetics of gifting, the CC asserts that passing along our ideas and inventions to future generations is a "driving force for human evolution."[5] Gifting is natural, a genetic propagation of collective knowledge, or the knowing of the commons. In this sense, the integrated processes of knowing, making, and gifting are consistent with the natural state of the commons. The commoners are consubstantial through the stuff that they pass along. And expertise thus is an organic matter. In the gene pool of common knowledge, illustrated by one of the CC's promotional graphics, a drop of content is readily conceivable as a drop of blood. When licensors gift the things that they have made, they participate in a natural process; as they do, they contribute substantively to the epigenetic edification of all who have access to digitized content. The organic material of the gift interacts with other materials—a photograph is mashed with another to create a political meme—as genetic materials from two parents result in the combined characteristics of their child.

By comparison, when the CC constructs gifting as a matter of philanthropy, the impetus is on individual givers' benevolence. The act of bequeathing licensed artifacts to future generations is an act not of genetic roulette but of generous intent. This makes gifting a cultural rather than natural process, wherein "cultural" refers to a ritualized intervention or formal structure. The reader may recall from chapter 2 the word "*deed*," borrowed from the language of estate planning, which contains certain restrictions for how artifacts circulate through the license infrastructure. The three-layered deed encodes licensed content with legal, technical, and commonly readable conditions; the deed dictates the terms of use, attaching, as it were, strings to the gift. And even though a deed is distinguishable rhetorically from a gene, both contain substantive information. Both participate in the gifting logos. The idea that the gifting logos facilitates an institutional endowment, and that this institution reflects generous individuals' choices, conflates intent and an elevated purview beyond genetics. Via the gifting logos, the CC implies a two-by-two grid wherein genetic inheritance aligns with what is natural, and the choice to contribute to the dowry of the digital commons aligns with what is unnatural, but in a good way. The gifting logos renders those who participate in it as intentionally cultured, sufficiently enlightened to make the choice to give.

In chapter 4 the rhetorical charge between the natural and the artificial energizes the idea of access. Specifically, it constructs access to natural space and access to cultural content as mutually implicative. In Sweden in 2006, the Pirate Party made access to cultural content and digital networks its central campaign promise. In so doing, it made extensive reference to a legal custom that resonated with its audience, *Allemansrätten*, the right of common access. Advocating for a cultural *Allemansrätt*, the Pirate Party effectively blended the natural and cultural. It insisted that just as Swedes have a right to forests and shorelines, so too do they have a right to digitized content. Importantly from a Swedish perspective, *Allemansrätten* is not only a right to natural resources but also a right that is generally perceived as naturally just, the natural order. With its advocacy, the Pirate Party harnessed the rhetorical tension between the naturalness of access and the artifice of microelectronic networks, computers, and binary code. In addition, it supplemented the ideal of access with other implications, such as the populist ideal of the people's access to elected leaders and the liberal democratic ideal of multiple parties' access to parliamentary inclusion and representation. With its policy program, its enactment of the gifting logos, the Pirate Party characterized obstructions to access, including and especially those imposed by the media industry, as unnatural. Copyright, according to the Pirate Party, stunts natural growth and common well-being.

In considering the rhetorical charge between nature and artifice, it is instructive to recall from chapter 1 my discussion of how life in the natural commons, and the commons generally, happens in the liminal space between what is familiar and what always remains elusive. I explain there that if we imagine a rural commoner in seventeenth-century England, we might imagine how he or she experiences both mystery and habit, enigmas and torpor. At times, life in the village is a continuous routine of familiar activities, people, and places. One's obligations are specified and one's tasks, following an apprenticeship pedagogy, are well mastered. And yet at the periphery of the village, where dense wilderness meets the commons habitat, the mysterious hovers like fog along the tree line. The unboundedness of the commons, which appears in scholarship on the natural as well as the cultural commons, is the source not only of contentious negotiations but of irreducible indeterminacy. That is, in territories without limits, inhabitants argue about governance, rights, and access. What has not been ordered entirely (by fences and proprietorship) exceeds full knowability. If we shift the perspective from the misty moors of the seventeenth century into the digital commons, we find again the dialectic of the mysterious and the habituated. In 2020, the daily routines that most of us maintain as we use digital networks, and the ways in which digital habits determine our lives, are familiar. They are quotidian, perhaps even automated (such as in the case of a social media news feed). Nevertheless, the digital commons has a seemingly impenetrable aspect, something out of sight. Many of us commoners have a sense that the machine is not transparent. The electronic networks and their interactions lie outside of our purview. Words like "*deep web*" and "*darknet*" are titillating precisely because they signify this sense of inaccessible strangeness.

As intriguing as the sources of mystery in various historical perspectives are, the mysterious and the mundane do not map neatly onto the natural and the artificial. Indeed, in the present moment it is difficult to say whether the natural or the artificial is more mysterious. And yet, given that the subject of this book is expertise, specifically as this term integrates knowing, making, and gifting, a worthwhile question is how the rhetorical practices of productive knowledge facilitate mastery, and in so doing, facilitate a sustainable life despite the perils of nature, culture, mystery, and habit. In chapter 3, for example, I demonstrate how archival expertise, the making of an institution in which knowledge is housed, masters whatever is curated in the archive. In filing cabinets and glass displays, knowable things are fixed. Likewise capturing a sense of what is and what could be, the Pirate Party ascends in chapter 4 by offering an interpretation of an uncertain state of political affairs. Its candidacy depends on naming and accounting for a crisis. In relation to conceptual pairs like natural/artificial and mysterious/familiar, thus, expertise is the *making sense* of something, which is to say that it is inventive. To make something unnatural seem natural (like access to a broadband infrastructure or digitized music) is to *make* it natural or to rhetorically give it over to an audience in a natural form. To transform something mysterious into something familiar is to *make* it knowable. The ambiguity is dealt with when an intelligible construct is invented and submitted for common consideration. Conversely, to make something as basic as silicon and metal wiring into a mystery is likewise a matter of rhetorical invention. Thus, the gifting logos wields the rhetorical tension between the opposing ideas of nature and artifice.

3. The gifting logos is abundant.

The gifting logos as a rhetoric of expertise places value on great quantity as inherently positive and prolific. "More is more" is the gifting logos's motto. With each case study in this book, I explicate this abundance as *copia*, the replicative production of rhetorical material. In chapter 2, for example, the CC boasts its success and entices prospective participants by detailing its copiousness. With grand and colorful figures and graphics, the *State of the Commons* draws attention to growing numbers: millions of licenses that tag images, texts, audio files, and videos.

The dominant message of the CC is that a massive amount of digital content in itself makes the overall project impressive. Similarly, in the Internet Archive (IA) expertise is signified by accumulation. The gifting logos is massive; where much is gathered, much is known, and much may be given to the commons. With reference to both the Wayback Machine's collection of web pages and the IA's holdings of books, films, and other artifacts, Kahle's team defines its purpose in terms of copious growth. Growth is presented as progress, and expertise is better the bigger it is. And, like the Pirate Party, the IA constructs access to copious materials as an end in itself. Expertise is a substance that can be increased by expanding its scope. For the Pirate Party, expansion is a political objective. Providing access to a network of digitized content is good, and the more access and the more content, the better.

In all three case studies, the gifting logos's emphasis on *copia* recognizes one meaning of access. In this meaning, which assumes that all things that are delivered are fully received, massive delivery cannot be anything but good. Indeed, expertise functions in such a way that the more of it is supplied to a node in the network, the more of it the node person possesses. Networked access to digitized content dominates, indeed obscures, questions of dispositional order and intelligibility. This means, for example, that in the Pirate Party's and the IA's discourses, a person who has the ability to click-to-open a document on a screen has access to the document, whether or not she or he can understand it, let alone engage actively with it. The tacit assumption is that a person with networked access to millions of artifacts has full access to them all. Any content that is available is accessible. In terms of expertise, this definition of access is significant, requiring attention within a theory of the gifting logos, especially insofar as it obviates other definitions. In chapter 3 I connect the IA's copious delivery with visitors' overwhelmed confusion by distinguishing between computational order, the algorithms that organize digitized content, and disposition, the rhetorical process of making sense. In chapter 4 I explain how the Pirate Party interlaces the benefits of access to communication networks with the populist ideal of access to political leaders. In its advocacy, the savant with a fast internet connection and the politically engaged citizen are interchangeable, connected through the ideal of access. What this position obfuscates is a consideration of what access (to networks of texts or networks of politicians) requires so as to lead to other things, such as education and democratic accountability. Thus, while the gifting logos concept has the capacity to manage interpretative and productive expertise, the combination of *copia* and access may foreclose some of this capacity.

It is here worth resisting the impulse to turn to a familiar equation of scarcity and value, which would classify that which is abundant as less valuable. This is the impulse that would have us ask, If ten thousand songs about heartache have been licensed by the CC and/or made available via the IA, how good can each one of them possibly be? The same impulse might prompt us to ask, If the IA has five thousand hours of AM radio broadcasting from Duluth about soil erosion, is providing global access to this collection important? If so, it is important primarily because until recently the collection was stored in shoeboxes in a basement? If expertise in the digital commons is about an integrated process of knowing, making, and gifting, and this process is geared toward abundance, what happens to the value of expertise? This last question is significant because one of the ways that expertise traditionally makes an intervention in public culture is by aligning certain individuals' and professions' knowledge with value. Doctors, for example, are valuable because, while most of us get sick at one time or another, few people know how to treat illness. According to the pervasive zero-sum perspective on expertise, more doctors would make "doctoring" less valuable in the system overall. My intent here is not to ridicule love songs, Minnesotans, or doctors, but rather to invite the reader to question what may seem like an obvious conclusion: that the abundant productivity and gift circulation of the digital commons means that expertise is less valuable in the digital commons, or for that matter, that expertise on- or offline is less valuable than it was before the emergence of the digital commons as a way of life. One of the enduring convictions among commons scholars and activists is that cultural resources like ideas are nonrivalrous, which is to say that they are not depleted by repeated use. If I tell a friend about a great idea, we both have it, whereas if I give my apple to a friend, only she gets to eat it. This assumption of sustainable cultural resources, and the ethics that come with it, are not to be dismissed. However, my contention is that the notion of a nonrivalrous resource may need more nuance in the context of the digital commons and abundant cultural creativity, especially regarding expertise and the relative value of productive knowledge.

In rhetorical scholarship, *copia* has long been associated with knowledge, specifically how a subject may be treated variously in multiple iterations and thereby understood with greater complexity. Erasmus's famous example of 195 ways to say, "Thank you for your letter" illustrates an effort to multiply an idea in order to assess its rhetorical tendencies, to suss out its potential. Through repetition, Erasmus explains, the intricate valences of meaning may be explored. Those who repeat, learn. In this kind of copious exercise, there is no meaningful distinction between how students of rhetoric repeat a sentiment in order to learn many ways of signifying it and how anyone (student or not) may repeat an idea in order to understand it fully. In either case, a trope is turned again and again, producing articulations and offering perspective. It is difficult to point to one or the other and call it "simple repetition" as opposed to a gradual development of an idea through symbolic rehearsal. The issue at stake is expertise: how something is made knowable (or learnable) through repetition that produces an abundant result. In digital networks, the scale and speed of *copia* are distinguishable from more traditional forms of abundantly productive repetition and the expertise that emerges from it. With speed and scope operating in tandem, so much is produced so fast that digital stuff effectively becomes immersive, a substance mediating between the digital commoners, who in turn make more of it.

4. The gifting logos is time-sensitive and progressivist.

The gifting logos as a cluster of rhetorical practices is necessarily attuned to kairos, sensitive to contextual time. It responds to the moments in which it functions. To start, gifting itself is a time-sensitive activity. A giver assesses an appropriative occasion for giving a gift and awaits a response, which could be immediate or delayed. The lag time of the response is, as Bourdieu explains, ambiguous, requiring careful analysis.[6] Whether the recipient is expected to respond with a performance of gratitude or a reciprocal gift, his or her timing has to connect the response to the original gifting action. If too much time passes in a gift exchange between the original action and the reciprocation, the latter may seem discontinuous with the former. Bourdieu's vivid illustration of this kind of delay is a revenge murder. But even in less extreme situations, an unrecognized gift is rhetorically troublesome. For someone who sends flowers to a friend and receives no acknowledgment, the lack of recognition may be little more than mildly offensive. However, in a framework in which cultural production is constituted through gifting, a delayed or absent response may be more significant. Indeed, it may indicate a failed intervention. For example, with the CC, an artifact may be tagged and submitted into circulation, awaiting reception and use by other participants in the digital network. Reception-as-acknowledgment is marked by reuse and resubmission. If, however, the artifact is never picked up or recirculated, it is an unsuccessful gift, a gift that nobody wants.

In chapter 2 I demonstrate that the kairos of the gifting logos as expertise may be thought of in relation to copyright, specifically its contingency on time. The basic tenet of copyright is that those who create material are entitled to enjoy the benefits of the creation for a limited amount of time. Expertise as created content, thus, is *timed*. The ways in which it is associated with its maker are timed, and so are the ways in which it may be used by others. Regardless of individual creators' intent or desire, however, copyright law insists that holders of copyright may at any point rescind whatever permissions they have granted for use of their material, including those permissions that seem to extend into an unspecified future. Their gifts may, in other words, be legally repossessed. And yet given the irrevocability of an idea that has been submitted to the commons, the gifting logos does not permit "take backs." Expertise that has been given cannot be ungiven, which in the rhetorical practice of the gifting logos means it cannot be unmade. Content that has been circulated cannot undo the trace or effects of its circulation, however brief, just as an idea cannot be un-had. For this reason, and because the contents of the CC may suddenly become proprietary, the gifting logos is indeterminate in perpetuity. In other words, it is indefinitely subject to flux. Those who take up the content with the intent of remaking and recirculating it do so with the awareness that the gift could at any time change legal status. Thus, recipients of gifted expertise are at risk not only legally but constitutively, acting with the logos.

Beyond its kairotic, contextual sensitivity, the gifting logos contains definitions of time in specific relations to what is known, made, and given to the commons. For example, in chapter 3 the archive of web pages is a time travel machine, moving travelers from the present to the past. The Wayback Machine is rhetorically constructed as a way to travel through the history of the World Wide Web. It hurls travelers through a cosmos of web captures, fragments, and perhaps even vague memories. Time, then, is a destination that is made up of digital bits. It is a distant invention, made accessible by retrieval technology. The machine knows the past the way a brick-and-mortar archive knows its collections. And it relegates time into a non-obstacle to accessing web history. Moreover, with the reference to the *Rocky and Bullwinkle* cartoon, the Wayback Machine promises an adventurous opportunity to find purpose in the past. Like most time travel stories, the Wayback Machine indicates that discovering a meaningful point of origin motivates an adjustment of the present and future. The idea is that as time travelers experience websites in their early versions, discovering simple designs and raw potential, they recognize what might have been or what might still be. The search for a potentially lost future gives urgent meaning to the present. Thus, in the archival project the gifting logos defines time as fully accessible. The integration of knowing, making, and gifting masters time.

The gifting logos's definition of time in the case of the Wayback Machine is focused as intensely on the future as on the past. And with respect to the future, what looms most ominously is the prospect of loss, the disappearance of data and links. The idea, simply put, is that digital information that is not archived will be irretrievably lost. It will fade into an unintelligible, unknowable blind spot. The networked commoners will not be able to access their own information once "link rot" and other disintegrative processes take over. Access, discussed previously, is threatened by the disappearance of networks and content; when the past of the World Wide Web cannot be accessed, it is in effect gone. Archiving thus protects the digital commons from time-as-decay. The gifting logos forecloses loss. It is a rhetorical habit, in which what is known ensures against existential amnesia. By generating a mass of digitized content, the Wayback Machine and the IA more generally *make* (knowledge of) the digital commons permanent. I argue in chapter 3 that by attending to the gift as an event, along with Heidegger, we might understand the time-contingent rhetoric of the gifting logos. In Heidegger's view, being is a gifting event. As "Rain rains," and "Being be's," so might we say, focusing on eventfulness, that "Being gifts." In light of this, the gift as an event forecloses the imminent nonbeing of digital data. Preservation of data in the archival commons is a gift against data loss. If being is a gifting event, then nonbeing is the risk or precarity that always threatens the gift. In the gifting logos, the epistemic habits of the digital commons are productive, keeping nonbeing at bay.

The urgency of the IA's preservation echoes in chapter 4, albeit with a different directive. There, too, the timing of the gifting logos is set to "urgent," a call for the commons to act as soon as possible lest something catastrophic happen. In the Pirate Party's campaigns, the catastrophe appears as a combination of clueless politicians, antiquated policies, and a malfunctioning telecommunication infrastructure. The party's argument, as noted previously, is that the commons must actively choose the right path for the future, electing leaders who understand the present and its inherent possibilities. The wrong path leads, according to the Pirate Party, to a tyranny of the copyright industry's unnatural regulations. Thus, the party gives the commons a political program with an "Act now!" time stamp. Seen from a political perspective, the gifting logos's sensitivity to time orients the givers' assessment of the situation and the recipients' expected actions. Recall the earlier example of the flowers sent from one friend to another. With the intent of sending flowers, a giver invents the message of the gift, discerning both its timing and the time frame of the anticipated response. For the Pirate Party, getting the timing right in 2006 was partly a matter of interpreting for the benefit of the commons an economic and social uncertainty. When the party emerged, the widespread uncertainty of the early 2000s had created a need for a political group to offer a definitive prognosis. In doing so, the party intervened via a political construct, giving itself and its plan to the commons. The party's mobilization of the gifting logos was kairotic, as was the task of reciprocity that it assigned to the commoners.

Each of the book's case studies indicates how the gifting logos is ultimately progressivist. It is evident in each chapter that if the right measures are taken by digital commoners in the present, the future is bright. In this future, digital commoners engage in networked productivity and continuous circulation. Cultural inventions, standardized in the form of binary bits, capture and disseminate lived experiences in a way that makes life intelligible. What is known is made and gifted. Thus, the rhetoric of expertise in the digital commons is in a particular sense opportunistic, intent on pursuing a prosperous future despite unpredictable circumstances. As Paulo Virno explains, deftly avoiding a moralistic rejection of opportunism, the multitude's opportunism is "marked by unexpected turns, perceptible shocks, permanent innovation, chronic instability."[7] Seen less as exploitational than as kairotic, then, opportunism is a feature of the gifting logos's positive outlook. Opportunism conditions life in the commons, where the material and temporal all-at-once of digital accumulation complicates both time (as in history) and timing (as in particular intervention). By being opportunistic, those who participate in the gifting logos orient themselves toward the rhetoric of possibility.

5. The gifting logos assumes a rhetorically playful posture toward its "others."

In a traditional sense, expertise is rhetorically serious business. Indeed, central to the rhetorical challenge of functioning as an expert in modern society is convincing others (peers and laypersons) to take you seriously. Seriousness is a rhetorical effect/affect, as is its opposite, however it is named: play, comedy, or parody. It is remarkable, therefore, that the gifting logos as a rhetoric of expertise repeatedly assumes a playful, not entirely sincere or serious posture. In its critiques of others, especially well-established alternatives, the gifting logos delivers an ostensibly playful performance. Of the case studies in this book, the most dramatic example of this performance is how the Pirate Party critiques other parties and politicians by glibly ridiculing them. They are made to seem hopelessly inept and out of touch with the younger generation. The prospect of these more traditional politicians at the helm appears comical. The Pirate Party's discourses are colloquial, demonstrating identification with "the people" and its language. Informality sets the Pirate Party's campaigning apart from the formality of traditional party politics. The very name, "Pirate Party," marks digital populism with an implied wink. There can be no doubt about whether this party would, if elected, operate as traditional parties do. And this is the playful irreverence of the gifting logos as wielded in certain circumstances: by giving the commons a political program, the party leads with a tongue-in-cheek promise not to continue with the government's business as usual. The political program defines the Pirate Party and the commons in the terms of a derisive attitude toward existing institutions. The party's constitutive act, in other words, makes governance something not to be taken too seriously. Or at least, seriousness itself must be reinvented, the Pirates suggest. The new seriousness, from the Pirate Party's perspective, applies to popular culture and the networks through which access to it is granted.

A similarly comedic note plays in the CC's discourses, particularly as these make reference to institutional authorities such as copyright. The suppressed implication of the CC website tutorials is that copyright is a legal stick in the mud and a creative bummer. It is incommensurate with the rich, lively, and inclusive habits of knowing and making that characterize the digital commons. Dutifully but halfheartedly gesturing toward the supremacy of the law of copyright, the CC orients its licenses to the law by depicting the former as vibrant and the latter as stagnant. Law is stifling but the CC is designed specifically to make culture accessible. The CC derides copyright, contrasting it with a different model of expertise, a cooler, "funner," younger way to think about cultural invention and circulation. Expertise, thus seen, is better when it is speedy and productive than when it is serious. Recall from chapter 2 the playful description of one of the three layers of the license deed, the legal code layer, which tags artifacts with "the kind of language and text formats that most lawyers know and love."[8] Whether or not most lawyers actually love a certain kind of legal code is beside the point of the phrase, which is instead to portray copyright lawyers in an unflattering light. The phrase casts lawyers and legal matters generally in a comedic role, something of a necessary nuisance. Against the contrast of these lawyers, the CC emerges as more commonsensical. Its ways of managing stuff, its model of expertise, indeed its enactment of the gifting logos, make sense to the commons.

In chapter 3 the playful irreverence of the gifting logos is most evident in the figure of Brewster Kahle himself. In media coverage, the visionary genius is a familiar character, including and especially from stories of internet start-ups. Kahle is precisely what one might expect, an eccentric technophile. But in the older, more academic frame of reference for archiving, Kahle appears as an outlier. He is no archivist, which is to say that he is rhetorically distinguishable from the expert of the traditional archive. What he lacks in historiographical experience and sweater-vest attire, he makes up for by being genial and approachable. In interviews, he plays the part of a dedicated and intelligent but ultimately regular guy, joking about how the IA's holdings exceed those of the Library of Congress several times over. For him, the joke is permissible because his project has in a comparative sense already won. And the humorous tone carries through commentary on the IA project; a reporter for the *New Yorker* writes that the Wayback Machine "is humongous, and getting humongouser."[9] In this remark, the scope of Kahle's archive is conveyed through his personal informality and, more fundamentally, through the style of a commons archive. Further, with Kahle's enthusiasm for an archive made up of old websites, many of which would hardly meet the quality standards of formal archiving, he embodies the ideal of the digital commons's content-as-knowledge. His machine, whimsically named after a cartoon, holds the wisdom of the digital commons. By not taking himself too seriously, Kahle personifies the gifting logos's orientation toward archival expertise. He invites digital commoners to join his venture, to make archives of their own. With this "anyone can do it" approach, the entry barrier to archival expertise is lowered by a playful rhetorical act.

What, then, does a rhetorical performance of play do for the gifting logos? What does a nonserious posture afford? My sense is that it brackets, or sets aside, two sets of questions that confront experts and expertise in the present moment. First, are the habits that function as expertise in the digital commons recognizable by that term from a traditional perspective on productive epistemology? Is the knowing and making that happens in the digital commons at all compatible with the metrics that have traditionally evaluated the merits of expertise? Is it justifiable to refer to the 'processes of invention of the digital commons as epistemic? Second, does rhetorically constructing an activity as a gifting activity make it so? Are the gifts of the digital commons, the stuff that the commoners make as they engage through the networks, *really* gifts? Can knowing and making be effectively integrated with gifting, or is the latter a façade for something else entirely? Throughout the book I have taken a rhetorician's approach to both sets of questions, which is to say that I presume the constitutive functions and effects of language. It matters that the epistemic practices of the digital commons are grounded in everyday experiences, and that those practices are made intelligible through the discourses of gifting. To affirm that it matters, the gifting logos uses play as a way to be permissibly critical of certain institutions and to be irreverently insistent on its own significance and value. With a meaningful wink, the gifting logos relieves the self-invented (self-inventing) experts of the digital commons of having to adopt the form of traditional experts; being not-too-serious, networked expertise eludes the judgment mechanisms of traditional expertise. Likewise, this posture avoids having to measure up to the conceptual impossibility of the gift. Gifting, thus conceived, does not have to be theoretical. Put another way, the gifting logos makes the gift a rhetorical event of common invention rather than an absolute ideal.

The gifting logos is the animating order of the rhetoric of expertise in the digital commons. It brings together the commons' habits of knowing and making, marking them with the idea of gifting. It directs productive epistemic practices and coordinates the giving and receiving nodes of multiple networks. In this continuous process, expertise is substantive, multidirectional, and mundane. It is what it makes, and it lives an intensely integrated life of everyday experiences. The accretions of this networked rhetorical invention, its products, substantiate the nodal relationships of the digital network. As they do, the multitude of the commons coalesces and articulates the being-together that allows intelligible contestation over political ends and a common good. That is, the gifting logos not only facilitates the creation of cultural artifacts like text, design, images, and music; it also indexes a constitutive interpretation of the multitude and its political circumstances in a way that is, in a word, givable.

As a rhetoric of expertise, the gifting logos must in a profound way be understood as *making sense*. In the networks of the digital commons, thus, expertise is different from what it was (and is) in a more traditional, analog context. It is continuous rather than episodic. It is common rather than professionalized. It is at once general and particular. Sense, and the way it is given from one (node) to another, is not separable from the sense maker, the sense made, or the contingencies of the making. And while the sense made (the stuff of expertise) is not beyond a market value system, it is made intelligible and viable in circulation through the logic of gifting. If the prototypical example of analog expertise is a doctor walking into an exam room or a professor up to a podium—both of whom would say, "I am an expert and I have expertise"—the prototypical example of expertise in/as the gifting logos happens when someone articulates an experience in digital form and submits it to the commons network, not just so that others may know something that they did not already, but to participate in the 'cultural productivity of the commons. Productive engagement is epistemic in the digital commons—this is my contention. We scholars of digital rhetoric and culture have much to gain by reimagining extant theories of epistemology for a twenty-first-century networked context.

What does the future hold for the gifting logos? Will it do good things for the commons? Will it challenge networked structures of control and exploitation? While resisting the temptation to conclude with sweeping statements and prescriptions, I might say that the digital commons would do well to improve its processing of the gifting logos as expertise. By this I mean that we need methods, of access, delivery, and interpretation. This, of course, means that we need teachers and reimagined pedagogies. The goal ought not to be that only "real" experts in a conventional sense are permitted to make digital stuff that circulates as expertise. Likewise, we should spend no time attempting to restore the word "*expertise*" by cutting away the epistemic productivity of digital commoners in their everyday practices, however trivial the artifacts thereof might seem. Expertise now lives its rhetorical life in the blinding speed and mind-blowing masses of the commons networks. Still, we might want to explore how to organize instances and outcomes of knowing-making-gifting. If we want to hold onto the ideal that participation and inclusion are good things, and within the register of gifting assume that gifts ought not to be dismissed out of hand, then we need a way to sort stuff. We need more efficient, more critical, and/or more ethical ways to manage what is known and what is made. If we increase the precision of the gifting logos's epistemic methods, we might be getting closer to the common good.

NOTES

INTRODUCTION

1. Marcus Boon, *In Praise of Copying* (Cambridge, MA: Harvard University Press, 2010), 5.
2. Boon, *In Praise of Copying*, 227–228.
3. E. Johanna Hartelius, *The Rhetoric of Expertise* (Lanham, MD: Lexington, 2010).
4. Protagoras is thought to have begun his text *Truth* with the following statement: "Of all things the measure is man, of things which are, that they are, of things which are not, that they are not." Ugo Zilioli, *Protagoras and the Challenge of Relativism: Plato's Subtlest Enemy* (Hampshire, UK: Ashgate, 2007), 5. In Plato's dialogue *Theaetetus*, which given the dearth of extant writings from Protagoras himself serves as a reenactment of his philosophy, Protagoras and Socrates explore the question "What is knowledge?" in relation to wisdom, perception, and truth. Myles Burnyeat, *The Theaetetus of Plato* (Indianapolis, IN: Hackett Publishing, 1990).
5. Giambattista Vico's epistemology is firmly situated in human practice, what he calls a "maker's theory of knowledge." In *The New Science*, Vico explains this *verum factum* principle by comparing the knowable inventions of humans to the unknowable creations of the divine. *The New Science of Giambattista Vico: Unabridged Translation of the Third Edition (1744)*, trans. Thomas G. Bergin and Max H. Fisch (Ithaca, NY: Cornell University Press, 1984), §331. In *The Study Methods of Our Time*, Vico orients the human/divine distinction to the notion of truth: "The principles of physics which are put forward as truths on the strength of the geometrical method are not really truths, but wear a semblance of probability. The method by which they were reached is that of geometry, but physical truths so elicited are not demonstrated as reliably as are geometrical axioms. We are able to demonstrate geometrical propositions because we create them." *On the Study Methods of Our Time*, trans. Elio Gianturco (Ithaca, NY: Cornell University Press, 1990), 23.

6. Robert L. Scott, "On Viewing Rhetoric as Epistemic," *Central States Speech Journal* 18, no. 1 (1967): 9–17. Many of us consider Scott's essay to be a catalyst in the subdisciplinary project focused on the rhetoric of inquiry, epistemology, and science.

7. Manuel Castells, ed., *The Network Society* (Cheltenham, UK: Edward Elgar, 2004).

8. Lewis Hyde, *The Gift: Creativity and the Artist in the Modern World* (New York: Vintage Books, 2007), 108. The book was first published in 1983 under the title *The Gift: Imagination and the Erotic Life of Property*.

9. See Diels-Kranz fragment 30, attributed to Heraclitus. W. K. C. Guthrie, *A History of Greek Philosophy* (Cambridge, UK: Cambridge University Press, 1962), 432. Philip Wheelwright, *Heraclitus* (New York: Atheneum, 1974), 37.

10. Martin Heidegger, *Early Greek Thinking*, trans. David Farrell Krell and Frank A. Capuzzi (New York: Harper and Row, 1975), 61.

11. Heidegger, *Early Greek Thinking*, 71.

12. With a similarly dual method, Douglas Eyman favors a sophistic perspective. He emphasizes rhetorical productivity, specifically "the relationship between rhetoric and knowledge production and meaning-making." Douglas Eyman, *Digital Rhetoric: Theory, Method, Practice* (Ann Arbor: University of Michigan Press, 2015), 17. Thinking of logos as I do (as both a praxis and a hermeneutic), Eyman explains, "The power of rhetoric, as I see it, is that it can be employed as both analytic method and guide for production of persuasive discourse—and it is both of these capacities that inform my understanding of digital rhetoric." *Digital Rhetoric*, 16.

13. Many if not most scholars and activists who write about the natural and cultural commons, particularly the past and present enclosures that privatize the commons, argue for the ecological and ethical value of shared resources. To them, establishing or restoring the commons as a form of governance is a moral imperative. For example, advocates of the open access movement tend to embrace parallels between the historical privatization of land and the increasing corporatization of digital resources. By contrast, my project is not driven by a technophile's faith in digital commons utopia; I comment further in chapter 1, "Networks."

CHAPTER 1

1. David Bollier, *Think Like a Commoner* (Gabriola Island, BC: New Society Publishers, 2014), 4–5.

2. Peter Linebaugh, *The Magna Carta Manifesto* (Berkeley: University of California Press, 2008), 303.

3. Lewis Hyde, *Common as Air* (New York: Farrar, Straus, and Giroux, 2010), 18.

4. Bollier, *Think Like a Commoner*, 15.

5. It must be noted that the private enclosure of land and natural resources is neither an event of the past nor confined to England. The Dawes Act of 1887 is an example of natural commons privatization in the United States. At present, land is appropriated globally by private organizations, including notably in the Amazon, where species and biological material are enclosed by the legal markers of property.

6. Derek Wall, *The Commons in History: Culture, Conflict, and Ecology* (Cambridge, MA: MIT Press, 2014), 74.

7. Garrett Hardin, "The Tragedy of the Commons," *Science* 162 (1968): 1244.

8. As one considers the possible merits of Hardin's perspective or gathers up what is left of it after numerous reputable critics have poked holes in his argument, it is important to recognize that Hardin had a distinguished career as a public voice of white nationalism. His controversial research in ecology is markedly inflected by his interest in eugenics and race, which informs his writings on immigration politics. He wrote prolifically for such far-right publications as *The Social Contract*, wherein he advocated nativist exclusionary policies. He also founded the anti-immigration group Californians for Population Stabilization, the name of which reveals how his notion of a commons "tragedy" intersects with his xenophobic protectionism.

9. Elinor Ostrom, *Governing the Commons: The Evolution of Institutions for Collective Action* (Cambridge, UK: Cambridge University Press, 1990), 17–20.

10. Ostrom, *Governing the Commons*, 24–25.

11. Fikret Berkes, David Feeny, Bonnie J. McCay, and James M. Acheson, "The Benefits of the Commons," *Nature* 340 (1989): 91–93; and Bollier, *Think Like a Commoner*, 27.

12. Hyde, *Common as Air*, 32–34. Stinted resources are regulated by the exact times, places, and ways in which they may be used. For example, if I plan to travel throughout the summer, I might invite my neighbors to use my pool and pick my strawberries. These are resources that would go to waste in my absence. Our understanding might be that use of the pool is permitted for the neighbors but not for their friends. And in exchange for my strawberries, which really would not be mine anyway but rather would rot, the assumption might be that the neighbors will pick weeds or water the garden.

13. For a discussion of how the debate on the commons follows the fault line of Hardin and Ostrom, see Wall, *Commons in History*, 73.

14. Linebaugh, *Magna Carta Manifesto*, 74–75.

15. Hyde, *Common as Air*, 37–39. Hyde's discussion of the implications of holding the perambulations during Ascension week is especially illuminating.

16. In chapter 4 the practice of perambulation reemerges in the form of the Swedish law and custom of *Allemansrätten*, the right of common access, which dictates that anyone is permitted to walk onto privately owned lands, forests, and shorelines. In the context of the Pirate Party's political campaign, which references *Allemansrätten* as an ideal, ownership does not dictate access; rather, access constitutes an alternate form of ownership through networked practice.

17. Bollier, *Think Like a Commoner*, 43.

18. Wall, *Commons in History*, 43–44.

19. One of my favorite examples of the cultural commons, illustrating the confounding of property structures, is the musical score to a children's taunt: "nana nana boo boo." This utterance, which is both transgenerational and internationally viable, eludes intellectual property rights, if not officially then certainly in practice.

20. Bollier, *Think Like a Commoner*, 141.

21. James Boyle, *The Public Domain: Enclosing the Commons of the Mind* (New Haven, CT: Yale University Press, 2008), 45.

22. Boyle, *Public Domain*, 47.

23. Against cynicism and the second enclosure movement, Boyle advocates what he calls *information environmentalism*. He situates this argument by explaining how

environmentalists originally had to create and publicly present the concept of the environment in order to counteract exploitation of natural resources. Boyle concludes: "We have to 'invent' the public domain before we can save it." Boyle, *Public Domain*, xv.

24. Michael Hardt and Antonio Negri, *Commonwealth* (Cambridge, MA: Harvard University Press, 2009), viii, 283–284.

25. Hardt and Negri, *Commonwealth*, 144.

26. David Harvey, "The Future of the Commons," *Radical History Review* 109 (2011): 104.

27. Barbara Warnick, "Two Systems of Invention: The Topics in the Rhetoric and the New Rhetoric," in *Rereading Aristotle's Rhetoric*, ed. Alan G. Gross and Arthur E. Walzer (Carbondale: Southern Illinois University Press, 2008), 108.

28. Beyond these primary sources extant from Aristotle and Cicero, the secondary literature on topoi, commonplaces, and rhetorical invention is too extensive to cite. As an introduction and foundation, the following are excellent: Michael Leff, "Topical Invention and Metaphoric Interaction," *Southern Speech Communication Journal* 48 (1983): 214–229; Michael Leff, "Up from Theory: Or I Fought the *Topoi* and the *Topoi* Won," *Rhetoric Society Quarterly* 36 (2006): 203–211; Carolyn R. Miller, "Aristotle's 'Special Topics' in Rhetorical Practice and Pedagogy," *Rhetoric Society Quarterly* 17, no. 1 (1987): 61–70; Carolyn R. Miller, "The Aristotelian *Topos*: Hunting for Novelty," in *Rereading Aristotle's Rhetoric*, ed. Alan G. Gross and Arthur E. Walzer (Carbondale: Southern Illinois University Press, 2008); William F. Nelson, "*Topoi*: Evidence of Human Conceptual Behavior," *Philosophy and Rhetoric* 2, no. 1 (1969): 1–11; and Karl R. Wallace, "*Topoi* and the Problem of Invention," *Quarterly Journal of Speech* 58, no. 4 (1972): 387–395.

29. To connect *doxa* as *sensus communis*, or conventional wisdom, with Vico's epistemological theory, see John D. Schaeffer, *Sensus communis: Vico, Rhetoric, and the Limits of Relativism* (London: Duke University Press, 1990).

30. Mari Lee Mifsud, *Rhetoric and the Gift: Ancient Rhetorical Theory and Contemporary Communication* (Pittsburgh, PA: Duquesne University Press, 2015), 71–72.

31. Paolo Virno, *A Grammar of the Multitude* (Los Angeles, CA: Semiotext(e) Foreign Agents Series, 2004), 76.

32. Virno, *Grammar of the Multitude*, 23.

33. Virno, *Grammar of the Multitude*, 21.

34. The term *multitude* is often associated with Hardt and Negri's three-part series on "the empire," in which it functions antinomically. According to Hardt and Negri, the multitude is "an open set of social singularities that are autonomous and equal, capable together, by articulating their actions on parallel paths in a horizontal network, of transforming society." Michael Hardt and Antonio Negri, *Commonwealth* (Cambridge, MA: Harvard University Press, 2009), 111. Given my focus on epistemic invention, the authors' emphasis on the multitude's productivity is especially relevant; they note that the multitude is "constituted by a process of making," arguing, "The self-transformation of the multitude in production, grounded in the expansion of the common, gives an initial indication of the direction of the self-rule of the multitude in the political realm." *Commonwealth*, 173, 177. While I find this point instructive, other aspects of Hardt and Negri's representation of the multitude are troubling. They characterize the multitude as an already energized

political organization while defining it, with reference to Rancière, as without rights. Their portrayal of the multitude is deeply romanticized, infused with what Crystal Bartolovich calls a "repellent and false [. . .] salt of the earth vocabulary." Crystal Bartolovich, "Organizing the (Un)Common," *Globalization Working Papers* 8. no. 6 (2008): 19.

35. Virno, *Grammar of the Multitude*, 22 (emphasis in original).
36. Virno, *Grammar of the Multitude*, 24.
37. Virno, *Grammar of the Multitude*, 106.
38. Virno, *Grammar of the Multitude*, 77.
39. Virno, *Grammar of the Multitude*, 42.
40. As I use the term here, *"general intellect"* refers to the vital fodder of the commons. This is a more constrained definition than the term has had in some of its primarily Marxist theoretical and critical history, the scope of which is beyond this note. Suffice it to say that thinkers like Virno, reflecting on Marxist positions on expertise, labor, and social knowledge, are keenly attuned to processes that monetize the multitude's general intellect. In his introduction to Virno's collection of lectures, Sylvère Lotringer contextualizes Virno's theory of the multitude beyond Spinoza. He explains how profoundly Virno's concept of the multitude and its capacities was affected by his political activism in the Italian Automist movement of the 1970s. Sylvère Lotringer, foreword to *A Grammar of the Multitude*, by Paolo Virno (Los Angeles, CA: Semiotext(e) Foreign Agents Series, 2004), 10–11. A more recent publication by McKenzie Wark situates general intellects—plural rather than singular—in relation to the forces of production in the twenty-first century. Wark explores intellectual labor that is principally funded and owned by academic institutions, the products of which are mediated in networks that extend to multiple publics. Surveying thinkers who have articulated various understandings of the general intellect, including Virno, Wark illustrates the impact of collaborative, practical knowledge and "living labor" in media habits outside the university. McKenzie Wark, *General Intellects: Twenty-One Thinkers for the Twenty-First Century* (New York: Verso, 2017).
41. Boyle, *Public Domain*, 5 (emphasis added).
42. Brian L. Ott, "Afterword: Digital Rhetoric at a Later Time," in *Theorizing Digital Rhetoric*, ed. Aaron Hess and Amber Davisson (New York: Routledge, 2018), 236 (emphasis added).
43. 43. Richard Lanham's widely cited discussion of stuff and fluff is relevant here, although it does not fit perfectly with the meaning of stuff that I am pursuing. Lanham's dichotomy commits him to a distinction between material and immaterial value, even as he inverts the relation. Lanham argues that in the attention economy of the digital era, stuff and fluff, or material goods and information, have swapped places in terms of superordinate value. For example, selling coffee is not about the beans but about the affects attached to the beans: the brand, the experience of brand identification, and so on. "Stuff has given way to fluff," he claims. Richard Lanham, *The Economics of Attention: Style and Substance in the Information Age* (Chicago: University of Chicago Press, 2006), 17. While I find his analysis compelling, I would also say that fluff is not only significant and valuable, but still intelligible as stuff: digital stuff.
44. Lawrence Lessig, *The Future of Ideas* (New York: Vintage Books, 2001), 249. Lessig explains the impact of making "circumvention technologies," which are designed to work

around the controls installed by owners of copyrighted content, illegal. Lawrence Lessig, *Free Culture: The Nature and Future of Creativity* (New York: Penguin Books, 2004), 151–159. He indicts the lobbyists behind the Digital Millennium Copyright Act, which contained "*legal code* intended to buttress *software code* which itself was intended to support the *legal code of copyright.*" *Free Culture*, 157 (emphasis in original).

45. Lessig, *Free Culture*, 8.

46. Manuel Castells, ed., *The Network Society* (Cheltenham, UK: Edward Elgar, 2004), 3.

47. Castells, *Network Society*, 39.

48. Castells, *Network Society*, 40, emphasis added.

49. Lessig identifies the architecture of the internet as the source of its innovative capacity. Lessig, *Future of Ideas*, 35. He explains that the original end-to-end network design facilitated a simple and neutral infrastructure, wherein information is produced at the periphery. Using the example of an electric grid, he notes that by plugging something into the grid (a toaster or an electric car), networked participants create value. The grid is a connective system for the transportation of resources. It facilitates invention by those who deploy its resources.

50. Yochai Benkler, *The Wealth of Networks* (New Haven, CT: Yale University Press, 2006), 7.

51. Benkler, *Wealth of Networks*, 1–3.

52. Benkler, *Wealth of Networks*, 63. Compared to Lessig's unbridled enthusiasm, Benkler is optimistic, but with an empirical orientation. Hoping to "render the optimism about the democratic advantages of the networked public sphere a fully specified argument," he writes, "There is no guarantee that networked information technology will lead to the improvements in innovation, freedom, and justice that I suggest are possible. That is a choice we face as a society." *Wealth of Networks*, 12, 18.

53. Benkler, *Wealth of Networks*, 81.

54. Benkler, *Wealth of Networks*, 152. Benkler comments on the notion of networked commons, limiting his definition to forms of property. The central question, he claims, regarding the institutional ecology of the digital commons, is "whether there will, or will not, be a core common infrastructure that is governed as a commons and therefor available to anyone who wishes to participate in the networked information environment outside of the market-based, proprietary framework." *Wealth of Networks*, 23.

55. Damien Smith Pfister, *Networked Media, Networked Rhetorics* (University Park: Pennsylvania State University Press, 2014), 9 (emphasis in original).

56. Pfister, *Networked Media*, 13.

57. Pfister, *Networked Media*, 175.

58. Pfister, *Networked Media*, 13.

59. Following a diligent discussion of public sphere deliberation, Pfister concludes that even if we should desire to put the concept of the public out to pasture, it is not going anywhere. He writes, "The idea of the public sphere is a legacy of modernity so firmly rooted in our intellectual traditions that resisting the term conceptually may well be futile." *Networked Media*, 48. My sense is that "network" pairs better with commons than with publics, and that the notion of a "networked public" is, if not oxymoronic, then potentially misleading for scholars of both digitality and rhetoric. Networks entail parallel rather than

serial connectivity, multinodal participation, and continuous productivity—all of which are difficult to conceive within the parameters of the traditional public. See Robert Glenn Howard's critical discussion of networks and vernacular "participatory media," specifically the limits of the concept of public. "The Vernacular Mode: Locating the Non-institutional in the Practice of Citizenship," in *Public Modalities: Rhetoric, Culture, Media, and the Shape of Public Life*, ed. Daniel C. Brouwer and Robert Asen (Tuscaloosa: University of Alabama Press, 2010), 241.

60. Pfister uses the softer phrase *"pragmatic spirit." Networked Media*, 14.

61. One exception are "whisper networks," a term that recently drew attention during the MeToo movement. Most simply, whisper networks transmit information informally, indirectly, and privately rather than publicly. In the MeToo example, transmitted information might include the names of alleged sexual harassment/abuse offenders. To the extent that whisper networks depend on interpersonal connections, circumlocution, and secrecy they are less efficient than forms of publication that present information openly and directly, such as in the crowdsourced spreadsheet initiative titled Shitty Media Men that appeared in 2017. This example illustrates in interesting ways how something that was originally a personal network (and thus inefficient from an information-distribution perspective) made strategic use of digital networks (designed for efficiency) and, as a result, the functional difference between personal networks and digital networks became evident.

62. The point of origin of the term *"digital rhetoric"* is generally thought to be Richard Lanham's essay "Digital Rhetoric: Theory, Practice, and Property," published in Myron C. Tuman's 1992 edited collection *Literacy Online: The Promise (and Peril) of Reading and Writing with Computers* (Pittsburgh: University of Pittsburgh Press, 1992). See also Tuman's *Wordperfect: Literacy in the Computer Age* (Pittsburgh: University of Pittsburgh Press, 1992). Reproduced a year later as a chapter of Lanham's *Electronic Word* (Chicago: University of Chicago Press), "Digital Rhetoric" argues that computers ought to be studied as rhetorical, rather than as machines of logical programming. The early history and genealogy of "digital rhetoric" reflect how scholars of literacy and composition focused on the significance of hypertext, while others focused on online advocacy and political discourse, and still others focused on the adaptation and amendment of literary and rhetorical theory. For foundational works on hypertext, see Jay David Bolter, *Writing Space: Computers, Hypertext, and the Remediation of Print* (Mahwah, NJ: Lawrence Erlbaum Associated, 1991); George P. Landow, *Hyper/Text/Theory* (Baltimore, MD: Johns Hopkins University Press, 1994); and George P. Landow, *Hypertext 3.0: Critical Theory and New Media in an Era of Globalization* (Baltimore, MD: Johns Hopkins University Press, 2006). Initial analyses of online advocacy and political discourse include Thomas W. Benson, "Rhetoric, Civility, and Community: Political Debate on Computer Bulletin Boards," *Communication Quarterly* 44, no. 3 (1996): 359–378; and Laura Gurak, *Persuasion and Privacy in Cyberspace: The Online Protests over Lotus Marketplace* (New Haven, CT: Yale University Press, 1997). Inaugural analyses of digital rhetorical theory include Gregory Ulmer, *Internet Invention: From Literacy to Electracy* (London: Longman, 2003); Barbara Warnick, *Critical Literacy in a Digital Era: Technology, Rhetoric, and the Public Interest* (New York: Routledge, 2001); Barbara Warnick, "Rhetorical Criticism of Public Discourse on the Internet: Theoretical Implications," *Rhetoric Society Quarterly* 28, no. 4 (1998): 73–84; James P. Zappen, "Digital

Rhetoric: Toward an Integrated Theory," *Technical Communication Quarterly* 14, no. 3 (2005): 319–325; and James P. Zappen, Laura J. Gurak, and Stephen Doheny-Farina, "Rhetoric, Community, and Cyberspace," *Rhetoric Review* 15, no. 2 (1997): 400–419.

63. Kathleen Welch, *Electric Rhetoric: Classical Rhetoric, Oralism, and a New Literacy* (MIT Press, 1999); and Collin G. Brooke, *Lingua Fracta: Toward a Rhetoric of New Media* (Hampton Press, 2009). Welch, who focuses more on television and video than on computers but anticipates my work on the rhetorical expertise of the digital commons, analyzes electric literacy as a "nonlinear, hyperlogical means of inquiry that links according to aural/oral/print features and not through a rational line." *Electric Rhetoric*, 106n17. Moreover, Welch's seminal project sets a precedent for using logos as the term of art for analyzing hypertextual rhetoric. *Electric Rhetoric*, 9.

64. Michele Kennerly and Damien Smith Pfister, eds., *Ancient Rhetorics & Digital Networks* (Tuscaloosa: University of Alabama Press, 2018), 2–3.

65. Hess and Davisson, *Theorizing Digital Rhetoric*, 2 (emphasis added).

66. Douglas Eyman, *Digital Rhetoric* (Ann Arbor: University of Michigan Press, 2015), 61.

67. Eyman, *Digital Rhetoric*, 34.

68. James Carey explains how "watershed moments" in the development of communication technologies reformat the ritualistic habits of everyday communication. In this reformatting, the myth of a better future with technology guides the common attitude toward adoption and adaptation of communication. James W. Carey, *Communication as Culture* (New York: Routledge, 1989). In the updated edition of his widely cited book, Carey writes, "An increasingly prevalent and popular brand of the futurist ethos is one that identifies electricity and electrical power, electronics and cybernetics, computers and information with a new birth of community, decentralization, ecological balance, and social harmony." *Communication as Culture: Essays on Media and Society* (New York: Routledge, 2009), 88. In chapter 3 of this book, this idea of technological sublimity and the great promise of future communication processes returns, with reference to Leo Marx, *The Machine in the Garden: Technology and the Pastoral Ideal in America* (New York: Oxford University Press, 1964).

69. On the theme of the continuous "newness" of communication technology, see Lisa Gitelman, *Always Already New* (Boston, MIT Press, 2006); and Carolyn Marvin, *When Old Technologies Were New: Thinking about Electric Communication in the Late Nineteenth Century* (New York: Oxford University Press, 1990). Marvin's analysis is especially instructive for my purposes, as she reads the historical emergence of communication technologies and public electricity networks alongside that of professionals whose technical expertise became a source of authority in the 1880s. In the chapter "Inventing the Expert," Marvin highlights the idea that access to expertise not only orients communities (of those in the know and those less so) to each other structurally but may be thought of as transmitted, or possibly gifted; in this transmission, Marvin demonstrates, the sociopolitical function of experts was established in a particular era under certain economic conditions. She writes, "One official boundary at which electrical insiders and outsiders met was negotiated in a currency of promises given by insiders to outsiders, that is, by experts to publics, and equally in expectations held by laymen concerning their *right to share* in an electric

prosperity made possible by public *recognition* and indulgence of expert ingenuity. Expert and popular literature alike monitored the rhetoric of *reciprocity*, watchful for any breach in the vague but binding bargain between experts and their publics in [sic] behalf of electrical progress" (16; emphasis added). In my analyses in the following chapters, which contextualize expertise in a more recent era, "right to share," "recognition," and "reciprocity" shift notably in meaning through digital networks and commons.

70. Rosalind Williams, "Afterword: An Historian's View on the Network Society," in *The Network Society*, ed. Manuel Castells (Cheltenham, UK: Edward Elgar, 2004), 434.
71. Castells, *Network Society*, 7.
72. Friedrich Nietzsche, *Thus Spoke Zarathustra*, in *The Portable Nietzsche*, trans. and ed. Walter Kaufmann (New York: Viking, 1976), 122.
73. Nietzsche, *Thus Spoke Zarathustra*, 130.
74. Nietzsche, *Thus Spoke Zarathustra*, 126 ("the people laugh"); and 133 ("jester").
75. Nietzsche, *Thus Spoke Zarathustra*, 218.
76. Nietzsche, *Thus Spoke Zarathustra*, 190.
77. The conversation between Zarathustra and the saint in Part One is especially remarkable when the latter insists that humans do not need gifts but rather help and relief from their toil. Nietzsche, *Thus Spoke Zarathustra*, 123. As Zarathustra has already told the saint that the gift he intends to bring is his wisdom, the saint implies that humans do not need wisdom, or at least that they need other gifts more. Zarathustra confirms this when he remarks that the gift he has in mind is unlikely to be well-received. Preparing finally to leave the saint, he asks, "What could I have to give you?" In place of an answer, Zarathustra says, "Let me go quickly lest I take something from you." Nietzsche, *Thus Spoke Zarathustra*, 124. The exchange concludes with a binary distinction: interlocutors either give or take something from one another.
78. Nietzsche, *Thus Spoke Zarathustra*, 186.
79. Nietzsche, *Thus Spoke Zarathustra*, 187.
80. Nietzsche, *Thus Spoke Zarathustra*, 201.
81. Nietzsche, *Thus Spoke Zarathustra*, 123.
82. Nietzsche, *Thus Spoke Zarathustra*, 289, 317.
83. Nietzsche, *Thus Spoke Zarathustra*, 167.
84. Richard White offers a compelling alternative to this bleak interpretation, arguing that gift giving reveals givers' attention to recipients' potential. Via Zarathustra's gift of wisdom, humans' gift to one another may be seen, he contends, not as selfish but as investments in others' spiritual possibilities. Richard White, "Nietzsche on Generosity and the Gift-Giving Virtue," *British Journal for the History of Philosophy* 24, no. 2 (2016): 349.
85. Nietzsche, *Thus Spoke Zarathustra*, 122.
86. Nietzsche, *Thus Spoke Zarathustra*, 218.
87. Nietzsche, *Thus Spoke Zarathustra*, 208.
88. Nietzsche, *Thus Spoke Zarathustra*, 170.
89. Marcel Mauss, *The Gift: Forms and Functions of Exchange in Archaic Societies* (Glencoe, IL: The Free Press, 1954), 1.
90. Mauss, *Gift*, 68.
91. Mauss, *Gift*, 45.

92. Mauss, *Gift*, 11–12 (emphasis added to reference earlier discussion of cultural resources in the digital commons).
93. Mauss, *Gift*, 22.
94. Mauss, *Gift*, 9.
95. Mauss, *Gift*, 57.
96. Mauss, *Gift*, 45.
97. Mauss, *Gift*, 4.
98. Mauss, *Gift*, 66.
99. Mauss, *Gift*, 74.
100. Mauss, *Gift*, 63.
101. Mauss, *Gift*, 69.
102. Mauss, *Gift*, 67.
103. Martin Heidegger, *Being and Time*, trans. Joan Stambaugh (Albany: State University of New York Press, 1996).
104. Joan Stambaugh, "introduction" to *On Time and Being*, trans. Joan Stambaugh (New York: Harper and Row, 1972), x.
105. Martin Heidegger, *On Time and Being*, trans. Joan Stambaugh (New York: Harper and Row Publishers, 1972), 3 (emphasis in original).
106. Heidegger, *On Time and Being*, 4.
107. Heidegger, *On Time and Being*, 4–5.
108. Heidegger, *On Time and Being*, 18.
109. Heidegger, *On Time and Being*, 17. Heidegger references his "Letter on Humanism," wherein he revisits central ideas from *Being and Time*, clarifying the theory of Dasein and positioning his claims relative to existentialism and the humanist tradition. He rejects the humanist tenets of Romantic and Christian worldviews, grounded in metaphysics, and "outfitting man with an immortal soul, the power of reason, or the character of a person." Martin Heidegger, "Letter on Humanism," in *Basic Writings*, ed. David Farrell Krell (New York: HarperCollins Publishers, 1993), 229.
110. Heidegger, *On Time and Being*, 6.
111. Heidegger, *On Time and Being*, 6.
112. Stambaugh, "introduction," ix, x.
113. Heidegger, *On Time and Being*, 19.
114. Heidegger, *On Time and Being*, 21.
115. Heidegger, *On Time and Being*, 17.
116. Heidegger, *On Time and Being*, 22.
117. Heidegger, *On Time and Being*, 22.
118. Heidegger, *On Time and Being*, 24.
119. Heidegger, *On Time and Being*, 12.
120. Lewis Hyde, *Gift: Creativity and the Artist in the Modern World* (New York: Vintage, 2007), xxi, 89, 110.
121. Hyde, *Gift*, 61.
122. Hyde, *Gift*, xvi.
123. Hyde, *Gift*, 187 (emphasis in original).
124. Hyde, *Gift*, xvi.
125. Hyde, *Gift*, 366.

126. Hyde, *Gift*, xix.
127. Hyde, *Gift*, 4.
128. Hyde, *Gift*, 91.
129. Hyde, *Gift*, 32.
130. Hyde, *Gift*, 33.
131. Hyde, *Gift*, 44.
132. Hyde, *Gift*, 145.
133. Hyde, *Gift*, xvi.
134. Hyde, *Gift*, 78.
135. Hyde, *Gift*, 360.
136. Hyde, *Gift*, 27 ("eros and logos") and 197 ("value assessment").
137. Hyde, *Gift*, 201.
138. Hyde, *Gift*, 196.
139. Jacques Derrida, "The Time of the King," in *Given Time: I. Counterfeit Money*, trans. Peggy Kamuf (Chicago: University of Chicago Press, 1992), 11.
140. Derrida, "Time of the King," 12.
141. Derrida, "Time of the King," 14.
142. Derrida, "Time of the King," 23.
143. Derrida, "Time of the King," 7.
144. Jacques Derrida, "The Madness of Economic Reason: A Gift without Present," in *Given Time: I. Counterfeit Money*, trans. Peggy Kamuf (Chicago: University of Chicago Press, 1992), 37.
145. Derrida, "Madness of Economic Reason," 37.
146. Derrida, "Time of the King," 24. Addressing gift exchange as a form of social manipulation, Derrida responds to Lewis Hyde's argument that gifts given within the family unit are unconditional. Derrida inverts Hyde's reading of family, revealing how nothing within it is unconditional. Derrida, "Time of the King," 17n8. See Hyde, *Gift*, 69.
147. Derrida, "Madness of Economic Reason," 59. For Derrida's discussion of how Mauss does not so much offer an apology as he "excuses himself" (see 59–62). Derrida's analysis of excuses continues in the last two essays of the volume, "'Counterfeit Money' I: Poetics of Tobacco" and "'Counterfeit Money' II: Gift and Countergift, Excuse and Forgiveness."
148. Derrida, "Madness of Economic Reason," 49.
149. Derrida, "Madness of Economic Reason," 49-50.
150. Derrida, "Madness of Economic Reason," 53.
151. Derrida, "Madness of Economic Reason," 66. For Mauss's argument about a return to "archaic" societies, see *Gift*, 67–69.
152. Derrida, "Time of the King," 13.
153. Derrida, "Time of the King," 9 (emphasis in original).
154. Derrida, "Madness of Economic Reason," 35.
155. Derrida, "Time of the King," 7 (emphasis in original).
156. Derrida, "Time of the King," 18.
157. Jacques Derrida, "'Counterfeit Money' I: Poetics of Tobacco," in *Given Time: I. Counterfeit Money*, trans. Peggy Kamuf (Chicago: University of Chicago Press, 1992), 91 ("immeasurable") and 30 ("untheorizable").

158. Derrida, "Time of the King," 19–21.

159. Michael J. Hyde, *The Life-Giving Gift of Acknowledgement* (West Lafayette, IN: Purdue University Press, 2006), xv, 10. Hyde's reference to the "call of conscience" is Heideggerian, citing the following translation: Martin Heidegger, *Being and Time*, trans. Edward Robinson and John MacQuarrie (New York: Harper and Row, 1962), 312–348. Because Hyde relies so heavily on the idiolect of Heideggerian theory, I do the same in this section. My earlier discussion of Heidegger supplies the reader with a basic orientation to the relevant concepts.

160. Hyde, *Life-Giving Gift*, 24–25

161. Hyde, *Life-Giving Gift*, 165; see also 61 for a more explicitly Heideggerian approach to this "saying of language."

162. The ambition of Hyde's theory of gifting is, in my assessment, compromised by his insistence on reciprocity. Claiming that God "demands acknowledgement" and "wants the favor [of the gift of life] returned" is a limiting interpretation of both creation and incarnation. It is, in other words, far from self-evident in Judeo-Christian faith. Also on the matter of reciprocity, Hyde departs from his mentor Calvin Schrag's principle that teaching is an altruistic gift for which no thanks are needed. As he explains, Schrag places teachers outside of the economic logic of debt and expectation. In my view, whether it is, as the liturgy goes, "right to give God thanks and praise" or, as Hyde says, "great teachers warrant heartfelt acknowledgement and remembrance," is beside the point. Hyde, *Life-Giving Gift*, 166. They do. But the gift aspect of teaching and of divine grace get lost in Hyde's account precisely when he is about to characterize them both as truly powerful.

163. Hyde, *Life-Giving Gift*, 66.

164. Hyde, *Life-Giving Gift*, 66.

165. Hyde, *Life-Giving Gift*, 74.

166. Hyde, *Life-Giving Gift*, 65.

167. Mifsud, *Rhetoric and the Gift*, 4.

168. Mifsud, *Rhetoric and the Gift*, 3.

169. Mifsud, *Rhetoric and the Gift*, 17 ("than the gift had been"); and 4 ("not amenable to figuration").

170. Mifsud, *Rhetoric and the Gift*, 33.

171. Mifsud, *Rhetoric and the Gift*, 33.

172. Mifsud, *Rhetoric and the Gift*, 79.

173. Mifsud, *Rhetoric and the Gift*, 69.

174. Mifsud, *Rhetoric and the Gift*, 71–72.

175. Mifsud, *Rhetoric and the Gift*, 140.

176. Mifsud, *Rhetoric and the Gift*, 141.

177. Mifsud, *Rhetoric and the Gift*, 141.

178. Mifsud, *Rhetoric and the Gift*, 140.

179. Mifsud, *Rhetoric and the Gift*, 96.

180. Mifsud, *Rhetoric and the Gift*, 104.

181. Mifsud, *Rhetoric and the Gift*, 11.

182. Ralph Waldo Emerson, "Gifts," in *The Logic of the Gift*, ed. Alan D. Schrift (New York: Routledge, 1997), 26.

183. Christina M. Geschwandtner, "The Excess of the Gift in Jean-Luc Marion," in *Gift and Economy: Ethics, Hospitality and the Market*, ed. Eric R. Severson (Newcastle, UK: Cambridge Scholars Publishing, 2012), 27.

184. John McAteer, "The Gifts of God for the People of God: Communion as Derrida's Impossible Gift," in *Gift and Economy: Ethics, Hospitality and the Market*, ed. Eric R. Severson (Newcastle, UK: Cambridge Scholars Publishing, 2012), 67.

185. An undercurrent of my project that surfaces here is how the gifting logos, particularly its progressivism, relates to the progressivist inflection of other models of the history and philosophy of science. At stake is not only what may be known about the universe (and/or the digital commons) and whether that knowledge gets better as history moves along, but also the relationship between expertise as produced through science and expertise as produced through the gifting logos. Simply put, the gifting logos as a rhetoric of expertise constructs its own history, comparable in interesting ways to the history of other epistemologies. Each narrates events in which ever-expanding knowledge is gained by heroes (who by definition seek the truth and the betterment of humanity) against various villains (who oppose and fail to recognize reality). Indeed, it may be more accurate to say that the gifting logos constructs a history in which its ways of knowing (and making and gifting) are a phase in the progress of technoculture. And though not all who engage with the gifting logos can be accurately caricatured as Whiggish, a certain triumphalism is palpable. If, as the example of the Pirate Party in chapter 4 suggests, digital technologies have *revolutionized* the production of culture, and that production might be understood as a networked rhetoric of expertise, as I contend, then various critiques of "revolutions" in the context of knowledge pertain. More simply put, the works of epistemology scholars like Steve Fuller become relevant, indicating the social (and, I would say, political) aspect of productive expertise. Considering the gifting logos as expertise, Fuller might note that beyond the macro-imaginaries of progress, wherein expertise gets better and better and the commons as a whole improves concomitantly, some rhetorical configurations (some rhetorical strategies of knowing-making-gifting) gain more adherence than others depending on sociological or contextual factors. In characterizing the gifting logos, I am compelled by Fuller's phrasing when he writes that "a scientist [expert] should be deciding on a general theory to which she would bind her colleagues." Steve Fuller, "Social Epistemology: A Quarter Century Itinerary," *Social Epistemology* 26, nos. 3–4 (2012): 268. In light of my Heraclitean understanding of logos, it would be apt to say that the gifting logos likewise binds digital commoners together in a network, and that the network regulates activity. Fuller might also say more simply that "experts," who through practice invent themselves as such, need a functional stance on the history of their enterprise. It stands to reason that in inventing oneself as an expert, one would be moved to do so while casting oneself as the fulfillment of a progressive trajectory. Steve Fuller, *Social Epistemology* (Bloomington: Indiana University Press, 1988), 185–188, 238.

CHAPTER 2

1. The legend told in *Stone Stoup* is about a man (usually a solider or vagrant) who comes to a town beset by hardship. In order to get a meal out of his stingy hosts, who are

hoarding stashes of food, the man brags that he knows how to cook a nourishing soup from nothing but a stone. Having dropped a single stone into a pot of boiling water, he convinces the townsfolk that the soup would be much tastier with a simple onion. Reluctantly or eagerly—there are various different accounts—a neighbor offers an onion from a hidden trove. The same procedure is repeated with carrots, potatoes, cream, and so on. The soup turns out to be delicious, and all share in the bounty. While the communalist moral of the story is fairly obvious, there are also more subtle motifs. The visitor who cooks the soup is in possession less of a recipe than of a performance; his art form, developed no doubt in the course of many long travels, and he either cons the townsfolk out of their savings or saves the town from its own fragmentation, depending on one's perspective. The latter frames the soup as the visitor's gift, sustaining not only hungry bellies but the townsfolks' sociality.

2. Ying Chang Compestine, *The Real Story of Stone Soup* (New York: Dutton Children's Books, 2007).

3. Capitalized, "Creative Commons" is the proper name of an organization. The lowercase "*commons*," for example in "*digital commons*," refers in this chapter and elsewhere in the book to the more general phenomenon, the aggregate of persons, places, and resources that is the subject of my investigation.

4. (1) Creative Commons, *The State of the Commons*, https://stateof.creativecommons.org/2015. For the accompanying data sheet, see https://stateof.creativecommons.org/2015/data.html#more-than-1-billion-cc-licensed-works-in-the-commons-as-of-2015; (2) Creative Commons, *The Power of Open*, http://thepowerofopen.org/assets/pdfs/tpoo_eng.pdf; (3) Creative Commons, http://creativecommons.org/; and (4) Lawrence Lessig, "Architecting Innovation," *Drake Law Review* 49 (2001): 397–405. Lawrence Lessig, "Copyright's First Amendment," *UCLA Law Review* 48 (2001): 1057–1073. Lawrence Lessig, "Dunwody Distinguished Lecture in Law: The Creative Commons," *Florida Law Review* 55 (2003): 763–777; Lawrence Lessig, *Free Culture: The Nature and Future of Creativity* (New York: Penguin Books, 2004); and Lawrence Lessig, *The Future of Ideas* (New York: Vintage Book, 2001).

5. For a history of copyright beyond the resources referenced directly in the next section, see Peter Decherney, *Hollywood's Copyright Wars: From Edison to the Internet* (New York: Columbia University Press, 2012); Jane C. Ginsburg, "How Copyright Got a Bad Name for Itself," *Columbia Journal of Law and the Arts* 26, no. 1 (2002): 1–6; David L. Lange, "Recognizing the Public Domain," *Law and Contemporary Problems* 44 (1981): 147–178; Joseph Loewenstein, *The Author's Due: Printing and the Prehistory of Copyright* (Chicago: University of Chicago Press, 2002); Lyman Ray Patterson, *Copyright in Historical Perspective* (Nashville: Vanderbilt University Press, 1968); Harry Ransom, *The First Copyright Statute* (Austin: The University of Texas Press, 1956); James Raven, *Free Print and Non-Commercial Publishing since 1700* (London and Burlington, VT: Ashgate Press, 2000); Siva Vaidhyanathan, *Copyrights and Copywrongs: The Rise of Intellectual Property and How It Threatens Creativity* (New York: New York University Press, 2001); and Martha Woodmansee, "The Genius and the Copyright: Economic and Legal Conditions of the Emergence of the 'Author,'" *Eighteenth Century Studies* 17, no. 4 (1984): 425–448. For an introduction to intellectual property in a historical perspective, see Jane Gaines, *Contested Culture: The Image, the Voice, and the Law* (Chapel Hill: University of North Carolina Press, 1991); Jane C. Ginsburg and Rochelle Dreyfuss, *Intellectual Property Stories* (New

York: Foundation Press, 2006); and Eva Hemmungs Wirten, *No Trespassing: Authorship, Intellectual Property Rights, and the Boundaries of Globalization* (Toronto: University of Toronto Press, 2004).

6. Joanna Kostylo, "From Gunpowder to Print: The Common Origins of Copyright and Patent," in *Privilege and Property: Essays on the History of Copyright*, ed. Ronan Deazley, Martin Kretschmer, and Lionel Bentley (Cambridge, UK: OpenBook Publishers, 2010), 25.

7. Oren Bracha, "Early American Printing Privileges: The Ambivalent Origins of Authors' Copyright in America," in *Privilege and Property: Essays on the History of Copyright*, ed. Ronan Deazley, Martin Kretschmer, and Lionel Bentley (Cambridge, UK: OpenBook Publishers, 2010), 97.

8. Mark Rose, *Authors and Owners: The Invention of Copyright* (Cambridge, MA: Harvard University Press, 1993), 11.

9. Venice in the fifteenth and sixteenth centuries was a vibrant center for artisans and craftsmen, whose technical expertise the Venetian authorities strategically sought to keep within the city. The guild system and local copyrights prevented ambitious individuals from breaking out on their own and moving trade secrets beyond the town. Of less concern to the privilege-granting authorities were the immaterial aspects of text, the idea beyond the fixed form, so long as no potentially insurgent message was propagated. In Usher's case, the arrangement with the not yet state of Massachusetts was a "win-win" in which a prominent local bore the expense of publishing public documents in exchange for the commercial privileges associated with printing technology.

10. Jody Greene, *The Trouble with Ownership: Literary Property and Authorial Liability in England, 1160–1730* (Philadelphia: University of Pennsylvania Press, 2005), 3.

11. Rose, *Authors and Owners*, 31.

12. Rose, *Authors and Owners*, 15.

13. Rose, *Authors and Owners*, 6. For an analysis of natural rights and the Lockean metaphor of the commons applied to digital culture, see Donald Fishman, "Reading John Locke in Cyberspace: Natural Rights and 'The Commons' in a Digital Age," *Free Speech Yearbook* 41 (2004): 39–42.

14. Paul Goldstein, *Copyright's Highway: The Law and Lore of Copyright from Gutenberg to the Celestial Jukebox* (New York: Hill and Wang, 1994), 43.

15. Greene, *Trouble with Ownership*, 5--. The word "*own*" is a rich point for scholars of copyright history, indexing the kinship between ownership-as-proprietorship and ownership-as-accountability. As an illustration, consider the phrase "to "own up" to one's mistakes. Greene, *Trouble with Ownership*, 4. See also William St. Clair, "Metaphors of Intellectual Property," in *Privilege and Property: Essays on the History of Copyright*, ed. Ronan Deazley, Martin Kretschmer, and Lionel Bentley (Cambridge, UK: OpenBook Publishers, 2010), 387.

16. *Intellectual property*, "an umbrella term encompassing copyright, patent law, trademarks, trade secrets, and industrial design," is a broader concept than copyright. Meredith L. McGill, "Copyright and Intellectual Property: The State of the Discipline," *Book History* 16 (2013): 388. I focus on copyright rather than intellectual property in this book, especially in this chapter, partly to highlight the significance of historical precedents and precursors. The following nested conceptual orientation might offer clarification: Intellectual property

is cultural material that someone owns, acting on this ownership in commerce; the World Intellectual Property Organization uses the phrase "creations of the mind." More specifically, copyright is a principle, instantiated in both laws and traditions, that reserves rights to cultural material for the material's creator, publisher, or owner. In short, intellectual property is protected nationally and internationally not only by copyright laws but also by patent laws and trademarks. By comparison, copyright is a complex institution whose history is an invaluable resource for understanding the initiatives of the digital commons.

17. Ronan Deazley, who locates the initial use of the term intellectual property in S. A. Plant's 1953 book *The New Commerce in Ideas and Intellectual Property*, makes a compelling case for distinguishing carefully between copyright, intellectual property, and other forms of property. *Rethinking Copyright: History, Theory, Language* (Cheltenham, UK: Edward Elgar, 2006), 132. In reference to a thick discussion of Jeremy Waldron's *The Right to Private Property*, Deazley attributes the "rampant expansionism" of proprietary restrictions to the "conceit and language of intellectual property as natural property right." *Rethinking Copyright*, 152. Deazley's concern is for the naturalization and reification of cultural ownership: "As we continue to embrace this reification of copyright, with its rhetorical paradigm of copyright as property right *qua* human right, and allow it to dominate copyright's future trajectory, we lose the opportunity to engage in other, arguably more appropriate forms of copyright discourse. One of the profoundly undesirable results of this conceptual juggernaut is that it operates to occlude other models of conceiving of, and talking about, intellectual property, at least within the realms of the policymaker, the legislature, and the judiciary." *Rethinking Copyright*, 160.

18. Meredith McGill, *American Literature and the Culture of Reprinting, 1834–1853* (Philadelphia: University of Pennsylvania Press, 2003).

19. McGill, *American Literature*, 47. McGill's analysis challenges the dominant view of literary culture in the antebellum era, which assumes that reprinting hindered both individual American authors' success and the formation of a national literary community. She writes, "Reprinting is not simply the antithesis of a legitimately national, original culture, neither are reprinted texts merely passive vehicles for the dissemination of European culture. In this case, reprinting is a sophisticated instrument for projecting an image of a nation that is at once colonial and imperial." *American Literature*, 23. In 1870, following the Civil War, copyright procedures were transformed to serve nationally unifying functions. The Library of Congress became the operative agency, collecting and archiving copies of texts for which copyrights were registered. The archive in this historical moment reflects both administrative efficiency and curatorial nationalism. For more on the archive and proprietary content, see chapter 3.

20. When the United States signed the Berne Convention in 1988, copyright became an internationally coordinated effort involving US courts.

21. See Timothy Armstrong's commentary on US copyright policy from 1976 to 1998 in "Shrinking the Commons: Termination of Copyright Licenses and Transfers for the Benefit of the Public," *Harvard Journal on Legislation* 47 (2010): 388–392.

22. In the 2002 Supreme Court oral arguments, Eldred was represented by Creative Commons founder Lawrence Lessig. For a discussion of Lessig's involvement with Eldred, see Marc Garcelon, "An Information Commons? Creative Commons and Public Access to

Cultural Creations," *New Media & Society* 11, no. 8 (2009): 1311–1318. Garcelon is optimistic about the democratic potential of the Creative Commons, particular in reference to the original Jeffersonian ideals of US copyright, including the "idea/expression dichotomy."

23. In the simplest terms, that the internet was designed as an end-to-end structure means that the complexity, value, and content of the enterprise as a whole happen at the periphery of the network, where the people sit at their screens. The grid or structure itself is simple, while the participants are complex. That is, the participants make complex digital things, using the simple network to disseminate what they make. This facilitates interaction and theoretically obstructs the kind of content-specific censorship that would allow some messages or applications to circulate in the grid but not others. Tim Berners-Lee, *Weaving the Web* (San Francisco: HarperSanFrancisco, 1999); and James Gillies, *How the Web Was Born: The Story of the World Wide Web* (Oxford and New York: Oxford University Press, 2000). For a discussion of the digital commons' network structure, see chapter 1, page 22.

24. The story of Unix, GNU('s not Unix), and GNU/Linux is beyond the scope of my treatment of Stallman here, as is further detail about the open source movement pertaining specifically to software code. See Gary Anthes, "Unix Turns 40: The Past, Present and Future of a Revolutionary OS," *Computerworld*, June 4, 2009, www.computerworld.com/article/2524456/linux/unix-turns-40--the-past--present-and-future-of-a-revolutionary-os.html. For Stallman's own reflections, see his self-published work, *Free Software, Free Society: Selected Essays of Richard M. Stallman* (Boston: Free Software Foundation, 2010), www.gnu.org/doc/fsfs-ii-2.pdf.

25. "*Open code*" and "*open source*" are not synonymous. Open source licenses do not require that derivative works be made openly available, as the GPL does for open code material. Thus, someone could be inspired by an open source program, turn pieces of it into new software, keep that code secret, and sell it for profit.

26. David Bollier, *Think Like a Commoner* (Gabriola Island, BC: New Society Publishers, 2014), 117; and Lessig, *Future of Ideas*, 12.

27. Joan Francesc Fondevila Gascón and Raúl López Garcia-Navas, "New Digital Production Models: The Consolidation of the Copyleft," in *Cultures of Copyright*, ed. Dánielle Nicole DeVoss and Martine Courant Rife (New York: Peter Lang, 2015), 67–70. Peter Suber, a prominent figure in the open access movement, chronicles its timeline at http://legacy.earlham.edu/~peters/fos/overview.htm. Kate Milberry and Steve Anderson offer a substantive if somewhat idealistic account of how the "free and open source software" movement resists corporate enclosure of the internet, "comprising a liberatory praxis that offers a roadmap to a more democratic media system and, more broadly construed, a more democratic society." "Open Sourcing Our Way to an Online Commons: Contesting Corporate Impermeability in the New Media Ecology," *Journal of Communication Inquiry* 33 (2009): 394.

28. As I note in chapter 1, advocates and scholars of the open access movement tend to seek and embrace long-spanning historical parallels, often with reference to the consequences of enclosures of the commons. The tragedy of the commons, argue Milberry and Anderson, is the tragedy of the corporate enclosure of the content layer of the internet, the World Wide Web, software, spaces, and services. "Open Sourcing Our Way," 396. According to Karl-Nikolaus Peifer, "The 'return of the commons' has a credible source in

the history of copyright itself. It is the information broker that may be conceived as the heart of a copyright theory rooted in the Enlightenment." "The Return of the Commons—Copyright History as a Common Source," in *Privilege and Property: Essays on the History of Copyright*, ed. Ronan Deazley, Martin Kretschmer, and Lionel Bentley (Cambridge, UK: OpenBook Publishers, 2010), 348. These efforts to historicize the commons typically share a vaguely political vision of how democratic or populist arrangements of the past may be revived. The unauthorized reprinting culture in the United States in the nineteenth century provides this line of thinking with abundant resources for romanticizing the civic impact of nonproprietary publishing. I am skeptical of this approach, which tends to justify policy in terms of an idealized reconstruction of the past. My analysis should not be interpreted as participating in historical analogism. Worth noting, as McGill does, is that Western "copyleft" advocates and contemporary indigenous movements that advocate for the commons (e.g., in Latin American tribal cultures) have in past decades diverged considerably on copyright issues. McGill, "Copyright and Intellectual Property," 417. The former strive to "limit or attenuate the hold of intellectual property over cultural creators," while the latter, responding to colonial exploitation and global capitalism, attempt to codify protections for indigenous/traditional/local knowledges, practices, and artifacts by classifying them as intellectual property.

29. Goldstein characterizes subscribers to the utilitarian model as copyright "pessimists" and to the natural rights model as "optimists." The optimists "view copyright's cup of entitlement as always half full, only waiting to be filled still further." The pessimists "accept that copyright owners should get some measure of control over copies as an incentive to produce creative works, but they would like copyright to extend only so far as is necessary to give this incentive, and treat anything more as an encroachment on the general freedom of everyone to write and say what they please." Goldstein, *Copyright's Highway*, 15. On the two models, see Susan Corbett, "Creative Commons Licenses, the Copyright Regime and the Online Community: Is There a Fatal Disconnect?," *Modern Law Review* 74 (2011): 511; Lewis Hyde, *Common as Air* (New York: Farrar, Straus, and Giroux, 2010), 48-50; and Deazley, *Rethinking Copyright*, 138.

30. Stephen Breyer, "The Uneasy Case for Copyright: A Study of Copyright in Books, Photocopies, and Computer Programs," *Harvard Law Review* 84, no. 2 (1970): 281–355. In this essay, the Supreme Court justice to be explicates the economic premises of American copyright law and rejects alternatives based on the natural rights model. One of the most famous responses to the article is Barry Tyerman's "The Economic Rationale for Copyright Protection for Published Books: A Reply to Professor Breyer," *UCLA Law Review* 18 (1971): 1100–1125.

31. The essay was translated to English in 1975. See Michel Foucault, "What Is an Author?," in *Criticism: Major Statements*, ed. Charles Kaplan and Willian Davis Anderson (Boston: Bedford/St. Martin's, 2000), 544–558.

32. Foucault, "What Is an Author?," 549. Although he does not engage Roland Barthes explicitly, Foucault's assumptions about the author's conceptual death are references to Barthes's essay "The Death of the Author," published just two years earlier. For an English translation of the essay, see Roland Barthes, *Image, Music, Text*, trans. Stephen Heath (New York: Hill and Wang, 1977), 142–148.

33. Foucault, "What Is an Author?" 547.

34. Foucault, "What Is an Author?" 551.

35. Greene, who claims that "no work on the history of authorship has had more influence than Foucault's essay," argues that the author function must be placed in the context of Foucault's claim that authors of transgressive discourses are penalized. Greene, *Trouble with Ownership*, 9. She responds to the problem of chronology that her thesis encounters: "Foucault is clear that 'penal appropriation' precedes the ownership of texts: the production of discourse, he writes, 'was a gesture fraught with risks before becoming goods caught up in a circuit of ownership.'" *Trouble with Ownership*, 10. According to Greene, Foucault implies that the privilege of ownership codified by the Statute of Anne "displaced" authors' liability to punishment, "getting rid of the risks formerly associated with textual production." *Trouble with Ownership*, 11. This is the point that Greene contests; as previously noted, her thesis is that precisely when authors were endowed with rights and were classified and registered as authors, authorship became precarious.

36. Ronan Deazley, Martin Kretschmer, and Lionel Bentley, eds., *Privilege and Property: Essays on the History of Copyright* (Cambridge, UK: OpenBook Publishers, 2010), 2, 15. See also Emily Apter, "What Is Yours, Ours, and Mine: Authorial Ownership and the Creative Commons," *October Magazine* 126 (2008): 92, 97.

37. He explains, "In speaking I attempt to communicate certain things to my hearer by getting him to recognize my intention to communicate just those things. I achieve the intended effect on the hearer by getting him to recognize my intention to achieve that effect, and as soon as the hearer recognizes what it is my intention to achieve, it is in general achieved." John R. Searle, *Speech Acts* (Cambridge, UK: Cambridge University Press, 1969), 43.

38. Stanley Cavell, *Philosophical Passages: Wittgenstein, Emerson, Austin, Derrida* (Cambridge, MA: Blackwell, 1995), 44.

39. It was originally written for a conference held in Montreal by the Congrès international des Sociétés de philosophie de langue francaise. The 1977 essay is reproduced in the book *Limited Inc.* (Evanston, IL: Northwestern University Press, 1988). References to it here include page numbers from the book.

40. Derrida, *Limited Inc.*, 36.

41. Derrida, *Limited Inc.*, 30–31.

42. Derrida, *Limited Inc.*, 8. For a helpful analysis of Searle's and Derrida's productive (mis)understandings of one another, see Gregory Ulmer, "Sounding the Unconscious," in *Glassary*, ed. John P. Leavey (Lincoln: University of Nebraska Press, 1986), 23–27. For further bibliographic information regarding the controversy, see Mark Alfino, "Another Look at the Derrida-Searle Debate," *Philosophy and Rhetoric* 24, no. 2 (1991): 144.

43. Jane Ginsburg, "A Tale of Two Copyrights: Literary Property in Revolutionary France and America," *Tulane Law Review* 64, no. 5 (1990): 1023. This resonates with McGill's description of the republican utilitarianism of antebellum reprinting culture (see "Property and the US Copyright Clause" and note 19).

44. Ginsburg, "A Tale of Two Copyrights," 8.

45. Ginsburg, "A Tale of Two Copyrights," 12.

46. Deazley, Kretschmer, and Bentley, *Privilege and Property*, 13.

47. Consider, for example, the odd and legally meaningless practice of annotating You-Tube videos with the disclaimer "No copyright infringement intended." Ben McCorkle, "Hindered Hope: Shepard Fairey, the Associated Press, and the Missed Opportunity to Help Clarify U.S. Copyright Law," in *Cultures of Copyright*, ed. Dánielle Nicole DeVoss and Martine Courant Rife (New York: Peter Lang, 2015), 61.

48. Fondevila Gascón and Garcia-Navas, "New Digital Production Models," 73.

49. The initiative was originally funded in large part by a grant from the Center for the Public Domain, whose chief representatives were the overnight-wealthy coders of the "dot-com" era.

50. Lessig, *Free Culture*, 10–12, 148–157; and Lessig, *Future of Ideas*, 98, 249.

51. David Bollier, *Viral Spiral* (New York: The New Press, 2008), 108.

52. The Creative Commons is not only comparable to these and similar initiatives in purpose, format, and various legalities, but also in many cases integrated with them. For example, the Wikimedia Commons database and the artifacts contained therein are licensed under the "Attribution-ShareAlike" tag combination.

53. All of the direct quotations in this block are from the CC's definitions of the licenses. See https://creativecommons.org/licenses/.

54. The "ShareAlike" dimension of this and several of the following combinations resonates with the aforementioned ethic of use dictated by Stallman's General Public License.

55. Since 2002 the Creative Commons has launched four versions of the suite, responding to the issue of international compatibility and users' calls for an option to license work anonymously. Cliff Morgan, "Making Your Article Freely Available: Some Clarifications about OnlineOpen and Creative Commons," *Bioessays* 32, no. (2010): 649. See also Matěj Myška, "The New Creative Commons 4.0 Licenses," *Grey Journal* 11 (2015): 58–62.

56. Armstrong, "Shrinking the Commons," 383.

57. Marcel Mauss, *The Gift: Forms and Functions of Exchange in Archaic Societies* (Glencoe, IL: The Free Press, 1954). Regarding Mauss's theory of gifting, see chapter 1, p. 28.

58. The manifesto *Speculate This!* (Durham, NC, and London: Duke University Press, 2013), by the anonymous writing cooperative Uncertain Commons, offers a compelling discussion of various forms of speculation. The authors argue that under the conditions of late capitalism, two semantic registers of "speculation" (cognitive forecasting and financial profiteering) intersect, particularly in the effort to minimize risk. Rejecting the elimination of risk and uncertainty, the authors propose that to speculate "affirmatively" is to "produce futures while refusing the foreclosure of potentialities." Affirmative speculation "unsettles in order to conjecture creatively" without thereby "suggesting the wild west of potentiation." It reaches "toward those futures that are already latent in the present, those possibilities that already exist embedded in the here and now, about human and nonhuman power, which is, in effect, the ability to become different from what is present." As I discuss in the following pages, the Creative Commons licensors seem to be operating somewhere between prediction, prescription, and potentiation of digital cultural practices.

59. See the preceding section's discussion of the two models of copyright, p. 50. Some of the challenges that CC has faced internationally are traceable to the issue of what rights an individual may intentionally surrender. Critics argue that CC may not be philosophically or legally suitable for countries that subscribe to the ideal of an inviolable relationship

between a creator and her or his creation. As Alexandra Giannopoulou notes in her critique of CC, the two major concerns in moral rights cultures is whether an inalienable right is suspendible as a result of individual choice and whether use of cultural material that compromises the original creator's reputation violates copyright's purpose, even when the creator has ostensibly agreed to such use. "The Creative Commons Licenses through Moral Rights Provisions in French Law," *International Review of Law, Computers and Technology* 28, no. 1 (2014): 60–80.

60. In reference to the "attribution" function, the CC has been accused of perpetuating and expanding individual rights to cultural content rather than stimulating collaborative production. Allison Fish argues that alternative proprietary forms, such as those offered by the CC, can never effectively produce a commons because they reproduce the public/private binary of modern law. She claims that such initiatives "produce a commons that is barren of social relationships and where informational objects are abandoned by creators." "The Place of 'Culture' in the Access to Knowledge Movement: Comparing Creative Commons and Yogic Theories of Knowledge Transfer," *Anthropology Today* 30, no. 5 (2014): 8.

61. Sociological studies of "collective knowledge production" and "content sharing" tend to connect the potential or perceived value of content with general reluctance against networked collaboration. They associate prospective participants' apprehension about collective production with the loss of individual distinction. When this research turns to the CC, it identifies the "Attribution" tag as providing reassurance. This tag singularizes the process of invention, guaranteeing participants credit. According to this research, participants who perceive either that what they are considering contributing may have offline value, or that the process itself of collective production insufficiently recognizes individual contributions, are apprehensive about the costs of participation. When the CC licenses are overlaid onto open production platforms (such as wikis), this "enforces an *identity preservation* strategy which requires the users of a work to acknowledge the original creators of the work, thereby increasing the visibility of the knowledge sharer in the community." Chen-Chung Liu, Chia-Ching Lin, Chun-Yi Chang, and Po-Yao Chao, "Knowledge Sharing among University Students Facilitated with a Creative Commons Licensing Mechanism: A Case Study in a Programming Course," *Educational Technology & Society* 17, no. 3 (2014): 157 (emphasis added). This research finds that the license "protects individual creations while encouraging remixing and deriving new creations from them. [. . .] All participants can share resources they created and utilise them to accomplish a personal-owned product through combining and deriving others' work." Chen-Chung Liu, Shu-Yuam Tao, Wei-Hung Chen, Sherry Y. Chen, and Baw-Jhiune Liu, "The Effects of a Creative Commons Approach on Collaborative Learning," *Behavior & Information Technology* 32, no. 1 (2013): 41. "Attribution" is the mechanism that assures participants that their individuality will not be lost in the deindividuated flux of the commons, that they will be credited for their gifts, and that any aggregating value rendered by multiple gifts will be traceable to a single node, a name. For an instructive, if somewhat uncritical, literature review of networked production and the Creative Commons, see Chen-Chung Liu, Chia-Ching Lin, Kuei-Yuam Deng, Ying-Tien Wu, and Chin-Chung Tsai, "Online Knowledge Sharing Experience with Creative Commons," *Online Information Review* 38 (2014): 680–696.

62. Lewis Hyde's celebration of the artist who "forgets" the market and "serve[s] his gifts on their own terms" is relevant here. *The Gift: Creativity and the Artist in the Modern World* (New York: Vintage Books, 2007), 360. As I explain in chapter 1, Hyde's distinction between true art's value and the market value of commodities is all but absolute. And insofar as the CC's cultural artifacts are declarative rather than subjunctive, and the market and the scene of giving are coinciding spaces, the simple binary of Lewis' model is undone.

63. This abundance effect is contested in legal scholarship that analyzes the CC initiative and copyright laws. That the organization's evidence of profit is anecdotal is less of a problem for these critics than that the issue of market demand is insufficiently addressed. Susan Corbett writes, "While the Creative Commons model is embraced by authors who are not dependent upon remuneration from their creativity but seek recognition or a wider audience for their creative works, such as teachers and researchers, it is not necessarily appropriate for individual authors who seek to earn their living through their creative works." "Creative Commons Licenses," 530. Bas Bloemsaat and Pieter Kleve characterize the potential impact of the CC as primarily awareness raising and argue that the licenses are unlikely to generate profit. To them, "CC may find some inroads into home-made content, but in general it seems more politically motivated than demand driven." "Creative Commons: A Business Model for Products Nobody Wants to Buy," *International Review of Law, Computers and Technology* 23 (2009): 248. It is striking how both interpretations of the CC's functionality implicitly confirm the gifting logos; content that is marked with the licenses enters the commons as gifts. To Corbett, authors who need to earn a living make licensed texts a sacrificial gift. To Bloemsaat and Kleve, gifts of cultural stuff are relatively valueless offline; donating them to the commons entails no lost revenue. Further, it is significant for my purposes that in the scholarship here represented by Corbett, Bloemsaat, and Kleve, gifts to the digital commons instantiate the giver's knowledge and experience in some specialized terrain. In the digital commons, which givers enter qua givers, gifts are cultural productions of expertise.

64. One of the highlighted stories in *The Power of Open* is about British photographer Jonathan Worth, who publicized a high-resolution image of science fiction writer and CC advocate Cory Doctorow, tagging it only with the "Attribution" tag. This made the image freely available for transformative use as well as commercial purposes. Worth comments, "The mode of information is the same, but the mode of distribution has changed. [. . .] It's like putting a message in a bottle and the tides can take it anywhere under its own steam and you can take advantage of those forces." For an analysis of digital data streams, logos, and flux, see my essay "Big Data and Global Knowledge: A Protagorean Analysis of the United Nations' Global Pulse," in *Ancient Rhetorics, Digital Networks*, ed. Michele Kennerly and Damien Smith Pfister (Tuscaloosa: University of Alabama Press, 2018).

65. Lessig, *Future of Ideas*, 39-40.

66. See my discussion of Heidegger's theory of the gift in chapter 1, p. 30. Reflecting on Heidegger's understanding of the gift as ontological, John McAteer proposes "that we think of gift as communion where what is given is the gift of being-with-the-other." "The Gifts of God for the People of God: Communion as Derrida's Impossible Gift," in *Gift and Economy: Ethics, Hospitality and the Market*, ed. Eric R. Severson (Newcastle, UK: Cambridge Scholars Publishing, 2012), 67. To simplify, not only is being a gift, and a given, but what is given is the being-with experience of community. McAteer continues, "The gift is

a communion that requires a recognition of the other as a distinct person both capable of giving to me and receiving from me." McAteer's approach is instructively applicable to my project insofar as he pursues "a third kind of gift" that is neither a favor—a coercive gesture—nor wholly/holy sacrificial, that is, entirely disinterested. Like McAteer, I am invested in accounting for the gift in rhetorical praxis and in realities beyond good and evil.

67. For a fuller treatment of Nietzsche's gift theory, see chapter 1, p. 27.

68. Creative Commons, *The State of the Commons* (emphasis added).

69. See chapter 1, p. 36.

70. Creative Commons, "About: What Can Creative Commons Do for Me?," http://creativecommons.org/about.

71. Creative Commons, "Team Open," http://teamopen.cc/sofya/ (emphasis added). Polyakov's project is an online archive of simple icons, publicized in "vector" format; they are free of charge and can be adapted and resized without loss of image quality.

72. Polyakov describes her project's implications: "Creative Commons makes it easier for people to put their ideas out there and share them with the world. [...] By sharing your creations and giving others permission to use them, you're actually expanding global knowledge. And that's pretty exciting." Creative Commons, "Team Open," http://teamopen.cc/sofya/.

73. Creative Commons, "Team Open," http://teamopen.cc/khalid/.

74. Creative Commons, "About: What Our Licenses Do," http://creativecommons.org/about.

75. Creative Commons, "About: What Can Creative Commons Do for Me?"

76. Creative Commons, *The Power of Open*. Remarkably, this perception of the CC as a gift that enters an unwieldy tension is reflected in scholarly commentary on Lessig's initiative. See for example Elizabeth Roxana Mass Araya and Silvana Aparecida Borsetti Gregorio Vidotti, "Creative Commons: A Convergence Model between the Ideal of Commons and the Possibilities of Creation in Contemporary Times, Opposed to Copyright Impediments," *Information Services and Use* 31, nos. 3–4 (2011): 108.

77. Lessig, "Architecting Innovation," 399–400, 403–404.

78. Lessig, "Dunwody Distinguished Lecture," 766; and Lessig, *Free Culture*, 148–157.

79. Creative Commons, *The State of the Commons*.

80. Lessig, "Copyright's First Amendment," 1069; and Lessig, *Free Culture*, 23–24.

81. This interpretation of an exigence in copyright culture and policy, to which the CC provides a fitting response, is reinforced in trade publications. See, for example, Wallys W. Conhaim, "Creative Commons Nurtures the Public Domain," *Information Today* 19 (2002): 52.

82. Creative Commons, "About: What Is Creative Commons?," http://creativecommons.org/about.

83. Creative Commons, "License Chooser," http://creativecommons.org/choose (emphasis added).

84. Creative Commons, "About: License Design and Rationale," http://creativecommons.org/about. The "NoDerivs" tag has been the subject of some criticism from radical advocates of open access and free culture. Critics argue that content cannot be free unless users are at liberty to modify the content without restrictions.

85. Creative Commons, *The State of the Commons*.

86. In the introduction to the *State of the Commons*, the CC is defined as a "global charity." Indeed, its tax classification is as a "charitable corporation," or a 501(c)(3), chartered in Massachusetts. Reinforcing the theme of charity, the *State of the Commons* showcases major philanthropic organizations that have adopted open license policies to ensure "that all grantees openly license any digital outputs of their work, an important shift that has had tremendous ripple effect." In this story of organizations and individuals who make good choices, any distinction between grants, charity, and gifts is difficult to discern.

87. The book was turned into a film (*Steal This Movie!*) about Hoffman's life. Years later, another film in two parts, titled *Steal This Film!*, chronicled the emergence of the Swedish "Pirate Party," which is the focus of chapter 4.

88. A related iteration of this complex of deliberate choices, digital actions, and systemic controls occurs in social media. Platforms like Facebook and Twitter host millions of users, whose production of data endows the sites with value. Put simply, what makes a site like Facebook pleasurable is not the site itself but what users discover about their "friends" when they log on. Value, as previously discussed, is created by (and traceable to) individuals. Names and profiles are the nodes wherein value is amassed. Social media platforms, then, as the infrastructure for this value, dispense limited control to users and retain structural control for themselves. (By comparison, recall how in early Anglo-American copyright history individuals were given privileges to publish useful texts like catechisms, maps, and almanacs, while the authorities pursued and punished instances of sedition and heresy. The little guys were given control over little things, while the big guys retained control over the big and dangerous things.) A user might choose to post a picture of her breakfast, comment on a friend's vacation story, repost an article from the *New York Times*, or "like" an artist. Facebook states explicitly, "You own all of the content and information you post on Facebook, and you can control how it is shared through your privacy and application settings." "Legal Terms," www.facebook.com/legal/terms/update. Over data that users tend to think of as content, such as text and images, users grant Facebook "a non-exclusive, transferable, sub-licensable, royalty-free, worldwide license to use any IP content that you [the user] post on or in connection with Facebook (IP License)." Important here is that Facebook and other platforms have little interest in what users think of as copyrightable content. They have little incentive to interfere with individual control of that content. The data that they do have motives to control are the data that many users think of as uninteresting or valueless, at least compared to the aforementioned content like texts and images. Social media platforms are interested in such things as when, from where, and with what device you log into your account; what kind of camera you use to take the pictures that you post; and what credit cards you use when you buy things from the same device. *This* information is worth tremendous amounts of money. The point of this detour into social media, whose legal and commercial relationships with the CC are tangential for my purposes, is that if gifting is contingent on choice, if choice implies control, and if ultimate control is perceived as beyond the participants of the digital commons, then gifting is a way to insist on creators' control over the created stuff. Facebook may control the data generated about me and by me, unbeknownst to me. But the CC tells me that I am in charge of how future users are going to engage with my music and photographs, as long as I choose to gift them. For an excellent analysis of data actions and the value thereof, see Timothy R. Amidon and

Jessica Reyman, "Authorship and Ownership of User Contributions on the Social Web," in *Cultures of Copyright*, ed. Dánielle Nicole DeVoss and Martine Courant Rife (New York: Peter Lang, 2015), 108–124.

89. Apter's contextualizing of Hoffman's political agenda thoughtfully bespeaks the much broader and older idea that art cannot be commerce. Apter, "What Is Yours," 104. With reference to Jacques Derrida and Edgar Allan Poe, she takes on the myth of literary originality and the notion that all symbol use is in some sense plagiarism. See page 51 of this chapter. Apter's analysis of how artistic influence functions is strikingly evocative of Nietzsche's theory of the gift. Both describe a process of coming to terms with and/or expelling alterity as it dwells within the giver or artist. To Apter, contagion among subjects "is an obvious point that psychoanalysis would not be alone in admitting. We constitute ourselves as autonomous subjects, but we continue to carry within us fragments that do not belong to us." "What Is Yours," 112.

90. Creative Commons, *The State of the Commons*.

91. Creative Commons, *The State of the Commons*. In a special issue of the *Cornell Law Review*, intellectual property scholars draw on models of the natural commons, Elinor Ostrom's research in particular, to theorize the cultural commons and their management. The authors articulate an analogous conceptual relationship that intersects on the idea of inheritance: "We inherit the natural physical environment—live within, use, interact with, and change it—and we pass it on to future generations. Similarly, we inherit, live within, use, interact with, change, and pass on an intellectual and cultural environment." Michael J. Madison, Brett M. Frischmann, and Katherine J. Strandburg, "Constructing Commons in the Cultural Environment," special issue, *Cornell Law Review* 95 (2010): 685.

92. Creative Commons, "About: Three 'Layers' of Licenses," http://creativecommons.org/about.

93. Creative Commons, "About: Three 'Layers' of Licenses."

94. Photo-sharing sites like Flickr and Google Picasa offer searchable photograph collections wherein the items are marked and made accessible by the CC licenses. Similarly, Ccmixter.org and OpSound.org are musical communities available for sampling and mash-up. RemixMyLit is a digital story anthology whose participants select, edit, and recontextualize stories. The NeuroCommons is a management platform making scientific research, particularly and most notably data sets, reusable.

95. As most commentaries on the CC note, the layers are where the influence of Stallman's GPL is most evident. Stallman's license was intended to facilitate, or perhaps even require, that software code that originated as "open source" and "open access" remain that way for future generations. In light of his commitment to "free culture," Stallman has criticized the Creative Commons licenses that are more restrictive than the "ShareAlike" tag, including and especially any license configurations that include the "NoDerivs" tag.

96. Creative Commons, *The State of the Commons*.

97. Creative Commons, *The State of the Commons*.

98. We might think of the "ShareAlike" tag, for example, as a gene that carries certain information, producing adaptations of a given strand in new embodiments. Lyrics to a song may be adapted from an original into new versions, and those versions move forward generationally, giving rise to more shared and adapted material.

99. On gifting and the pool metaphor, see Hyde, *Gift*, 96.

100. This dot-graph is accompanied by a reference to the "global pool of content," illustrating the relationship between a pool and drops, or dots.

101. Notably, this model of cultural production resonates with the policy rationale behind "fair use" and its "transformative" impact on copyrighted material. Transformative use of cultural artifacts is a legally protected form of copyright violation, justifiable to the extent that it generates more artifacts. A satirical reinterpretation of a play or a book cannot make its point without reproducing some of the original. See US Supreme Court rulings in *Suntrust v. Houghton Mifflin Co.*, 268 F.3d 1257 (11th Cir. 2001), and *Campbell v. Acuff-Rose Music, Inc.*, 510 U.S. 569 (1994). Journalists and critics cannot offer analyses of cultural artifacts without excerpting them. Teachers at all levels use copyrighted material in the classroom; more important, students do so to develop their own ideas, indeed their own cultural stuff. This is the idea behind, for example, the ancient *Progymnasmata* exercises. When courts use "transformative" as a standard to assess whether someone adapted, or simply reproduced, copyrighted material, they rely on the same notion that animates the CC's license for "derivative" use. Transformative and derivative use of cultural stuff is permissible, indeed encouraged, insofar as it generates more stuff. See Goldstein, *Copyright's Highway*, 5, 20, 34.

102. See Mifsud's description of rhetoric in giving as "requir[ing] not investment and savings but a spending of excess, creation of and through waste, and production of surplus." *Rhetoric and the Gift: Ancient Rhetorical Theory and Contemporary Communication* (Pittsburgh, PA: Duquesne University Press, 2015), 145.

103. Pierre Bourdieu, excerpt from *The Logic of Practice*, in *The Logic of the Gift*, ed. Alan D. Schrift (New York: Routledge, 1997), 199.

104. Pierre Bourdieu, "Marginalia: Some Additional Notes on the Gift," in *The Logic of the Gift*, ed. Alan D. Schrift (New York: Routledge, 1997), 232.

105. Armstrong, "Shrinking the Commons," 360, 365.

106. Armstrong, "Shrinking the Commons," 360.

107. Armstrong writes, "Nothing in the Copyright Act contemplates a voluntary extinguishment of the rights vested by the statute in the creator of a work, and the courts have been highly reluctant to find copyright abandonment." "Shrinking the Commons," 396. He continues, "There appears to be little the author can do *ex ante* to make her own dedication of a work to the public domain perpetual and irrevocable." "Shrinking the Commons," 410. Despite characterizing copyright reform as not "presently politically feasible," Armstrong's recommendation is that Congress "enact new legislation expressly authorizing authors to make a nonwaivable, irrevocable dedication of their works, in whole or in part, to the use and benefit of the public—a possibility that the Patent Act expressly recognizes but the Copyright Act presently does not." "Shrinking the Commons," 417, 359.

108. Deazley, *Rethinking Copyright*, 109 (emphasis in original).

109. Heraclitus is credited by Plato as having said that one can never step into the same river twice. And while flux is central to a Heraclitean understanding of logos, it is characterized by him as forceful, oppositional, and fiery, rather than gently trickling. See Heraclitus fragment 91 of Diels-Kranz and W. K. C. Guthrie, *A History of Greek Philosophy* (Cambridge, UK: Cambridge University Press, 1962), 432, 472. I establish the Heraclitean basis of my understanding of logos in introduction, p. 5.

CHAPTER 3

1. See chapter 1, pp. 30–31.
2. In this material I examine especially the self-definitional blog posts with the tags "Wayback Machine," "Web Archive," and "Archive Version 2."
3. For commentary on my use of the term *"stuff,"* see chapter 1, p. 21.
4. The chapter responds to several recent calls for sustained disciplinary discussions of what archival work (digital and brick and mortar) entails for scholars of rhetoric. And although it is addressed primarily to rhetorical scholars invested in the archive, the chapter also speaks to those who are expanding the definition of *"archiving"* and those scholars beyond rhetoric who direct their efforts toward digital archives' characteristic logos.
5. Michel Foucault, *The Archeology of Knowledge*, trans. A. M. Sheridan (New York: Vintage Books, 2010), 129. On Foucault's understanding of the archive, see also Carolyn Steedman, *Dust: The Archive and Cultural History* (New Brunswick, NJ: Rutgers University Press, 2001), 2–6.
6. Recall from chapter 2 that on the other side of the ocean, the US Congress in 1790 acted on its constitutional authority to pass the Copyright Act. This legislation resonated with the ideals of the revolutionary moment, securing certain exclusive rights for authors of "maps, charts, and books" to encourage public learning. Public learning as an ideal must in this moment be thought of in relation to nation building.
7. Regarding the development of academic historiography in the nineteenth century, see Ernst Breisach, *Historiography: Ancient, Medieval, and Modern* (Chicago: University of Chicago Press, 1994); Richard Johnson et al., eds., *Making Histories: Studies in History-Writing and Politics* (London: Hutchinson, 1982); and Paul Veyne, *Writing History: Essay on Epistemology*, trans. Mina Moore-Rinvolucri (Middletown, CT: Wesleyan University Press, 1984).
8. Malea Powell, "Dreaming Charles Eastman," in *Beyond the Archives: Research as a Lived Process*, ed. Gesa E. Kirsch and Liz Rohan (Carbondale: Southern Illinois University Press, 2008). See also Gail Y. Okawa's chapter "Unbundling," on pages 93–106 in the same volume.
9. Steedman, *Dust*, 69, 9. Examining the relationship between knowledge and bureaucratic power, Steedman offers a thoughtful discussion of Michel Foucault and Jacques Derrida.
10. Max Weber, *The Protestant Ethic and the Spirit of Capitalism*, trans. Talcott Parsons (New York: Charles Scribner's Sons, 1958), 957.
11. Weber, *Protestant Ethic*, 957.
12. Arlette Farge, *The Allure of the Archives*, trans. Thomas Scott-Railton (New Haven, CT: Yale University Press, 2013), 6.
13. Farge, *Allure of the Archives*, 32.
14. Steedman, *Dust*, 29 (emphasis in the original).
15. Lynée Lewis Gaillet, "Archival Survival: Navigating Historical Research," in *Working in the Archives*, ed. Alexis E. Ramsey, Wendy B. Sharer, Barbara L'Eplattenier, and Lisa S. Mastrangelo (Carbondale: Southern Illinois Press, 2010), 29.
16. Elizabeth (Betsy) Birmingham, "'I See Dead People': Archive, Crypt, and an Argument for the Researcher's Sixth Sense," in *Beyond the Archives: Research as a Lived*

Process, ed. Gesa E. Kirsch and Liz Rohan (Carbondale: Southern Illinois University Press, 2008), 144.

17. Farge, *Allure of the Archives*, 4.

18. David Gold, "The Accidental Archivist," in *Beyond the Archives: Research as a Lived Process*, ed. Gesa E. Kirsch and Liz Rohan (Carbondale: Southern Illinois University Press, 2008), 15.

19. Jacques Derrida, *Archive Fever*, trans. Eric Prenowitz (Chicago: University of Chicago Press, 1995), 100.

20. Derrida, *Archive Fever*, 81.

21. Derrida, *Archive Fever*, 55, 91.

22. Steedman, *Dust*, 4.

23. Barbara Biesecker, "Of Historicity, Rhetoric: The Archive as Scene of Invention," *Rhetoric and Public Affairs* 9, no. 1 (2006): 124.

24. Biesecker, "Of Historicity, Rhetoric," 126.

25. Derrida, *Archive Fever*, 17, 55 (emphasis in original).

26. Gesa E. Kirsch and Liz Rohan, eds., *Beyond the Archives: Research as a Lived Process* (Carbondale: Southern Illinois University Press, 2008), 73–80.

27. Davis W. Houck, "On or About June 1988," *Rhetoric and Public Affairs* 9, no. 1 (2006): 132–137. On presidential archiving and secrecy, see also Mary Stuckey's contribution to the same special issue of *Rhetoric and Public Affairs*, "Presidential Secrecy: Keeping Archives Open," in "Forum on the Politics of Archival Research," special issue, *Rhetoric and Public Affairs* 9, no. 1 (2006): 138–144.

28. Cara Finnegan, "What Is This a Picture Of? Some Thoughts on Images and Archives," *Rhetoric and Public Affairs* 9, no. 1 (2006): 116–123. Finnegan encourages scholars to consider the agency not only of our interpretive methods but of the archive itself.

29. Tarez Samra Graban, "Emergent Taxonomies: Using Tension and Forum to Organize Primary Texts," in *Working in the Archives*, ed. Alexis E. Ramsey, Wendy B. Sharer, Barbara L'Eplattenier, and Lisa S. Mastrangelo (Carbondale: Southern Illinois Press, 2010), 207. Regarding provenance, see Sammie Morris and Shirley Rose's discussion of *respect des fonds*, or "respect for the group," with reference to the ideals of the French Revolution. Sammie L. Morris and Shirley K. Rose, "Invisible Hands: Recognizing Archivists' Work to Make Record Accessible," in *Working in the Archives*, ed. Alexis E. Ramsey, Wendy B. Sharer, Barbara L'Eplattenier, and Lisa S. Mastrangelo (Carbondale: Southern Illinois Press, 2010), 55–60. To direct attention to archivists' "invisible hands," Morris and Rose explain that "unlike file clerks, archivists base their actions on not only their practical training for processing collections and describing them but also the theoretical foundation of the archives profession" (70). In digital archives, wherein relationships among artifacts are hyperlinked, provenance has special significance. Compared to card catalogs, accordion folders, and boxes, hyperlinks are easy to establish, revise, and layer. In traditional archives, provenance is curated among artifacts produced by the same creator. In the digital context, however, provenance may be translated to apply to other hyperlinked clusters as well, including those established by the person who retrieves data from multiple sources and thereby creates new coherence. Janine Solberg calls this virtual "proximity," or "nearness," based on retrieval patterns. Janine Solberg, "Googling the Archive: Digital Tools and the

Practice of History," *Advances in the History of Rhetoric* 15, no. 1 (2012): 67–68. Provenance with respect to users' habits presumes that archival objects are created not only by some original historical figure, and not only by the archivist who arranges them, but also by the retriever of data. For this reason, provenance as a principle must be examined in the digital environment with reference to the constant "reset-ability" of participatory access. As Alexis Ramsey explains, digitally archived materials may be accessed and configured, which is to say they are pliable to experimental invention. Alexis E. Ramsey, "Viewing the Archives: The Hidden and the Digital," in *Working in the Archives*, ed. Alexis E. Ramsey, Wendy B. Sharer, Barbara L'Eplattenier, and Lisa S. Mastrangelo (Carbondale: Southern Illinois Press, 2010), 86–87. A digital thing, then, may be dissolved into its component parts when the user/producer of the digital archive is done for the day. Like a videogame simulation, the interface is reset. The pieces of data go back to the place in the archive from whence they were retrieved. Later in the chapter I discuss this playful configuring and resetting with reference to the digital flâneur.

30. Katherine E. Tirabassi, "Journeying into the Archives: Exploring the Pragmatics of Archival Research," in *Working in the Archives*, ed. Alexis E. Ramsey, Wendy B. Sharer, Barbara L'Eplattenier, and Lisa S. Mastrangelo (Carbondale: Southern Illinois Press, 2010), 171–177.

31. Lisa Mastrangelo and Barbara L'Eplattenier, "Stumbling in the Archives," in *Beyond the Archives: Research as a Lived Process*, ed. Gesa E. Kirsch and Liz Rohan (Carbondale: Southern Illinois University Press, 2008), 163–164.

32. Lewis Gaillet, "Archival Survival," 35 (emphasis added). For a discussion of research methods and historiography in rhetoric and composition, see Cheryl Glenn and Jessica Enoch, "Drama in the Archives: Rereading Methods, Rewriting History," *College Composition and Communication* 61, no. 2 (2009): 321–342; Alexis E. Ramsey-Tobienne, "Archives 2.0: Digital Archives and the Formation of New Research Methods," *Peitho* 15, no. 1 (2012): 4–29; and a special issue of *Advances in the History of Rhetoric* 15 (2012).

33. Lori Ostergaard, "Open to the Possibilities: Seven Tales of Serendipity in the Archives," in *Working in the Archives*, ed. Alexis E. Ramsey, Wendy B. Sharer, Barbara L'Eplattenier, and Lisa S. Mastrangelo (Carbondale: Southern Illinois Press, 2010), 40–41. Note how the notion of an unexpected find presumes a process of access that resists preconceptions; this is consistent with the experience of flanerie discussed in the analysis.

34. See Ostergaard, "Open to the Possibilities," 251.

35. Farge, *Allure of the Archives*, 48.

36. Powell, "Dreaming Charles Eastman," 116–117.

37. Susan Wells's widely cited chapter on the gifts of archival work for scholars of rhetoric and composition demonstrates how archives resist knowledge as a totalizing conclusion, or what she refers to as "closure." "Claiming the Archive for Rhetoric and Composition," in *Rhetoric and Composition As Intellectual Work*, ed. Gary A. Olson (Carbondale: Southern Illinois University Press, 2002), 58–59. She offers a perspective on the earlier conversation linking political power with archival epistemology, indicating that archival scholars do not in fact control the substances of the archive. Rhetorician and compositionist Wendy Hayden compellingly extends Wells's argument to undergraduate pedagogy, arguing that students in a range of courses and disciplines benefit from working with

archives. Specifically, she explores how students adapt to the complexities of archival access methods. "And Gladly Teach: The Archival Turn's Pedagogical Turn," *College English* 80, no. 2 (2017): 133–158. Her discussion of how archival work facilitates both the discovery of personal connections and a sense of social cohesion is of special significance for my purposes in this chapter. "'Gifts' of the Archives: A Pedagogy for Undergraduate Research," *College Composition and Communication* 66, no. 3 (2015): 416–417.

38. Diana Taylor, *The Archive and the Repertoire* (Durham, NC: Duke University Press, 2003).

39. Taylor, *Archive and the Repertoire*, 20, 24. Furthermore, the way in which archival scholars write about the immersive experience of working among the stacks troubles Taylor's distinction, wherein the repertoire but not the archive requires live and embodied presence. See for example Gold, "Accidental Archivist," 15.

40. Mike Featherstone, "Archive," *Theory, Culture & Society* 23, nos. 2–3 (2006): 594.

41. Steedman, *Dust*, 80–81, 124–125. Steedman's claim that time in the archive is slowed down, in which she references Bachelard's assumption that time inside the home is compressed, presents a pertinent question: Is time in the digital archive compressed and accelerated?

42. Gaston Bachelard, *The Poetics of Space*, trans. Maria Jolas (Boston: Beacon Press, 1994), 5.

43. Not surprisingly, the difference between the archive that provides a lot of digital access and the archive that does not often coincides with funding structures.

44. Ramsey, "Viewing the Archives," 87.

45. Quentin Hardy, "Lend Ho!," *Forbes*, October 29, 2009, www.forbes.com/forbes/2009/1116/opinions-brewster-kahle-google-ideas-opinions.html; and Andy Potts, "Brewster Kahle Wants to Create a Free, Online Collection of Human Knowledge: It Sounds Impossibly Idealistic—but He Is Making Progress," *Economist*, March 5, 2009, www.economist.com/node/13174399.

46. Internet Archive, "About the Internet Archive," accessed September 13, 2018, https://archive.org/about/; Jeff Kaplan, "Wayback Machine Has 85 Billion Archived Webpages," *Internet Archive Blog*, December 5, 2006, https://blog.archive.org/2006/12/05/wayback-machine-has-85-billion-archived-webpages/; and Alexis Rossi, "Fixing Broken Links on the Internet," *Internet Archive Blog*, October 25, 2013, https://blog.archive.org/2013/10/25/fixing-broken-links/.

47. Joseph Janes, "Internet Librarian: Nowhere to Hide," *American Libraries* 35, no. 8 (September 2004): 72.

48. Internet Archive, "About the Internet Archive"; and JCG, "20,000 Hard Drives on a Mission," *Internet Archive Blog*, October 25, 2016, https://blog.archive.org/2016/10/25/20000-hard-drives-on-a-mission/.

49. Mark Graham, "No More 404s! Resurrect Dead Web Pages with our New Firefox Add-on," *Internet Archive Blog*, August 9, 2016, https://blog.archive.org/2016/08/09/no-more-404s-resurrect-dead-web-pages-with-our-new-firefox-add-on/.

50. Potts, "Brewster Kahle Wants to Create"; and Lisa Rein, "Brewster Kahle on the Internet Archive and People's Technology," *Open P2P*, January 22, 2004, www.openp2p.com/pub/a/p2p/2004/01/22/kahle.html.

51. Richard Koman, "How the Wayback Machine Works," *XML.com*, January 21, 2002, www.xml.com/pub/a/ws/2002/01/18/brewster.html.

52. JCG, "20,000 Hard Drives." The quotation is the author's response to a comment from a reader.

53. Brewster Kahle, "How Google Threatens Books," *Washington Post*, May 19, 2009, www.washingtonpost.com/wp-dyn/content/article/2009/05/18/AR2009051802637.html. See also Kahle's commentary on Google's digital books efforts in Hardy, "Lend Ho!" When asked about his personal motives, indeed what the point is of the IA and the Wayback Machine, Kahle replies, "The obvious answer is because these commercial entities [Google, Amazon, Apple] charge for access to some information, whereas non-profit archives are generally free." "Lost in Cyberspace," *Economist*, September 1, 2012, www.economist.com/node/21560992. As a gift to the commons, the IA is both free like free beer *and* free like free speech, as in Stallman's adage (see chapter 2, p. 50).

54. Internet Archive, "About the Internet Archive."

55. Rena Marie Pacella, "Where Data Lives," *Popular Science*, November 2011, 56.

56. Becky Hogge, "Brewster Kahle: On the Egghead Who Hopes to Create a Permanent Record of All Human Knowledge," *New Statesman*, October 17, 2005, 26.

57. Koman, "How the Wayback Machine Works." The article concludes, "You wouldn't think with 100 terabytes of stuff already that you would need to encourage the creation of more content."

58. Rein, "Brewster Kahle on the Internet Archive."

59. Jeff Kaplan, "Wayback Machine Comes to Life in New Home," *Internet Archive Blog*, April 24, 2009, https://blog.archive.org/2009/04/24/wayback-machine-comes-to-life-in-new-home-2/.

60. See chapter 2, pp. 45–46.

61. Judy Tong, "Responsible Party—Brewster Kahle: A Library of the Web, On the Web," *New York Times*, September 8, 2002, www.nytimes.com/2002/09/08/business/responsible-party-brewster-kahle-a-library-of-the-web-on-the-web.html?pagewanted=1&register=google.

62. Internet Archive, "About the Internet Archive."

63. Internet Archive, "About the Internet Archive."

64. Carolyn Steedman, "The Space of Memory: In an Archive," *History of the Human Sciences* 11, no. 4 (1998): 72.

65. Hogge, "Brewster Kahle," 26.

66. Reid Goldsborough, "Internet Posts Can Take on a Very Long Life of Their Own," *Community College Week*, March 24, 2008, 14.

67. Koman, "How the Wayback Machine Works."

68. Internet Archive, "About the Internet Archive: Why the Archive Is Building an 'Internet Library.'" Note here the strong resonance with the generational aspects of the gifting logos of the Creative Commons. As I demonstrate in chapter 2, the CC's approach, which is just as romantic as the IA's, establishes a kind of determinism for future users.

69. David Kesmodel, "Lawyers' Delight: Old Web Material Doesn't Disappear; Wayback Machine and Google Archive Billions of Pages, Including Deleted Ones," *Wall Street Journal*, July 27, 2007, www.wsj.com/articles/SB112242983960797010.

70. Jill Lepore, "The Cobweb: Can the Internet Be Archived?" *New Yorker*, January 26, 2015, www.newyorker.com/magazine/2015/01/26/cobweb.

71. Sanjay K. Arora, Yin Li, Jan Youtie, and Philip Shapira, "Using the Wayback Machine to Mine Websites in the Social Sciences: A Methodological Resource," *Journal of the Association for Information Science and Technology* 67, no. 8 (2016): 1905. Offering a tutorial for social scientists, the article supplies a "step-by-step description of how the analyst can design a research project using archived websites" (1904). The authors present a methodological discussion of how the Wayback Machine has been used primarily "over the past decade in computer science, information retrieval, and library and archival fields" (1905).

72. Internet Archive, "About the Internet Archive: Future Libraries—How People Envision Using Internet Libraries."

73. Internet Archive, "About the Internet Archive: Why the Archive Is Building an 'Internet Library'" (emphasis added). I am here smudging the distinction between the IA's collections of digitized materials, which were originally created in hard copy, and the "born digital" materials stored in the Wayback Machine. Doing so reproduces and draws attention to the IA's own rhetorical practices, which tend to fashion this rhetorical smudging strategically. Hardly anyone would refute that the IA's photographic collections give access to the documents of history; some of the photographs are seventy-five years old. The question at hand, however, is whether the contents of the WayBack Machine may be classified as historical.

74. In reference to this complexity, Nick Szydlowski asks, "What is the copy of record: one of the print editions, or a particular iteration of a constantly updated online edition?" "Archiving the Web: It's Going to Have to Be a Group Effort," *Serials Librarian* 59, no. 1 (2010): 38. Szydlowski investigates why for many years blog content was not archived. The response that he offers, and uses to examine the significance of the Wayback Machine, is that for years the internet was not recognized as a primary publishing medium. He contrasts this with the attitude of the contemporary moment, when, "every year, state and federal agencies publish thousands of documents directly to the Web without issuing print versions. These documents are important to many libraries' collections, not only for the information they contain, but because they represent the continuation of series that libraries have collected over many years" (37).

75. Steedman, "The Space of Memory," 73.

76. Internet Archive, "About Internet Archive."

77. Koman, "How the Wayback Machine Works."

78. Jenny Rice traces this exuberance to conspiracy theories and big data initiatives, both of which thrive on the promise of massive evidence. Using the Aristotelian concept of *megethos* (magnitude) rather than *copia*, Rice thoughtfully demonstrates how abundance—or what she calls "the power of more"—functions rhetorically and aesthetically, rather than explicitly as standards of epistemic validity. Jenny Rice, "The Rhetorical Aesthetic of More: On Archival Magnitude," *Philosophy and Rhetoric* 50, no. 1 (2017): 29. With reference to the aggregating speed and magnitude of contemporary archiving, she writes, "*Megethos* may thus be understood as an aesthetic inflection of a quantitative mass that gives a sense of weightiness, a sense that sustains the epistemic without relying on epistemology to structure it" (32). Further, Rice's careful explication of the "activity itself of *building*, of

accumulating and sticking together" (42) in the rhetorical invention of archival magnitude informs my earlier distinction between archival expertise in curating a collection and in method of access to the collection. In addition, Rice's analysis of the significance of an aesthetic experience of creating coherence sheds light on what I analyze in the paragraph to follow, the Archive-It project. On *megethos* and its place in Aristotelian persuasion, see also Thomas B. Farrell, "Sizing Things Up: Colloquial Reflections as Practical Wisdom," *Argumentation* 12, no. 1 (1998): 1–14. Debra Hawhee cites Aristotle's discussion of the aesthetic experiences generated by *megethos* gathered in coherent configuration. She considers magnitude in terms of weight, metaphorical and literal, which bears on the earlier example of web pages and micrograms. See p. 81 in this chapter. Debra Hawhee, *Rhetoric in Tooth and Claw* (Chicago: University of Chicago Press, 2017), 55–56.

79. Shirley Duglin Kennedy, "When Good Links Go Bad," *Information Today*, November 2014, 8; and Greg R. Notess, "Surviving Rot and Finding the Online Past," *Online Searcher*, March/April 2014, 66, www.thefreelibrary.com/Surviving+rot+and+finding+the +online+past-a0372555782.

80. James Purdy, who extends Susan Wells's argument about the three gifts of archiving to digital archives, adds three new gifts: integration, customization, and accessibility. His explanation of how consuming and producing the digital data of an archival repository is applicable here. "Three Gifts of Digital Archives," *Journal of Literacy & Technology* 12, no. 3 (2011): 37–39.

81. Internet Archive, "Internet Archive Projects: Building Libraries Together," https://archive.org/projects/.

82. Jefferson, "10 Years of Archiving the Web Together," *Internet Archive Blog*, October 25, 2016, https://blog.archive.org/2016/10/25/10-years-of-archiving-the-web-together/. Note the parallel between the organic metaphor of seeded propagation and the gene metaphor of inheritance in chapter 2.

83. "Internet Archive Founder Turns to New Information Storage Device—The Book," *Guardian*, August 1, 2011, www.theguardian.com/books/2011/aug/01/internet-archive -books-brewster-kahle.

84. Taylor, *Archive and the Repertoire*, 20.

85. Taylor, in *Archive and the Repertoire*, makes passing references to "young people's" experiences with digital culture (xix) and the function of digital networks and interconnectivity (89), which "eludes embodiment" (16).

86. Leo Marx, *The Machine in the Garden: Technology and the Pastoral Ideal in America* (New York: Oxford University Press, 1964), 198.

87. For more on this unending dream, see, for example, James W. Carey, *Communication as Culture* (New York: Routledge, 1989).

88. Lisa Gitelman, *Always Already New* (Boston: MIT Press, 2006); and Brent J. Malin, *Feeling Mediated* (New York: New York University Press, 2014).

89. An IA blog post from 2009 announces, "Today the new machine came to life, so if you're using the service, you are using a 20′ by 8′ by 8′ 'machine' that sits in Santa Clara, courtesy of Sun Microcomputer." Kaplan, "Wayback Machine Comes to Life."

90. Note that traditional archive scholars similarly comment on the excess of the archive, describing an experience of being overpowered. In such commentaries, collections

are characterized as overwhelming in relation both to the archivist's categorical efforts and the scholar's attempt to access a sufficient portion of the archive in a manageable way. On this point, the archive and the machine are brought together.

91. Lepore, "The Cobweb."

92. Internet Archive, "About the Internet Archive: Why the Archive Is Building an 'Internet Library.'"

93. John Joyce, "The Wayback Machine: A Glimpse of Cultural Memories from 10 Billion Web Pages," *Scientific Computing and Instrumentation*, October 2002, 16.

94. Jeff Kaplan, "New Firefox Add-on for Searching the Wayback Machine," *Internet Archive Blog*, June 8, 2010, https://blog.archive.org/2010/06/08/new-firefox-add-on-for-searching-the-wayback-machine/.

95. Tong, "Responsible Party."

96. Koman, "How the Wayback Machine Works."

97. See also Yasmin AlNoamany, Ahmed AlSum, Michele C. Weigle, and Michael L. Nelson, "Who and What Links to the Internet Archive," *International Journal on Digital Libraries* 14 (2014): 101; and Dan Tynan, "30 Things You Didn't Know You Could Do on the Internet," *PCWorld*, July 2005, 76.

98. William Powell, "Time Machine," *TD*, March 2002, 25.

99. "Remembrances of Sites Past," *Newsweek* 138, no. 20 (2001): 73.

100. Powell, "Time Machine," 26.

101. Barry Brummett, *Clockwork Rhetoric: The Language and Style of Steampunk* (Jackson: University Press of Mississippi, 2014).

102. Potts, "Brewster Kahle Wants to Create."

103. Regarding archiving and "doors of the future," see Derrida, *Archive Fever*, 69–73. The IA staff prefers the metaphorical "window on the past." Internet Archive, "About the Internet Archive: Future Libraries—How People Envision Using Internet Libraries."

104. According to Featherstone the archive in digital culture is less a physical place to store records than "a virtual site facilitating immediate *transfer*." Featherstone, "Archive," 595 (emphasis added).

105. Colin Gifford Brooke uses this metaphor of pizza (and newspapers) in his analysis of new media and the rhetorical canon, wherein he juxtaposes delivery as circulation and delivery as performance. Colin Gifford Brooke, *Lingua Fracta* (Cresskill, NJ: Hampton Press, 2009), 170.

106. Internet Archive, "About the Internet Archive." Regarding noise and access to information, see Arora, Youtie, and Shapira, "Using the Wayback Machine," 1910.

107. For an important discussion of how archival processing may be obstructing archival research, see Mark A. Greene and Dennis Meissner, "More Product, Less Process: Revamping Traditional Archival Processing," *American Archivist* 68 (2005): 208–263. Working with the hypothesis that archivists devote excessive resources to processing, Meissner and Greene "articulate a new set of arrangement, preservation, and description guidelines that 1) expedites getting collection materials into the hands of users; 2) assures arrangement of materials adequate to user needs; 3) takes the minimal steps necessary to physically preserve collection materials; and 4) describes materials sufficient to promote use" (212–213).

108. Explicating its methods and procedures as a bona fide archive, the IA openly discusses the practical considerations of storage and preservation: "Web data is received and stored in archive format of 100-megabyte ARC files made up of many individual files." Internet Archive, "About the Internet Archive: Storage and Preservation." In the same text, the staff expresses caution regarding the "consequences of accidents and data degradation and maintaining the accessibility of data as formats become obsolete." The challenges of storage and preservation obtain whether an archive contains digital artifacts or antique manuscripts. A significant difference between the two, however, is that the digital archive's central function is to enact the gifting logos through constant and rapid flow. The classical archival ideal of access is magnified and accelerated, which necessarily has an impact on the materials themselves.

109. The value that traditional archival scholars ascribe to a certain level of disorder, or "mess" inside the archive, raises questions about the sterility of a mathematical non-mess. If the scholarly tradition that relies on unanticipated discoveries in archives migrates into algorithmic hyper-organization, does the inventive potential of the archive dry up? If software code eradicates the lost cardboard box left behind accidentally in the cleaning closet, is the digital archive foreclosing certain hermeneutic opportunities? See Jennifer Clary-Lemon, "Archival Research Processes: A Case for Material Methods," *Rhetoric Review* 33, no. 4 (2014): 398.

110. Responding to the persistent requests, the IA introduced in October 2016 a service in beta form that allows users to search "homepages of over 361 Million websites preserved in the Wayback Machine just by typing in keywords that describe these sites (e.g., 'new york times' [sic])." Vinay Goel, "Beta Wayback Machine—Now with Site Search!," *Internet Archive Blog*, October 24, 2016, https://blog.archive.org/2016/10/24/beta-wayback-machine-now-with-site-search/. Regarding search engines and archives, see Elizabeth Yakel, "Searching and Seeking in the Deep Web: Primary Sources on the Internet," in *Working in the Archives*, ed. Alexis E. Ramsey, Wendy B. Sharer, Barbara L'Eplattenier, and Lisa S. Mastrangelo (Carbondale: Southern Illinois Press, 2010), 113. While the web pages of the Wayback Machine are not keyword searchable, portions of the digitized books in the IA's collection are searchable by the books' contents. Brenton, "Searching through Everything," *Internet Archive Blog*, June 15, 2011, https://blog.archive.org/2016/10/26/searching-through-everything/.

111. Mark Graham, "FAQs for Some New Features Available in the Beta Wayback Machine," *Internet Archive Blog*, October 24, 2016, https://blog.archive.org/2016/10/24/faqs-for-some-new-features-available-in-the-beta-wayback-machine/. Regarding search processes and access, see also Notess, "Surviving Rot," 66.

112. As noted in the "Archival Knowing" section, provenance is an archival principle of configuration traceable to invention. It "protect[s] the integrity and authenticity of archival records as evidence by retaining the nature of the relationship that exists among records by the same creator." Morris and Rose, "Invisible Hands," 55. This relationship, although it may be said to exist independently in some historical or pseudometaphyiscal sense, must in the archive be invented. The invention or making of provenance reflects expert archivists' knowledge of the documents and of how they may be understood, individually and as a constellation. In the digital archive, provenance is invented by the acts of retrieval executed

by members of the digital commons, who would seem not be to archival experts in the conventional sense. The cohesion of provenance is thus potentially shifted from among items created by the same person to items retrieved by the same person in a certain pattern of access. By this reasoning, provenance informs my analysis in chapter two, specifically the discussion of how multiple CC artifacts licensed by the same person may be traceable to an individual network node where symbolic value pools. Worth noting is that the participatory dynamic of provenance in the digital archive affords a bridge, again, between the digital archive as an archive per se and what Taylor calls a repertoire, wherein participants engage directly with the ritual and the material. Regarding provenance and the IA, see Lepore, "The Cobweb."

113. Lewis Gaillet, "Archival Survival," 29.

114. Mari Lee Mifsud, *Rhetoric and the Gift: Ancient Rhetorical Theory and Contemporary Communication* (Pittsburgh, PA: Duquesne University Press, 2015), 71–72.

115. In this chapter I refer to the flâneur as "he" in part because the construct itself is so thoroughly masculine, steeped in the philosophy and culture of a particular modernity. Flânerie is an experience of a privileged "he" regardless of the individual practitioner. Walter Benjamin, *The Writer of Modern Life: Essays on Charles Baudelaire*, ed. Michael W. Jennings, trans. Howard Eiland, Edmund Jephcott, Rodney Livingston, and Harry Zohn (Cambridge, MA: The Belknap Press of Harvard University Press, 2006), 68.

116. Steedman offers a compelling reflection on the Flâneur and the Historian as characters of a nineteenth-century drama centered on identity. Steedman, "The Space of Memory," 73, original capitalization. The Historian, she argues, searches the past for identity and purpose, while the Flâneur searches the Parisian arcade. Both are defined in relation to labor and the intensity of their investment, or lack thereof.

117. Benjamin, *Writer of Modern Life*, 157.

118. Janes, "Internet Librarian," 72.

119. Joyce, "The Wayback Machine: A Glimpse," 16.

120. Koman, "How the Wayback Machine Works."

121. "Remembrances of Sites Past."

122. Janes, "Internet Librarian," 72.

123. It is instructive to think of flânerie as a mode of access to digital archives in light of the conditions of interiority and exteriority, or the public and private. As I discuss in the " Archival Knowing" section, there is intimacy to the archive, a sense that archival space is the space of home. This "home-ness" exists beyond the archive's function as the administrator of official records, a public matter. It reflects the archive's containment not only of records but of memory. Benjamin's flâneur, whose urban "dwelling place" is intensely public, is noticeably comfortable transforming the boulevard into an *intérieur*. Benjamin, *Writer of Modern Life*, 68, 85. For the flâneur, the street is intimate; the public is private. He is at liberty to roam, and none of the things that he encounters in the arcade are off limits. He interacts as he pleases. In the IA/Wayback Machine, access is possible from the data retriever's literal home. He or she can make an everyday habit of visiting the IA website, there strolling about and clicking at will. Browsing is an "at-home" form of leisure.

124. Media artist Paul Miller (aka DJ Spooky) reflects on his performance at the IA's twentieth anniversary, noting, "Playing with the Archive is a kind of digital analytics of the

subconscious impulse to collage. It's also really fun." Caitlin Olson, "The New Memory Palace," *Internet Archive Blog*, October 25, 2016, https://blog.archive.org/2016/10/25/the-new-memory-palace/. Miller describes the impulsive process: "Where to start? Sir Tim Berners-Lee's speech inaugurating the internet back when he came up with the term the 'Semantic Web?' The first recordings from Edison? That could be cool. [...] Grab some clips of Cory Doctorow talking about the upcoming war on open computing and mix it with Parliament Funkadelic? Sure. Take the first 'sound heard around the world,' the telemetry signals guiding the Sputnik satellite as it swirled around planet Earth to become our first orbital artificial moon? Cool. Why not? Take a speech from Margaret Sanger, the woman who started Planned Parenthood, and mix it with Public Enemy? Cool." Miller concludes with a reference to cultural production as gifting: "The Archive is a mirror of infinite recombinant potential. I hope that its gift of free culture and free exchange creates a place where we will be comfortable with what is almost impossible to guess comes next."

125. Ramsey, "Viewing the Archives," 86.

126. Rein, "Brewster Kahle on the Internet Archive."

127. Internet Archive, "About the Internet Archive: Why the Archive Is Building an 'Internet Library.'"

128. Jason Scott, "I CAN HAZ MEME HISTORY??," *Internet Archive Blog*, October 25, 2016, https://blog.archive.org/2016/10/25/i-can-haz-meme-history/.

129. Mark Boster, "Patt Morrison Asks: The Internet Archive's Brewster Kahle," *Los Angeles Times*, January 28, 2012, www.latimes.com/opinion/opinion-la/la-oe-morrison-brewster-kahle-20120128-column.html.

130. Joyce, "The Wayback Machine: A Glimpse," 16.

131. Jessica Dye, "Web Site Sued for Controversial Trip into Internet Past," *Econtent Magazine*, October 2005, www.econtentmag.com/Articles/News/News-Feature/Web-Site-Sued-For-Controversial-Trip-into-Internet-Past-14182.htm.

132. Powell, "Time Machine," 26.

133. Kahle, "Lost in Cyberspace."

134. Internet Archive, "About the Internet Archive: Future Libraries—How People Envision Using Internet Libraries."

135. Internet Archive, "About the Internet Archive."

136. "Internet Archive Founder Turns to New Information."

137. Potts, "Brewster Kahle Wants to Create."

138. Martin Heidegger, *Early Greek Thinking*, trans. David Farrell Krell and Frank A. Capuzzi (New York: Harper and Row Publishing, 1975), 61.

139. Heidegger, *Early Greek Thinking*, 62.

140. Heidegger, *Early Greek Thinking*, 71.

141. Steedman, *Dust*, 81.

CHAPTER 4

1. Regarding unauthorized publications and literary piracy, see chapter 2, pp. 48–49.

2. With 0.63 percent of the national vote, the party fell short of the 4 percent mark required for a seat in Riksdagen.

3. The party's second candidate, Amelia Andersdotter, was granted a seat in December 2009.

4. Bertil Bengtsson, *Allemansrätten: Vad Säger Lagen?* (Solna, Sweden: Naturvårdsverket Tryckindustri, 2004), 6, www.naturvardsverket.se/Documents/publikationer/620-8161-6.pdf

5. "Skapa en Allemansrätt för kunskap och kultur, och därmed gynna hela samhällets utveckling." Piratpartiet, "Principprogram Version 3.4," https://web.archive.org/web/20100923231330/http://www.piratpartiet.se:80/principer. Here and elsewhere in the chapter I include the original Swedish, which I translate in the main text to English. To the extent possible, my translations retain the grammatical idiosyncrasies of the original.

6. Benjamin Arditi, *Politics on the Edges of Liberalism: Difference, Populism, Revolution, Agitation* (Edinburgh: Edinburgh University Press, 2007), 100–101.

7. Jacques Rancière, *Disagreement: Politics and Philosophy* (Minneapolis: University of Minnesota Press, 1999), 138. Rancière defines a "consensus democracy" as a "regime in which the parties are presupposed as already given" (102).

8. Via Plato and Aristotle, Rancière distinguishes *politeia* from *politeiaï*. *Disagreement*, 63–64. He writes, "Politics exists when the natural order of domination is interrupted by the institution of a part of those who have no part." *Disagreement*, 11. In his third thesis on politics, he explains, "Politics is a specific rupture in the logic of arche." Jacques Rancière, "Ten Theses on Politics," *Theory and Event* 5, no. 3 (2001): n.p. For reference, see my etymological treatment in chapter 3 of *arche* as the original meaning pertaining to "archive" on page 72.

9. Ernesto Laclau, *On Populist Reason* (New York: Verso, 2005), 74.

10. Cas Mudde and Cristóbal Rovira Kaltwasser, eds., *Populism in Europe and the Americas: Threat or Corrective for Democracy?* (New York: Cambridge University Press, 2010), 1–5. For a history and rhetorical analysis of American populism in the late nineteenth century, see Michael Kazin, *The Populist Persuasion: An American History* (Ithaca, NY: Cornell University Press, 1995).

11. Donald MacRae, "Populism as an Ideology," in *Populism: Its Meanings and National Characteristics*, ed. Ghita Ionescu and Ernest Gellner (London: Weidenfeld and Nicolson, 1969), 155.

12. Francisco Panizza, ed., *Populism and the Mirror of Democracy* (London: Verso, 2005), 12, 22.

13. Mudde and Kaltwasser, *Populism in Europe and the Americas*, 8. The purpose of Mudde and Kaltwasser's collection is to assess with reference to representations of the general will how "populism can be both a corrective and a threat to democracy" (16). They find that populism may erode democratic governance with its "lack of respect of public contestation," undermining the efficacy of institutions (21, 206). Regarding political discontent and antipolitical attitudes, see Gianpietro Mazzoleni, "Populism and the Media," in *Twenty-First Century Populism: The Spectre of Western European Democracy*, ed. Daniele Albertazzi and Duncan McDonnell (New York: Palgrave Macmillan, 2008), 51.

14. Robert R. Barr, "Populists, Outsiders and Anti-establishment Politics," *Party Politics* 15 (2009): 32; and Peter Wiles, "A Syndrome, Not a Doctrine: Some Elementary Theses on Populism," in *Populism: Its Meanings and National Characteristics*, ed. Ghita Ionescu and Ernest Gellner (London: Weidenfeld and Nicolson, 1969), 167.

15. Sir Bernard Crick, "Populism, Politics and Democracy," *Democratization* 12 (2005): 626.

16. Kazin, *Populist Persuasion*, 13; and Peter Worsley, "The Concept of Populism," in *Populism: Its Meanings and National Characteristics*, ed. Ghita Ionescu and Ernest Gellner (London: Weidenfeld and Nicolson, 1969), 241.

17. A worthwhile connection might be made here between the populist ideals of producerism and what has been called the "makers' movement." The makers' movement is a decentralized networked community of artisans, entrepreneurs, DYI (do-it-yourself) enthusiasts, and/or tech autodidacts. As Joan Voight explains, "Makers tap into an American admiration for self-reliance and combine that with open-source learning, contemporary design and powerful personal technology like 3-D printers. The creations, born in cluttered local workshops and bedroom offices, stir the imaginations of consumers numbed by generic, mass-produced, made-in-China merchandise." "Meet Your Maker: Which Big Brands Are Courting the Maker Movement, and Why," *Adweek* 55, no. 11 (2014): 23. While at least one stereotype of these makers is that they work alone—this is the image of a commoner (digital or traditional) toiling in solitude over a workbench or a keyboard—they have also been significantly aided by internet communication networks, social media, and crowdsourcing platforms. Writes Simmi Singh, "The maker movement is a cultural phenomenon that celebrates shared experimentation, iterative learning, and discovery through connected communities that build together, while always emphasizing creativity over criticism." "Lessons from the Maker Movement," *MIT Sloan Management Review* (Summer 2018), https://sloanreview.mit.edu/article/lessons-from-the-maker-movement/. For members of the makers' movement, integrating processes of knowing, making, and gifting constitutes a commons of inventors.

18. Angus Stewart thoughtfully examines populism as both nostalgic for tradition and hostile to traditional establishments, ascribing to it a "Janus quality." "The Social Roots," in *Populism: Its Meanings and National Characteristics*, ed. Ghita Ionescu and Ernest Gellner (London: Weidenfeld and Nicolson, 1969), 186. Populism, Stewart notes, emerges in response to the "development crises" of modernism. Attempting to account for this crisis, Stuart Hall casts "Entrepreneurial Man" as the main character in the neoliberal drama. "The Great Moving Nowhere Show," *Marxism Today*, November–December 1998, 9–11. Entrepreneurial Man, he suggests, supersedes the idea of the citizen and the community member. He—it is indeed a masculine figure—possesses a capacity that can flourish only when the old constraints of postwar social democracy have been removed, a process that Hall aligns with Thatcherism in the United Kingdom. "The Neo-liberal Revolution," *Cultural Studies* 25 (2011): 705–728. As I indicate with reference to producerism, Hall's entrepreneurial character is populism's idea of fulfilled human potential, specifically in the neoliberal historical moment.

19. Steven Levitsky and James Loxton, "Populism and Competitive Authoritarianism: The Case of Fujimori's Peru," in *Populism in Europe and the Americas: Threat or Corrective for Democracy?*, ed. Cas Mudde and Cristóbal Rovira Kaltwasser (New York: Cambridge University Press, 2010), 162.

20. Richard Hofstadter, "North America," in *Populism: Its Meanings and National Characteristics*, ed. Ghita Ionescu and Ernest Gellner (London: Weidenfeld and Nicolson, 1969), 18.

21. Alfio Mastrapaolo, "Politics against Democracy: Party Withdrawal and Populist Breakthrough," in *Twenty-First Century Populism: The Spectre of Western European Democracy*, ed. Daniele Albertazzi and Duncan McDonnell (New York: Palgrave Macmillan, 2008), 33.

22. Hofstadter, "North America," 20.

23. Michael Oakeshott, *The Politics of Faith and the Politics of Skepticism*, ed. Timothy Fuller (New Haven, CT: Yale University Press, 1996), 23–24. See also Kazin, *Populist Persuasion*, 2.

24. Oakeshott, *Politics of Faith*, 29.

25. Margaret Canovan, "Trust the People! Populism and the Two Faces of Democracy," *Political Studies* 47 (1999): 6. See also Arditi's commentary on Oakeshott and Canovan in *Politics on the Edges of Liberalism*, 44–46.

26. Jack Hayward, ed., Élitism, Populism, and European Politics (Oxford: Clarendon Press, 1996), 20. This collection of essays is the outcome of a conference held at Oxford University's Institute of European Studies in 1993. The conference, which inaugurated an annual event, addressed the question, "Are European Élites Losing Touch with Their Peoples?"

27. Hofstadter, "North America," 17.

28. Kenneth Minogue, "Populism as a Political Movement," in *Populism: Its Meanings and National Characteristics*, ed. Ghita Ionescu and Ernest Gellner (London: Weidenfeld and Nicolson, 1969), 206.

29. MacRae, "Populism as an Ideology," 156.

30. Hofstadter, "North American," 17.

31. Laclau, *Populist Reason*, 108.

32. Laclau, *Populist Reason*, 74.

33. Laclau, *Populist Reason*, 74.

34. Ernesto Laclau, "Populism: What's in a Name?," in *Populism and the Mirror of Democracy*, ed. Francisco Panizza (London: Verso, 2005), 33.

35. Laclau, *Populist Reason*, 47 (emphasis added).

36. Laclau, *Populist Reason*, 95, 85 (emphasis added).

37. Panizza, *Populism and the Mirror*, 3 (emphasis added).

38. Lloyd Bitzer, "The Rhetorical Situation," *Philosophy and Rhetoric* 1, no. 1 (1968): 6.

39. Daniele Albertazzi and Duncan McDonnell, eds., *Twenty-First Century Populism: The Spectre of Western European Democracy* (New York: Palgrave Macmillan, 2008), 6; and Canovan, "Trust the People," 4.

40. Arditi, *Politics on the Edges*, 60–65. With reference to Freud, Derrida, and Hamlet, Arditi characterizes populism as a "spectre" that haunts democracy. The specter occupies three modalities, the first of which is political representation. He proposes that populism and democracy can coexist "when populists see representative government as something more than either empty formalism or a poor substitute of direct democracy, and when traits of the populist mode of representation become regular components of liberal democratic politics" (61). See also Benjamin Arditi, "Populism as an Internal Periphery of Democratic Politics," in *Populism and the Mirror of Democracy*, ed. Francisco Panizza (London: Verso, 2005), 81.

41. Arditi remarks that the word *representation*, rather than *style* or *aesthetic*, instructively "maintains a family resemblance with both style and rhetoric but also connects populism with mainstream politics." "Populism, or Politics at the Edges of Democracy," *Contemporary Politics* 9 (2003): 21. See also *Politics on the Edges*, 62.

42. Panizza, *Populism and the Mirror*, 11.

43. Panizza, *Populism and the Mirror*, 12–13.

44. Hayward, Élitism, Populism, and European Politics, 21–25. Ironically, Hayward's lucid analysis of European populism concludes that in well-established representative democracies like Scandinavia, populism does not gain support.

45. Tom Mackie, "Parties and Elections," in *Governing the New Europe*, ed. Jack Hayward and Edward C. Page (Oxford University Press, 1995), 176–182.

46. Paul A. Taggart, *The New Populism and the New Politics: New Protest Parties in Sweden in a Comparative Perspective* (London: Macmillan Press, 1996), 152–153.

47. Dennis Westlind, *The Politics of Popular Identity: Understanding Recent Populist Movements in Sweden and the United States* (Lund, Sweden: Lund University Press, 1996), 132.

48. Arditi, *Politics on the Edges*, 27.

49. It is noteworthy that what was considered a rightwing political position in Sweden in 1991 would eventually become recognizable as an iteration of transnational neoliberalism.

50. Jens Rydgren, "Sweden: The Scandinavian Exception," in *Twenty-First Century Populism: The Spectre of Western European Democracy*, ed. Daniele Albertazzi and Duncan McDonnell (New York: Palgrave Macmillan, 2008), 149.

51. Regarding the Sweden Democrats' ascent to parliamentary status and other parties' responses to its xenophobic agenda, Rydgren writes, "The mainstream parties in Sweden have effectively erected a *cordon sanitaire* against the Sweden Democrats, [who have] found it very difficult to create a respectable façade." "Sweden: The Scandinavian Exception," 146, 149. Regarding the ideological connections between Sweden's populist movements, it should be noted, as Rydgren does, that New Democracy's restrictive immigration policy directly contributed to making immigration a political subject in the 1991 election. The party's advocacy may not have been as openly aggressive as that of the Sweden Democrats,' but its critique of the welfare state targeted immigrants explicitly. In the 2018 national election, wherein the European refugee crises figured centrally, the Sweden Democrats became the third largest party in the parliament.

52. Westlind, *Politics of Popular Identity*, 139.

53. As an illustration of trope turning for the purpose of political articulation, "*greven och betjänten*" is a reference to a British comedy sketch from the 1920s by Lauri Wylie originally titled "*Dinner for One.*" Well-known and usually televised in Sweden on New Year's Eve under the title "*Grevinnan och Betjänten*," the sketch is about a wealthy widow with a high-pitched, nasal voice and her butler who, during a dinner ritual, becomes increasingly intoxicated.

54. Taggart, *New Populism and the New Politics*, 33.

55. Gianfranco Pasquino, "Populism and Democracy," in *Twenty-First Century Populism: The Spectre of Western European Democracy*, ed. Daniele Albertazzi and Duncan McDonnell (New York: Palgrave Macmillan, 2008), 21.

56. Worsley, "The Concept of Populism," 245.

57. "Polisen drog då nämligen ur pluggen inte enbart för servrarna som delar ut helt lagliga s.k. torrentfiler, utan också för den politiska organisationen Piratbyrån som är fristående från organisationen Piratebay. En politisk organisation som försöker påverka hur de etablerade partierna skall ta upp dessa frågor i valrörelsen 2006." Mika Sjöman, "Rättsövergreppen Frodas när Pirater Jagas inför Valet 2006," https://web.archive.org/web/20061014152559/http:// etc.se/artikel/12699/raettsoevergreppen-frodas-naer-pirater-jagas-infoer-valet-2006.

58. "Med möjligheten till fildelning har vi idag en fantastisk chans att ge alla ett socialt medborgarskap, d.v.s. allmän tillgång till en modern variant av folkbibliotek."

59. "Fildelning är något positivt för samhället och för medborgarna. [...] Internet fyller idag samma funktion som folkbiblioteken gjorde för hundra år sedan. Det är något positivt och nyttigt för samhällsutvecklingen." Piratpartiet, *Valmanifest 2006*, http://mediekritik.lege.net/doc/Piratpartiets_valmanifest_2006.pdf, 3.

60. "Vi pirater är en rörelse med en ideologi. [...] Vår ideologi i fildelningsfrågan menar jag bör jämföras med varför folkbildning och folkbibliotek finns." Mika Sjöman, "Grundkurs i Piratideologi för Liza Marklund," https://web.archive.org/web/20061014152619/http://etc.se/artikel/12776/grundkurs-i-piratideologi-foer-liza-marklund#c000424.

61. "Den grundläggande värderingen [är] att alla medborgare ska ha fri tillgång till kulturen. Det är minst lika viktigt för Sveriges utveckling idag som för ungefär hundra år sedan när folkbiblioteken skapades." Sjöman, "Grundkurs."

62. "Vi kräver en folkligt förankrad immaterialrätt som skall berika enskilda människors liv, möjliggöra ett sunt företagarklimat, skapa en Allemansrätt för kunskap och kultur, och därmed gynna hela samhällets utveckling." The literal translation of the Swedish word for *intellectual property* is "immaterial right." Piratpartiet, "Principprogram," http://web.archive.org/web/20061014033401/http://www2.piratpartiet.se/principer. The 2010 "Program of Principles" restates the demand nearly verbatim.

63. "Immaterialrätterna är ett sätt att lagstifta om materiella egenskaper för immateriella värden. Idéer, kunskap och information är av naturen icke-exklusiva, deras gemensamma värde ligger i att de kan delas och spridas."

64. The 2006 election manifesto contains a slogan that metaphorically connects a path that one might walk in the woods while taking advantage of *Allemansrätten* with the path that the party envisions for Sweden's political future: "Sweden and Europe have everything to gain from choosing the path of openness." "Sverige och Europa har allt att vinna på att välja öppenhetens väg." Piratpartiet, *Valmanifest 2006*, 4. In Swedish, "öppenhetens väg" conjures an image of a trail or path in a natural and open-air setting. In addition, it plays on the ideas of transparency, or matters that are discussed openly; and of inclusivity, wherein the national parliament might be open to new participants.

65. "Dagens upphovsrätt är i obalans. Ett samhälle där kultur och kunskap är fri och åtkomlig för alla på lika villkor gynnar hela samhället. Vi hävdar att ett utbrett och systematiskt missbruk av dagens upphovsrätt aktivt motverkar dessa syften genom att det begränsar både utbudet av kultur och tillgången till kultur." Piratpartiet, "Principprogram." After the 2009 European Parliamentary election, the same sound-bite was circulated widely. The 2010 "Program of Principles" reiterates the same message of imbalance.

66. The 2006 "Program of Principles" contains a claim regarding a return to copyright origins: "Upphovsrätten behöver återföras till sitt ursprung."

67. "Den tekniska utvecklingen har gjort att Sverige och Europa står inför ett vägskäl. Den nya tekniken erbjuder fantastiska möjligheter att sprida kultur och kunskap över hela världen till nästan ingen kostnad alls. Men den gör det också möjligt att bygga ett övervakningssamhälle av aldrig skådat slag." Piratpartiet, *Valmanifest 2006*, 2.

68. "Vi är på väg mot ett samhälle, där alla övervakas elektroniskt 24 timmar om dygnet." Piratpartiet, "Politik," https://web.archive.org/web/20090628232505/http://www.piratpartiet.se:80/politik.

69. "Vi befinner oss i ett kontrollsamhälle där praktiskt taget alla registreras och övervakas." Piratpartiet, "Principprogram Version 3.4."

70. In most episodes of *Black Mirror*, twenty-first-century media technologies and networks punish humans for their hubris, sloth, selfishness, and indifference to others. The drama frequently turns (tropologically) on the conveniences of technology and its terrifying and ostensibly inevitable consequences. Conley and Burroughs analyze the political possibilities of the program via the affective experience of technological voyeurism and the "traumatic twist." Donovan Conley and Benjamin Burroughs, "*Black Mirror*, Mediated Affect and the Political," *Culture, Theory and Critique* 60 (2019): 140–143.

71. "Konflikten [...] kommer att växa i hela världen till dess att vi antingen har ett så repressivt informationssamhälle att man inte får ha egna åsikter eller att informationstekniken hamnar i medborgarnas händer." Henrik Ståhl, "EU-valet Avgörande för Piratpartiets Tillväxt," www.svd.se/eu-valet-avgorande-for-piratpartiets-tillvaxt.

72. "Vi har en revolution just nu, mitt framför ögonen på oss, som för kultur och kunskap till allmänheten i en större omfattning än när biblioteken kom." Piratpartiet, "Piratpartiet Kommenterar Pirate-Bay-Rättegången"https://web.archive.org/web/20090309174136/http://www.piratpartiet.se:80/nyheter/piratpartiet_kommenterar_pirate_bay_rattegangen.

73. "Tack vare den nya tekniken befinner oss nu i informationssamhället. Det är viktigt att vi tar vara på dess fantastiska möjligheter, både på ett personligt plan och på ett samhälleligt plan." Piratpartiet, *Valmanifest 2010: Kunskap*, https://blog.mmn-o.se/wp-content/uploads/2010/08/valmanifest-kunskap-2010.pdf, 2.

74. "Tack vare den nya tekniken är det i dag möjligt för alla att ta del av en närmast oändlig kulturskatt." Piratpartiet, *Valmanifest 2010: Kultur*, https://blog.mmn-o.se/wp-content/uploads/2010/08/valmanifest-kultur-2010.pdf, 2.

75. "Vi lever i en tid som är unik i mänsklighetens historia. Aldrig tidigare har så många haft möjlighet att kommunicera så lätt med varandra. Aldrig tidigare har så många haft tillgång till så mycket kunskap. Aldrig tidigare har spridande av information bidragit till så många så snabba tekniska, kulturella och ekonomiska framsteg, och dessutom öppnat nya förutsättningar och möjligheter för delaktighet och demokrati." Piratpartiet, "Principprogram," http://www.piratpartiet.se/principprogram/.

76. Thomas M. Malaby's study of technoliberalism is instructive on this point, specifically his understanding of the complicated notion of emergence. His ethnographic analysis of Linden Lab's virtual reality environment Second Life suggests that certain self-governance forms are treated as just a result of their emergence. *Making Virtual Worlds: Linden Lab and Second Life* (Ithaca, NY: Cornell University Press, 2009), 104. According to technoliberalism, Malaby argues, "the emergent properties of complex interactions enjoy a certain degree of rightness just by virtue of being emergent" (56). In short, what is there is good. To question this goodness is to reveal one's failure to recognize what is there.

77. Or, as Jenny Rice writes in her analysis of archival magnitude and the aesthetic experience of emergent mass, "More is not only more; more is better." Jenny Rice, "The Rhetorical Aesthetic of More: On Archival Magnitude," *Philosophy and Rhetoric* 50 (2017): 28. See chapter 3, note 78.

78. "Flera av oss unga nu känner att vi håller på att förlora större delen av vårt digitala kulturliv. Och i vårt liv spelar det roll." Sjöman, "Grundkurs" (emphasis added).

79. "Vi har stofiler från en gammal industri som utvecklingen springer ifrån, som spenderar sina sista slantar på att försöka stoppa den tekniska utvecklingen." Piratpartiet Nyhetsgruppen, "Piratpartiet Kommenterar."

80. "Liza, du borde lyssna på dina barn. Du är sur och bakåtsträvande, precis som dinosaur . . . jag menar mediamogulerna."

81. "Läste hennes krönika och den gav en dålig smak av gammalt och förstenat tänkande."

82. "Ett tips, lyssna på dina barn istället för att förbjuda dom. Det kan ju vara så att dom förstår något som du inte förstår. [. . .] Tiderna förändras. Hys inte rädsla för förändring, bara för att du inte än har förstått/vill förstå fördelarna. Den rädsla du påvisar resulterar, som dina barn så klokt uttrycker det endast till bakåtsträvande."

83. "Det är nog sant att ångmaskinstillverkarna fick en del problem när förbränningsmotorn introducerades men var hade vi varit idag om den hade hindrats med lagstiftning?"

84. "Självklart blir folk som traditionellt försörjt sig på ett system arga när de inte kan göra det längre. Spinnarna blev arga när spinnmaskinerna kom på 1800-talet. En ny uppfinning gör vissa människor överflödiga."

85. Regarding the articulation of a political subjectivity, see my discussion of Laclau, see pages 111–112.

86. "Miljontals klassiska verk, sånger, filmer och konstverk hålls gisslan i mediabolagens valv, inte tillräckligt efterfrågade av deras fokusgrupper för att det ska löna sig att ge ut dem men potentiellt för lukrativa för att släppas fria. Vi vill göra alla dessa verk fria och tillgängliga för envar, innan filmernas celluloid förstörs av tidens tand." Piratpartiet, "Principprogram Version 3.4."

87. Note how similar this image of a vault is to the discourses of the Internet Archive and the Wayback Machine; see chapter 3. There, too, the gifting logos uses the idea of a treasure, integrating knowing, making, and gifting via the trope of access.

88. "Fildelningen har under sin korta tid begränsat mediabolagens topplistors kontroll över det populära. Det skrämmer dem." Sjöman, "Grundkurs."

89. "De enda som inte blir glada är de feta skivbolagsbossarna som förlorar miljarder på en marknad som inte längre är deras." Sjöman, "Rättsövergreppen Frodas."

90. "Den allt hårdare tillämpningen av en föråldrad upphovsrätt skapar inte bara integritetsproblem, utan även problem för kulturen. [På så sätt] bidrar upphovsrättsindustrin och de lagförslag och lagar de stödjer till att stympa den kulturella återväxten." Piratpartiet, *Valmanifest 2010: Kultur*, 2.

91. "Upphovsrättsindustrin motarbetar systematiskt alla försök att trampa upp nya stigar i kulturlandskapet."

92. "Deltagarkulturen ska främjas. Gränserna mellan kreatör och publik har suddats ut. I dag skapar vi alla kultur genom att skriva en blogg, kommentera någon annans blogg,

lägga upp filmer på YouTube, etc. Det ställer helt nya krav på hur vi definierar begreppet kultur. Deltagarkultur behandlas i dag ofta styvmoderligt som en andra klassens kultur. Piratpartiet anser att deltagarkulturen istället ska lyftas fram som ett föredöme." Piratpartiet, *Valmanifest 2010: Kultur*, 3.

93. "Internet innebär att vi inte längre är hänvisade till en kulturell kanon som bestämts uppifrån." Piratpartiet, *Valmanifest 2010: Kultur*, 2.

94. "Dessvärre har mycket av kulturen, precis som kunskapen, under större delen av historien varit ett privilegium för ett fåtal. De senaste årens tekniska utveckling skapar emellertid stora möjligheter för allt fler att både uppleva, utöva och försörja sig på kultur. [...] Aldrig tidigare har unga svenskar haft så många olika musikstilar i sina samlingar. Aldrig har det varit så lätt att få tag på udda filmtitlar." Piratpartiet, "Principprogram," http://www.piratpartiet.se/principprogram/.

95. "Terrorister kan attackera det öppna samhället, men bara regeringar kan avskaffa det." Piratpartiet, *Valmanifest 2006*, 2.

96. "Mycket av den dåliga lagstiftning som går igenom gör det mest för att de etablerade partierna inte förstår sig på internet och den nya tekniken. De har inte tänkt igenom konsekvenserna av att bygga upp ett kontrollsamhälle för att bevara det gamla, istället för att bejaka den nya tidens möjligheter." Piratpartiet, *Valmanifest 2006*, 7.

97. "Demokratin förutsätter ett starkt skydd för den personliga integriteten." Piratpartiet, "Principprogram," http://www.piratpartiet.se/principprogram/.

98. "Brevhemligheten skall upphöjas till en generell kommunikationshemlighet. Det skall alltså bli förbjudet att avlyssna andras telefonsamtal, läsa annans e-post, SMS eller andra meddelanden på samma sätt som det idag är förbjudet att läsa någon annans brev, oavsett tekniken och vem som tillhandahåller den."

99. Värnet om den enskildes privatliv är lagfäst i Sveriges grundlag. Ur denna grundläggande rätt springer flera andra viktiga mänskliga rättigheter som yttrande och åsiktsfrihet, informationsfrihet, rätten till kultur och rätten till personlig utveckling." Piratpartiet, "Principprogram Version 3.4."

100. "För att ett samhälle ska kunna växa kulturellt och teknologiskt, så måste medborgare ha en garanterad rätt till privatliv." Piratpartiet, "Politik."

101. Regarding the populist gemeinschaft, see page 101.

102. "Det enda vi är intresserade av är värnet av det öppna samhället och demokratin, att marschen mot kontrollsamhället avbryts, och att kulturen och kunskapen släpps fria." Piratpartiet, *Valmanifest 2006*, 4.

103. "Vi är det enda parti som aldrig kommer att kompromissa bort det fria och öppna samhället till förmån för någon annan fråga. [...] Det är vi ensamma om i svensk politik." Piratpartiet, *Valmanifest 2006*, 4.

104. "Vi menar att rätten till bredband är lika självklar som rätten till rinnande vatten, el och avlopp. Man ska inte diskrimineras och utestängas från det moderna samhället bara för att man bor på ett visst ställe i landet." Piratpartiet, *Valmanifest 2010: Kunskap*, 3.

105. "Den tekniska utvecklingen har också lett till en utjämning av tillgången till kunskap. [...] Miljoner barn och ungdomar, som tidigare inte hade möjlighet att få utbildning, har nu tillgång till hela mänsklighetens samlade kunskap. Om ingen annan utbildning finns tillgänglig har de möjlighet att utbilda sig själva. Den informationstekniska revolutionen och den fria tillgången till kunskap och kultur ger därigenom många människor

nya möjligheter att själv ta kontrollen över sina liv." Piratpartiet, "Principprogram," http://www.piratpartiet.se/principprogram/.
106. Rancière, *Disagreement*, 16.
107. Rancière, *Disagreement*, 26.

CHAPTER 5

1. Lessig writes, "I am fanatically pro-market." *The Future of Ideas* (New York: Vintage Books, 2001), 6.
2. See chapter 4, note 62.
3. J. L. Austin, *How to Do Things with Words* (Cambridge, MA: Harvard University Press, 1975), 14, 54.
4. Friedrich Nietzsche, *Thus Spoke Zarathustra*, in *The Viking Portable Nietzsche*, trans. and ed. Walter Kaufmann (New York: Viking, 1976), 186–187.
5. See chapter 2, note 98.
6. Pierre Bourdieu, excerpt from *The Logic of Practice*, in *The Logic of the Gift*, ed. Alan D. Schrift (New York: Routledge, 1997), 199. See chapter 2, p. XX.
7. Paolo Virno, *A Grammar of the Multitude* (Los Angeles, CA: Semiotext(e) Foreign Agents Series, 2004), 86.
8. See chapter 2, p. XX.
9. Jill Lepore, "The Cobweb: Can the Internet Be Archived?," *New Yorker*, January 26, 2015, www.newyorker.com/magazine/2015/01/26/cobweb.

BIBLIOGRAPHY

Albertazzi, Daniele, and Duncan McDonnell, eds. *Twenty-First Century Populism: The Spectre of Western European Democracy*. New York: Palgrave Macmillan, 2008.
Alfino, Mark. "Another Look at the Derrida-Searle Debate." *Philosophy and Rhetoric* 24, no. 2 (1991): 143–152.
AlNoamany, Yasmin, Ahmed AlSum, Michele C. Weigle, and Michael L. Nelson. "Who and What Links to the Internet Archive." *International Journal on Digital Libraries* 14, nos. 3–4 (2014): 101–115.
Amidon, Timothy R., and Jessica Reyman. "Authorship and Ownership of User Contributions on the Social Web." In *Cultures of Copyright*, edited by Dánielle Nicole DeVoss and Martine Courant Rife, 108–124. New York: Peter Lang, 2015.
Anthes, Gary. "Unix Turns 40: The Past, Present and Future of a Revolutionary OS." *Computerworld*, June 4, 2009. www.computerworld.com/article/2524456/linux/unix-turns-40--the-past--present-and-future-of-a-revolutionary-os.html.
Apter, Emily. "What Is Yours, Ours, and Mine: Authorial Ownership and the Creative Commons." *October Magazine* 126 (2008): 92, 97.
Araya, Elizabeth Roxana Mass, and Silvana Aparecida Borsetti Gregorio Vidotti, "Creative Commons: A Convergence Model between the Ideal of Commons and the Possibilities of Creation in Contemporary Times, Opposed to Copyright Impediments." *Information Services and Use* 31, nos. 3–4 (2011): 101–109.
Arditi, Benjamin. *Politics on the Edges of Liberalism: Difference, Populism, Revolution, Agitation*. Edinburgh: Edinburgh University Press, 2007.
———. "Populism as an Internal Periphery of Democratic Politics." In *Populism and the Mirror of Democracy*, edited by Francisco Panizza, 72–98. London: Verso, 2005.
———. "Populism, or Politics at the Edges of Democracy." *Contemporary Politics* 9 (2003): 21.
Armstrong, Timothy. "Shrinking the Commons: Termination of Copyright Licenses and Transfers for the Benefit of the Public." *Harvard Journal on Legislation* 47 (2010): 359–423.

Arora, Sanjay K., Yin Li, Jan Youtie, and Philip Shapira. "Using the Wayback Machine to Mine Websites in the Social Sciences: A Methodological Resource." *Journal of the Association for Information Science and Technology* 67, no. 8 (2016): 1904–1915.

Austin. *How to Do Things with Words.* Cambridge, MA: Harvard University Press, 1975.

Bachelard, Gaston. *The Poetics of Space.* Translated by Maria Jolas. Boston: Beacon Press, 1994.

Barr, Robert R. "Populists, Outsiders and Anti-establishment Politics." *Party Politics* 15, no. 1 (2009): 29–48.

Barthes, Roland. "The Death of the Author." In *Image, Music, Text,* translated by Stephen Heath, 142–148. New York: Hill and Wang, 1977.

Bartolovich, Crystal. "Organizing the (Un)Common." *Globalization Working Papers* 8, no. 6 (2008): 19.

Bengtsson, Bertil. *Allemansrätten: Vad Säger Lagen?* Solna, Sweden: Naturvårdsverket Tryckindustri, 2004. www.naturvardsverket.se/Documents/publikationer/620-8161-6.pdf.

Benjamin, Walter. *The Writer of Modern Life: Essays on Charles Baudelaire.* Edited by Michael W. Jennings. Translated by Howard Eiland, Edmund Jephcott, Rodney Livingston, and Harry Zohn. Cambridge, MA: The Belknap Press of Harvard University Press, 2006.

Benkler, Yochai. *The Wealth of Networks.* New Haven, CT: Yale University Press, 2006.

Benson, Thomas W. "Rhetoric, Civility, and Community: Political Debate on Computer Bulletin Boards." *Communication Quarterly* 44, no. 3 (1996): 359–378.

Berkes, Fikret, David Feeny, Bonnie J. McCay, and James M. Acheson. "The Benefits of the Commons." *Nature* 340 (1989): 91–93.

Berners-Lee, Tim. *Weaving the Web.* San Francisco: HarperSanFrancisco, 1999.

Biesecker, Barbara. "Of Historicity, Rhetoric: The Archive as Scene of Invention." *Rhetoric and Public Affairs* 9, no. 1 (2006): 124–131.

Birmingham, Elizabeth (Betsy). "'I See Dead People': Archive, Crypt, and an Argument for the Researcher's Sixth Sense." In *Beyond the Archives: Research as a Lived Process,* edited by Gesa E. Kirsch and Liz Rohan, 139–146. Carbondale: Southern Illinois University Press, 2008.

Bitzer, Lloyd. "The Rhetorical Situation." *Philosophy and Rhetoric* 1, no. 1 (1968): 1–14.

Bloemsaat, Bas, and Pieter Kleve. "Creative Commons: A Business Model for Products Nobody Wants to Buy." *International Review of Law, Computers and Technology* 23 (2009): 237–249.

Bloom, Lynn Z. "Deep Sea Diving: Building an Archive as the Basis for Composition Studies Research." In *Working in the Archives,* edited by Alexis E. Ramsey, Wendy B. Sharer, Barbara L'Eplattenier, and Lisa S. Mastrangelo, 278–289. Carbondale: Southern Illinois University Press, 2010.

Bollier, David. *Think Like a Commoner.* Gabriola Island, BC: New Society Publishers, 2014.

———. *Viral Spiral.* New York: The New Press, 2008.

Bolter, Jay David. *Writing Space: Computers, Hypertext, and the Remediation of Print.* Mahwah, NJ: Lawrence Erlbaum Associates, 1991.

Boon, Marcus. *In Praise of Copying.* Cambridge, MA: Harvard University Press, 2010.

Boster, Mark. "Patt Morrison Asks: The Internet Archive's Brewster Kahle." *Los Angeles Times*, January 28, 2012. www.latimes.com/opinion/opinion-la/la-oe-morrison-brewster-kahle-20120128-column.html.

Bourdieu, Pierre. *The Logic of Practice*, in *The Logic of the Gift*, edited by Alan D. Schrift, 190–230. New York: Routledge, 1997.

———. "Marginalia: Some Additional Notes on the Gift." In *The Logic of the Gift*, edited by Alan D. Schrift, 231–243. New York: Routledge, 1997.

Boyle, James. *The Public Domain: Enclosing the Commons of the Mind*. New Haven, CT: Yale University Press, 2008.

Bracha, Oren. "Early American Printing Privileges: The Ambivalent Origins of Authors' Copyright in America." In *Privilege and Property: Essays on the History of Copyright*, edited by Ronan Deazley, Martin Kretschmer, and Lionel Bentley, 89–114. Cambridge, UK: OpenBook Publishers, 2010.

Breisach, Ernst. *Historiography: Ancient, Medieval, and Modern*. Chicago: University of Chicago Press, 1994.

Brenton. "Searching through Everything." *Internet Archive Blogs*, June 15, 2011. https://blog.archive.org/2016/10/26/searching-through-everything/.

Breyer, Stephen. "The Uneasy Case for Copyright: A Study of Copyright in Books, Photocopies, and Computer Programs." *Harvard Law Review* 84, no. 2 (1970): 281–351.

Brooke, Collin G. *Lingua Fracta: Toward a Rhetoric of New Media*. New York: Hampton Press, 2009.

Brooke, Colin Gifford. *Lingua Fracta*. Cresskill, NJ: Hampton Press, 2009.

Brummett, Barry. *Clockwork Rhetoric: The Language and Style of Steampunk*. Jackson: University Press of Mississippi, 2014.

Burnyeat, Myles. *The Theaetetus of Plato*. Indianapolis, IN: Hackett Publishing, 1990.

Canovan, Margaret. "Trust the People! Populism and the Two Faces of Democracy." *Political Studies* 47, no. 1 (1999): 2–16.

Carey, James W. *Communication as Culture*. New York: Routledge, 1989.

———. *Communication as Culture: Essays on Media and Society*. New York: Routledge, 2009.

Castells, Manuel, ed. *The Network Society*. Cheltenham, UK: Edward Elgar, 2004.

Cavell, Stanley. *Philosophical Passages: Wittgenstein, Emerson, Austin, Derrida*. Cambridge, MA: Blackwell, 1995.

Clary-Lemon, Jennifer. "Archival Research Processes: A Case for Material Methods." *Rhetoric Review* 33, no. 4 (2014): 381–402.

Compestine, Ying Chang. *The Real Story of Stone Soup*. New York: Dutton Children's Books, 2007.

Conhaim, Wallys W. "Creative Commons Nurtures the Public Domain." *Information Today* 19 (2002): 52.

Conley, Donovan, and Benjamin Burroughs. "*Black Mirror*, Mediated Affect and the Political." *Culture, Theory and Critique* 60, no. 2 (2019): 139–153.

Corbett, Susan. "Creative Commons Licenses, the Copyright Regime and the Online Community: Is There a Fatal Disconnect?" *Modern Law Review* 74, no. 4 (2011): 503–531.

Creative Commons. Accessed January 29, 2015. http://creativecommons.org/.
———. "About: License Design and Rationale." Accessed January 29, 2015. http://creativecommons.org/about.
———. "About: Three 'Layers' of Licenses." Accessed January 29, 2015. http://creativecommons.org/about.
———. "About: What Can Creative Commons Do for Me?" Accessed January 29, 2015. http://creativecommons.org/about.
———. "About: What Is Creative Commons?" Accessed January 29, 2015. http://creativecommons.org/about.
———. "About: What Our Licenses Do." Accessed January 29, 2015. http://creativecommons.org/licenses.
———. "License Chooser." Accessed January 29, 2015. http://creativecommons.org/choose.
———. *The Power of Open.* 2011. http://thepowerofopen.org/assets/pdfs/tpoo_eng.pdf.
———. *The State of the Commons.* 2015. https://stateof.creativecommons.org/2015/.
———. *The State of the Commons* data sheet. 2015. https://stateof.creativecommons.org/2015/data.html#more-than-1-billion-cc-licensed-works-in-the-commons-as-of-2015.
———. "Team Open." Accessed January 29, 2015. http://teamopen.cc/khalid/.
Crick, Sir Bernard. "Populism, Politics and Democracy." *Democratization* 12, no. 5 (2005): 625–632.
Deazley, Ronan. *Rethinking Copyright: History, Theory, Language.* Cheltenham, UK: Edward Elgar, 2006.
Deazley, Ronan, Martin Kretschmer, and Lionel Bentley, eds. *Privilege and Property: Essays on the History of Copyright.* Cambridge, UK: OpenBook Publishers, 2010.
Decherney, Peter. *Hollywood's Copyright Wars: From Edison to the Internet.* New York: Columbia University Press, 2012.
Derrida, Jacques. *Archive Fever.* Translated by Eric Prenowitz. Chicago: University of Chicago Press, 1995.
———. "'Counterfeit Money' I: Poetics of Tobacco." In *Given Time: I. Counterfeit Money,* translated by Peggy Kamuf, 71–107. Chicago: University of Chicago Press, 1992.
———. "Limited Inc abc." In *Limited Inc.,* translated by Samuel Weber, 29–107. Evanston, IL: Northwestern University Press, 1988.
———. "The Madness of Economic Reason: A Gift without Present." In *Given Time: I. Counterfeit Money,* translated by Peggy Kamuf, 34–70. Chicago: University of Chicago Press, 1992.
———. "The Time of the King." In *Given Time: I. Counterfeit Money,* translated by Peggy Kamuf, 1–33. Chicago: University of Chicago Press, 1992.
Dye, Jessica. "Web Site Sued for Controversial Trip into Internet Past." *Econtent Magazine* October 2005. www.econtentmag.com/Articles/News/News-Feature/Web-Site-Sued-For-Controversial-Trip-into-Internet-Past-14182.htm.
Emerson, Ralph Waldo. "Gifts." In *The Logic of the Gift,* edited by Alan D. Schrift, 25–27. New York: Routledge, 1997.
Eyman, Douglas. *Digital Rhetoric: Theory, Method, Practice.* Ann Arbor: University of Michigan Press, 2015.
Facebook. "Legal Terms." Accessed August 8, 2016. www.facebook.com/legal/terms/update.

Farge, Arlette. *The Allure of the Archives*. Translated by Thomas Scott-Railton. New Haven, CT: Yale University Press, 2013.
Farrell, Thomas B. "Sizing Things Up: Colloquial Reflections as Practical Wisdom." *Argumentation* 12, no. 1 (1998): 1–14.
Featherstone, Mike. "Archive." *Theory, Culture & Society* 23, nos. 2–3 (2006): 591–596.
Finnegan, Cara. "What Is This a Picture of? Some Thoughts on Images and Archives." *Rhetoric and Public Affairs* 9, no. 1 (2006): 116–123.
Fish, Allison. "The Place of 'Culture' in the Access to Knowledge Movement: Comparing Creative Commons and Yogic Theories of Knowledge Transfer." *Anthropology Today* 30, no. 5 (2014): 7–10.
Fishman, Donald. "Reading John Locke in Cyberspace: Natural Rights and 'The Commons' in a Digital Age." *Free Speech Yearbook* 41 (2004): 34–54.
Foucault, Michel. *The Archeology of Knowledge*. Translated by A. M. Sheridan. New York: Vintage, 2010.
———. "What Is an Author?" In *Criticism: Major Statements*, edited by Charles Kaplan and Willian Davis Anderson, 544–558. Boston: Bedford/St. Martin's, 2000.
Fuller, Steve. *Social Epistemology*. Bloomington: Indiana University Press, 1988.
———. "Social Epistemology: A Quarter Century Itinerary." *Social Epistemology* 26, no. 3–4 (2012): 267–283.
Gaillet, Lynée Lewis. "Archival Survival: Navigating Historical Research." In *Working in the Archives*, edited by Alexis E. Ramsey, Wendy B. Sharer, Barbara L'Eplattenier, and Lisa S. Mastrangelo, 28–39. Carbondale: Southern Illinois Press, 2010.
Gaines, Jane. *Contested Culture: The Image, the Voice, and the Law*. Chapel Hill: University of North Carolina Press, 1991.
Garcelon, Marc. "An Information Commons? Creative Commons and Public Access to Cultural Creations." *New Media & Society* 11, no. 8 (2009): 1307–1326.
Gascón, Joan Francesc Fondevila, and Raúl López Garcia-Navas. "New Digital Production Models: The Consolidation of the Copyleft." In *Cultures of Copyright*, edited by Dánielle Nicole DeVoss and Martine Courant Rife, 64–74. New York: Peter Lang, 2015.
Geschwandtner, Christina M. "The Excess of the Gift in Jean-Luc Marion." In *Gift and Economy: Ethics, Hospitality and the Market*, edited by Eric R. Severson, 20–32. Newcastle, UK: Cambridge Scholars Publishing, 2012.
Giannopoulou, Alexandra. "The Creative Commons Licenses through Moral Rights Provisions in French Law." *International Review of Law, Computers and Technology* 28, no. 2 (2014): 60–80.
Gillies, James. *How the Web Was Born: The Story of the World Wide Web*. Oxford and New York: Oxford University Press, 2000.
Ginsburg, Jane. "A Tale of Two Copyrights: Literary Property in Revolutionary France and America." *Tulane Law Review* 64, no. 5 (1990): 991–1031.
Ginsburg, Jane C. "How Copyright Got a Bad Name for Itself." *Columbia Journal of Law and the Arts* 26, no. 1 (2002): 1–16.
Ginsburg, Jane C., and Rochelle Dreyfuss. *Intellectual Property Stories*. New York: Foundation Press, 2006.
Gitelman, Lisa. *Always Already New*. Boston: MIT Press, 2006.

Glenn, Cheryl, and Jessica Enoch. "Drama in the Archives: Rereading Methods, Rewriting History." *College Composition and Communication* 61, no. 2 (2009): 321–342.

Goel, Vinay. "Beta Wayback Machine—Now with Site Search!" *Internet Archive Blogs*, October 24, 2016. https://blog.archive.org/2016/10/24/beta-wayback-machine-now-with-site-search/.

Gold, David. "The Accidental Archivist." In *Beyond the Archives: Research as a Lived Process*, edited by Gesa E. Kirsch and Liz Rohan, 13–19. Carbondale: Southern Illinois University Press, 2008.

Goldsborough, Reid. "Internet Posts Can Take on a Very Long Life of Their Own." *Community College Week*, March 24, 2008, 14.

Goldstein, Paul. *Copyright's Highway: The Law and Lore of Copyright from Gutenberg to the Celestial Jukebox*. New York: Hill and Wang, 1994.

Graban, Tarez Samra. "Emergent Taxonomies: Using Tension and Forum to Organize Primary Texts." In *Working in the Archives*, edited by Alexis E. Ramsey, Wendy B. Sharer, Barbara L'Eplattenier, and Lisa S. Mastrangelo, 206–219. Carbondale: Southern Illinois University Press, 2010.

Graham, Mark. "FAQs for Some New Features Available in the Beta Wayback Machine." *Internet Archive Blogs*, October 24, 2016. https://blog.archive.org/2016/10/24/faqs-for-some-new-features-available-in-the-beta-wayback-machine/.

———. "No More 404s! Resurrect Dead Web Pages with Our New Firefox Add-on." *Internet Archive Blogs*, August 9, 2016. https://blog.archive.org/2016/08/09/no-more-404s-resurrect-dead-web-pages-with-our-new-firefox-add-on/.

Greene, Jody. *The Trouble with Ownership: Literary Property and Authorial Liability in England, 1160–1730*. Philadelphia: University of Pennsylvania Press, 2005.

Greene, Mark A., and Dennis Meissner. "More Product, Less Process: Revamping Traditional Archival Processing." *American Archivist* 68 (2005): 208–263.

Gurak, Laura. *Persuasion and Privacy in Cyberspace: The Online Protests over Lotus Marketplace*. New Haven, CT: Yale University Press, 1997.

Guthrie, W. K. C. *A History of Greek Philosophy*. Cambridge, UK: Cambridge University Press, 1962.

Hall, Stuart. "The Great Moving Nowhere Show." *Marxism Today*, November–December 1998, 9–14.

Hall, Stuart. "The Neo-liberal Revolution." *Cultural Studies* 25 (2011): 705–728.

Hardin, Garrett. "The Tragedy of the Commons." *Science* 162 (1968): 1243–1248.

Hardt, Michael, and Antonio Negri. *Commonwealth*. Cambridge, MA: Harvard University Press, 2009.

Hardy, Quentin. "Lend Ho!" *Forbes*, October 29, 2009. www.forbes.com/forbes/2009/1116/opinions-brewster-kahle-google-ideas-opinions.html.

Harmon, Elliot. "Sofya Polyakov (Team Open)." http://teamopen.cc/sofya/.

Hartelius, E. Johanna. *The Rhetoric of Expertise*. Lanham, MD: Lexington, 2010.

Hartelius, Johanna. "Big Data and Global Knowledge: A Protagorean Analysis of the United Nations' Global Pulse." In *Ancient Rhetorics, Digital Networks*, edited by Michele Kennerly and Damien Smith Pfister, 67–87. Tuscaloosa: University of Alabama Press, 2018.

Harvey, David. "The Future of the Commons." *Radical History Review* 109 (2011): 101–107.

Hawhee, Debra. *Rhetoric in Tooth and Claw*. Chicago: University of Chicago Press, 2017.
Hayden, Wendy. "And Gladly Teach: The Archival Turn's Pedagogical Turn." *College English* 80, no. 2 (2017): 133–158.
———. "'Gifts' of the Archives: A Pedagogy for Undergraduate Research." *College Composition and Communication* 66, no. 3 (2015): 416–417.
Hayward, Jack, ed. Élitism, *Populism, and European Politics*. Oxford: Clarendon Press, 1996.
Heidegger, Martin. *Being and Time*. Translated by Edward Robinson and John MacQuarrie. New York: Harper and Row, 1962.
Heidegger, Martin. *Being and Time*. Translated by Joan Stambaugh. Albany: State University of New York Press, 1996.
———. *Early Greek Thinking*. Translated by David Farrell Krell and Frank A. Capuzzi. New York: Harper and Row, 1975.
———. "Letter on Humanism." In *Basic Writings*, edited by David Farrell Krell, 213–266. New York: HarperCollins, 1993.
———. *On Time and Being*. Translated by Joan Stambaugh. New York: Harper and Row, 1972.
Hess, Aaron, and Amber Davisson. *Theorizing Digital Rhetoric*. New York: Routledge, 2018.
Hofstadter, Richard. "North America." In *Populism: Its Meanings and National Characteristics*, edited by Ghita Ionescu and Ernest Gellner, 9–27. London: Weidenfeld and Nicolson, 1969.
Hogge, Becky. "Brewster Kahle: On the Egghead Who Hopes to Create a Permanent Record of All Human Knowledge." *New Statesman*, October 17, 2005, 26.
Houck, Davis W. "On or About June 1988." *Rhetoric and Public Affairs* 9, no. 1 (2006): 132–137.
Howard, R. G. "The Vernacular Mode: Locating the Non-institutional in the Practice of Citizenship." In *Public Modalities: Rhetoric, Culture, Media, and the Shape of Public Life*, edited by Daniel C. Brouwer and Robert Asen, 240–261. Tuscaloosa: University of Alabama Press, 2010.
Hyde, Lewis. *Common as Air*. New York: Farrar, Straus, and Giroux, 2010.
———. *The Gift: Creativity and the Artist in the Modern World*. New York: Vintage, 2007.
Hyde, Michael J. *The Life-Giving Gift of Acknowledgement*. West Lafayette: Purdue University Press, 2006.
Internet Archive. "About the Internet Archive." Accessed September 13, 2018. https://archive.org/about/.
———. "About the Internet Archive: Future Libraries—How People Envision Using Internet Libraries." Accessed November 3, 2016 at https://archive.org/about/.
———. "About the Internet Archive: Storage and Preservation." Accessed November 3, 2016 at https://archive.org/about/.
———. "About the Internet Archive: Why the Archive Is Building an 'Internet Library.'" Accessed November 3, 2016 at https://archive.org/about/.
———. "Internet Archive Projects: Building Libraries Together." Accessed January 31, 2017. https://archive.org/projects/.

"Internet Archive Founder Turns to New Information Storage Device—The Book," *Guardian*, August 1, 2011. www.theguardian.com/books/2011/aug/01/internet-archive-books-brewster-kahle.

Janes, Joseph. "Internet Librarian: Nowhere to Hide." *American Libraries* 35, no. 8 (September 2004): 72.

JCG. "20,000 Hard Drives on a Mission." *Internet Archive Blogs*, October 25, 2016. https://blog.archive.org/2016/10/25/20000-hard-drives-on-a-mission/.

Jefferson. "10 Years of Archiving the Web Together." *Internet Archive Blogs*, October 25, 2016. https://blog.archive.org/2016/10/25/10-years-of-archiving-the-web-together/.

Johnson, Richard, et al., eds. *Making Histories: Studies in History-Writing and Politics*. London: Hutchinson, 1982.

Joyce, John. "The Wayback Machine: A Glimpse of Cultural Memories from 10 Billion Web Pages." *Scientific Computing and Instrumentation*, October 2002, 16.

Kahle, Brewster. "How Google Threatens Books." *Washington Post*, May 19, 2009. www.washingtonpost.com/wp-dyn/content/article/2009/05/18/AR2009051802637.html.

———. "Lost in Cyberspace." *Economist*, September 1, 2012. www.economist.com/node/21560992.

Kaplan, Jeff. "New Firefox Add-on for Searching the Wayback Machine." *Internet Archive Blogs*, June 8, 2010. https://blog.archive.org/2010/06/08/new-firefox-add-on-for-searching-the-wayback-machine/.

Kaplan, Jeff. "Wayback Machine Comes to Life in New Home." *Internet Archive Blogs*, April 24, 2009. https://blog.archive.org/2009/04/24/wayback-machine-comes-to-life-in-new-home-2/.

———. "Wayback Machine Has 85 Billion Archived Webpages." *Internet Archive Blogs*, December 5, 2006. https://blog.archive.org/2006/12/05/wayback-machine-has-85-billion-archived-webpages/.

Kazin, Michael. *The Populist Persuasion: An American History*. Ithaca, NY: Cornell University Press, 1995.

Kennedy, Shirley Duglin. "When Good Links Go Bad." *Information Today*, November 2014, 8–16.

Kennerly, Michele, and Damien Smith Pfister, eds. *Ancient Rhetorics & Digital Networks*. Tuscaloosa: University of Alabama Press, 2018.

Kesmodel, David. "Lawyers' Delight: Old Web Material Doesn't Disappear; Wayback Machine and Google Archive Billions of Pages, Including Deleted Ones." *Wall Street Journal*, July 27, 2007. www.wsj.com/articles/SB112242983960797010.

Kirsch, Gesa E., and Liz Rohan, eds. *Beyond the Archives: Research as a Lived Process*. Carbondale: Southern Illinois University Press, 2008.

Koman, Richard. "How the Wayback Machine Works." *XML.com*, January 21, 2002. www.xml.com/pub/a/ws/2002/01/18/brewster.html.

Kostylo, Joanna. "From Gunpowder to Print: The Common Origins of Copyright and Patent." In *Privilege and Property: Essays on the History of Copyright*, edited by Ronan Deazley, Martin Kretschmer, and Lionel Bentley, 21–50. Cambridge, UK: OpenBook Publishers, 2010.

Laclau, Ernesto. *On Populist Reason*. New York: Verso, 2005.

———. "Populism: What's in a Name?" In *Populism and the Mirror of Democracy*, edited by Francisco Panizza, 32–49. London: Verso, 2005.
Landow, George P. *Hyper/Text/Theory*. Baltimore, MD: Johns Hopkins University Press, 1994.
———. *Hypertext 3.0: Critical Theory and New Media in an Era of Globalization*. Johns Hopkins University Press, 2006.
Lange, David L. "Recognizing the Public Domain." *Law and Contemporary Problems* 44 (1981): 147–178.
Lanham, Richard. "Digital Rhetoric: Theory, Practice, and Property." In *Literacy Online: The Promise (and Peril) of Reading and Writing with Computers*, edited by Myron C. Tuman, 221–243. Pittsburgh, PA: University of Pittsburgh Press, 1992.
———. *The Economics of Attention: Style and Substance in the Information Age*. Chicago: University of Chicago Press, 2006.
———. *Electronic Word*. Chicago: University of Chicago Press, 1993.
Leff, Michael. "Topical Invention and Metaphoric Interaction." *Southern Speech Communication Journal* 48 (1983): 214–229.
———. "Up from Theory: Or I Fought the *Topoi* and the *Topoi* Won." *Rhetoric Society Quarterly* 36 (2006): 203–211.
Lepore, Jill. "The Cobweb: Can the Internet Be Archived?" *New Yorker*, January 26, 2015. www.newyorker.com/magazine/2015/01/26/cobweb.
Lessig, Lawrence. "Architecting Innovation." *Drake Law Review* 49 (2001): 397–405.
———. "Copyright's First Amendment." *UCLA Law Review* 48 (2001): 1057–1073.
———. "Dunwody Distinguished Lecture in Law: The Creative Commons." *Florida Law Review* 55 (2003): 763–777.
———. *Free Culture: The Nature and Future of Creativity*. New York: Penguin, 2004.
———. *The Future of Ideas*. New York: Vintage, 2001.
Levitsky Steven, and James Loxton. "Populism and Competitive Authoritarianism: The Case of Fujimori's Peru." In *Populism in Europe and the Americas: Threat or Corrective for Democracy?*, edited by Cas Mudde and Cristóbal Rovira Kaltwasser, 160–181. New York: Cambridge University Press, 2010.
Linebaugh, Peter. *The Magna Carta Manifesto*. Berkeley: University of California Press, 2008.
Liu, Chen-Chung, Chia-Ching Lin, Chun-Yi Chang, and Po-Yao Chao. "Knowledge Sharing among University Students Facilitated with a Creative Commons Licensing Mechanism: A Case Study in a Programming Course." *Educational Technology & Society* 17, no. 3 (2014): 154–167.
Liu, Chen-Chung, Chia-Ching Lin, Kuei-Yuam Deng, Ying-Tien Wu, and Chin-Chung Tsai. "Online Knowledge Sharing Experience with Creative Commons." *Online Information Review* 38 (2014): 680–696.
Liu, Chen-Chung, Shu-Yuam Tao, Wei-Hung Chen, Sherry Y. Chen, and Baw-Jhiune Liu. "The Effects of a Creative Commons Approach on Collaborative Learning." *Behavior & Information Technology* 32, no. 1 (2013): 37–51.
Loewenstein, Joseph. *The Author's Due: Printing and the Prehistory of Copyright*. Chicago: University of Chicago Press, 2002.

Lotringer, Sylvère. Foreword to *A Grammar of the Multitude*, by Paolo Virno, 7–19. Los Angeles, CA: Semiotext(e) Foreign Agents Series, 2004.
Mackie, Tom. "Parties and Elections." In *Governing the New Europe*, edited by Jack Hayward and Edward C. Page, 166–195. Oxford University Press, 1995.
MacRae, Donald. "Populism as an Ideology." In *Populism: Its Meanings and National Characteristics*, edited by Ghita Ionescu and Ernest Gellner, 153–165. London: Weidenfeld and Nicolson, 1969.
Madison, Michael J., Brett M. Frischmann, and Katherine J. Strandburg. "Constructing Commons in the Cultural Environment." Special issue, *Cornell Law Review* 95 (2010): 657–709.
Malaby, Thomas M. *Making Virtual Worlds: Linden Lab and Second Life*. Ithaca, NY: Cornell University Press, 2009.
Malin, Brent J. *Feeling Mediated*. New York: New York University Press, 2014.
Marvin, Carolyn. *When Old Technologies Were New: Thinking about Electric Communication in the Late Nineteenth Century*. New York: Oxford University Press, 1990.
Marx, Leo. *The Machine in the Garden: Technology and the Pastoral Ideal in America*. New York: Oxford University Press, 1964.
Mastrangelo, Lisa, and Barbara L'Eplattenier. "Stumbling in the Archives." In *Beyond the Archives: Research as a Lived Process*, edited by Gesa E. Kirsch and Liz Rohan, 161–170. Carbondale: Southern Illinois University Press, 2008.
Mastrapaolo, Alfio. "Politics against Democracy: Party Withdrawal and Populist Breakthrough." In *Twenty-First Century Populism: The Spectre of Western European Democracy*, edited by Daniele Albertazzi and Duncan McDonnell, 30–48. New York: Palgrave Macmillan, 2008.
Mauss, Marcel. *The Gift: Forms and Functions of Exchange in Archaic Societies*. Glencoe, IL: The Free Press, 1954.
Mazzoleni, Gianpietro. "Populism and the Media." In *Twenty-First Century Populism: The Spectre of Western European Democracy*, edited by Daniele Albertazzi and Duncan McDonnell, 49–64. New York: Palgrave Macmillan, 2008.
McAteer, John. "The Gifts of God for the People of God: Communion as Derrida's Impossible Gift." In *Gift and Economy: Ethics, Hospitality and the Market*, edited by Eric R. Severson, 59–74. Newcastle, UK: Cambridge Scholars Publishing, 2012.
McCorkle, Ben. "Hindered Hope: Shepard Fairey, the Associated Press, and the Missed Opportunity to Help Clarify U.S. Copyright Law." In *Cultures of Copyright*, edited by Dánielle Nicole DeVoss and Martine Courant Rife, 54–63. New York: Peter Lang, 2015.
McGill, Meredith. *American Literature and the Culture of Reprinting, 1834–1853*. Philadelphia: University of Pennsylvania Press, 2003.
McGill, Meredith L. "Copyright and Intellectual Property: The State of the Discipline." *Book History* 16 (2013): 387–427.
Mifsud, Mari Lee. *Rhetoric and the Gift: Ancient Rhetorical Theory and Contemporary Communication*. Pittsburgh, PA: Duquesne University Press, 2015.
Milberry, Kate, and Steve Anderson. "Open Sourcing Our Way to an Online Commons: Contesting Corporate Impermeability in the New Media Ecology." *Journal of Communication Inquiry* 33, no. 4 (2009): 393–412.

Miller, Carolyn R. "The Aristotelian *Topos*: Hunting for Novelty." In *Rereading Aristotle's Rhetoric*, edited by Alan G. Gross and Arthur E. Walzer, 130–147. Carbondale: Southern Illinois University Press, 2008.

———. "Aristotle's 'Special Topics' in Rhetorical Practice and Pedagogy." *Rhetoric Society Quarterly* 17, no. 1 (1987): 61–70.

Minogue, Kenneth. "Populism as a Political Movement." In *Populism: Its Meanings and National Characteristics*, edited by Ghita Ionescu and Ernest Gellner, 197–211. London: Weidenfeld and Nicolson, 1969.

Morgan, Cliff. "Making Your Article Freely Available: Some Clarifications about Online-Open and Creative Commons." *Bioessays* 32, no. 8 (2010): 648–649.

Morris, Sammie L., and Shirley K. Rose. "Invisible Hands: Recognizing Archivists' Work to Make Record Accessible." In *Working in the Archives*, edited by Alexis E. Ramsey, Wendy B. Sharer, Barbara L'Eplattenier, and Lisa S. Mastrangelo, 51–78. Carbondale: Southern Illinois Press, 2010.

Mudde, Cas, and Cristóbal Rovira Kaltwasser, eds. *Populism in Europe and the Americas: Threat or Corrective for Democracy?* New York: Cambridge University Press, 2010.

Myška, Matěj. "The New Creative Commons 4.0 Licenses." *Grey Journal* 11 (2015): 58–62.

Nelson, William F. "*Topoi*: Evidence of Human Conceptual Behavior." *Philosophy and Rhetoric* 2, no. 1 (1969): 1–11.

Nietzsche, Friedrich. *Thus Spoke Zarathustra*. In *The Portable Nietzsche*. Translated and edited by Walter Kaufmann. New York: Viking, 1976.

Notess, Greg R. "Surviving Rot and Finding the Online Past." *Online Searcher*, March/April 2014, 66. www.thefreelibrary.com/Surviving+rot+and+finding+the+online+past-a0372555782.

Oakeshott, Michael. *The Politics of Faith and the Politics of Skepticism*. Edited by Timothy Fuller, 23–24. New Haven, CT: Yale University Press, 1996.

Okawa, Gail Y. "Unbundling." In *Beyond the Archives: Research as a Lived Process*, edited by Gesa E. Kirsch and Liz Rohan, 93–106. Carbondale: Southern Illinois University Press, 2008.

Olson, Caitlin. "The New Memory Palace." *Internet Archive Blogs*, October 25, 2016. https://blog.archive.org/2016/10/25/the-new-memory-palace/.

Ostergaard, Lori. "Open to the Possibilities: Seven Tales of Serendipity in the Archives." In *Working in the Archives*, edited by Alexis E. Ramsey, Wendy B. Sharer, Barbara L'Eplattenier, and Lisa S. Mastrangelo, 40–41. Carbondale: Southern Illinois University Press, 2010.

Ostrom, Elinor. *Governing the Commons: The Evolution of Institutions for Collective Action*. Cambridge, UK: Cambridge University Press, 1990.

Ott, Brian L. "Afterword: Digital Rhetoric at a Later Time." In *Theorizing Digital Rhetoric*, edited by Aaron Hess and Amber Davisson, 234–239. New York: Routledge, 2018.

Pacella, Rena Marie. "Where Data Lives." *Popular Science*, November 2011, 52–56.

Panizza, Francisco, ed. *Populism and the Mirror of Democracy*. London: Verso, 2005.

Pasquino, Gianfranco. "Populism and Democracy." In *Twenty-First Century Populism: The Spectre of Western European Democracy*, edited by Daniele Albertazzi and Duncan McDonnell, 15–29. New York: Palgrave Macmillan, 2008.

Patterson, Lyman Ray. *Copyright in Historical Perspective.* Nashville, TN: Vanderbilt University Press, 1968.
Peifer, Karl-Nikolaus. "The Return of the Commons—Copyright History as a Common Source." In *Privilege and Property: Essays on the History of Copyright,* edited by Ronan Deazley, Martin Kretschmer, and Lionel Bentley, 347–358. Cambridge, UK: OpenBook Publishers, 2010.
Pfister, Damien Smith. *Networked Media, Networked Rhetorics.* University Park: Pennsylvania State University Press, 2014.
Piratpartiet. "Piratpartiet Kommenterar Pirate-Bay-Rättegången." Last modified March 3, 2009. Accessed April 25, 2017. https://web.archive.org/web/20090309174136/http://www.piratpartiet.se:80/nyheter/piratpartiet_kommenterar_pirate_bay_rattegangen.
———. "Politik." Last modified June 28, 2009. Accessed April 25, 2017. www.piratpartiet.se:80/politik.
———. "Principprogram." Accessed April 25, 2017. www.piratpartiet.se/principprogram/.
———. "Principprogram." Last modified January 5, 2006. Accessed April 25, 2017. http://web.archive.org/web/20061014033401/http://www2.piratpartiet.se/principer.
———. *Valmanifest 2006.* Accessed April 30, 2018. http://mediekritik.lege.net/doc/Piratpartiets_valmanifest_2006.pdf.
———. *Valmanifest 2010: Kultur.* Accessed April 30, 2018. https://blog.mmn-o.se/wp-content/uploads/2010/08/valmanifest-kultur-2010.pdf.
———. *Valmanifest 2010: Kunskap.* Accessed April 30, 2018. https://blog.mmn-o.se/wp-content/uploads/2010/08/valmanifest-kunskap-2010.pdf.
Plant, S. A. *The New Commerce in Ideas and Intellectual Property.* London: The Athlone Press, 1953.
Potts, Andy. "Brewster Kahle Wants to Create a Free, Online Collection of Human Knowledge. It Sounds Impossibly Idealistic—but He Is Making Progress." *Economist,* March 5, 2009. www.economist.com/node/13174399.
Powell, Malea. "Dreaming Charles Eastman." In *Beyond the Archives: Research as a Lived Process,* edited by Gesa E. Kirsch and Liz Rohan, 115–127. Carbondale: Southern Illinois University Press, 2008.
Powell, William. "Time Machine." *TD,* March 2002, 25.
Purdy, James. "Three Gifts of Digital Archives." *Journal of Literacy & Technology* 12, no. 2 (2011): 24–49.
Ramsey, Alexis E. "Viewing the Archives: The Hidden and the Digital." In *Working in the Archives,* edited by Alexis E. Ramsey, Wendy B. Sharer, Barbara L'Eplattenier, and Lisa S. Mastrangelo, 79–90. Carbondale: Southern Illinois University Press, 2010.
Ramsey-Tobienne, Alexis E. "Archives 2.0: Digital Archives and the Formation of New Research Methods." *Peitho* 15 (2012): 4–29.
Rancière, Jacques. *Disagreement: Politics and Philosophy.* Minneapolis: University of Minnesota Press, 1999.
———. "Ten Theses on Politics." *Theory and Event* 5, no. 3 (2001): n.p.
Ransom, Harry. *The First Copyright Statute.* Austin: University of Texas Press, 1956.
Raven, James. *Free Print and Non-Commercial Publishing since 1700.* London and Burlington, VT: Ashgate Press, 2000.

Rein, Lisa. "Brewster Kahle on the Internet Archive and People's Technology." *Open P2P*, January 22, 2004. www.openp2p.com/pub/a/p2p/2004/01/22/kahle.html.
"Remembrances of Sites Past." *Newsweek* 138, no. 20 (2001): 73.
Rice, Jenny. "The Rhetorical Aesthetic of More: On Archival Magnitude." *Philosophy and Rhetoric* 50, no. 1 (2017): 26–49.
Rose, Mark. *Authors and Owners: The Invention of Copyright*. Cambridge, MA: Harvard University Press, 1993.
Rossi, Alexis. "Fixing Broken Links on the Internet." *Internet Archive Blogs*, October 25, 2013. https://blog.archive.org/2013/10/25/fixing-broken-links/.
Rydgren, Jens. "Sweden: The Scandinavian Exception." In *Twenty-First Century Populism: The Spectre of Western European Democracy*, edited by Daniele Albertazzi and Duncan McDonnell, 135–150. New York: Palgrave Macmillan, 2008.
Schaeffer, John D. *Sensus communis: Vico, Rhetoric, and the Limits of Relativism*. London: Duke University Press, 1990.
Scott, Jason. "I CAN HAZ MEME HISTORY??" *Internet Archive Blogs*, October 25, 2016. https://blog.archive.org/2016/10/25/i-can-haz-meme-history/.
Scott, Robert L. "On Viewing Rhetoric as Epistemic." *Central States Speech Journal* 18, no. 1 (1967): 9–17.
Searle, John R. *Speech Acts*. Cambridge, UK: Cambridge University Press, 1969.
Singh, Simmi. "Lessons from the Maker Movement." *MIT Sloan Management Review*, Summer 2018. Accessed March 8, 2019. https://sloanreview.mit.edu/article/lessons-from-the-maker-movement/.
Sjöman, Mika. "Grundkurs i Piratideologi för Liza Marklund." Last modified June 12, 2006. Accessed February 15, 2017. https://web.archive.org/web/20061014152619/http://etc.se/artikel/12776/grundkurs-i-piratideologi-foer-liza-marklund#c000424.
———. "Rättsövergreppen Frodas när Pirater Jagas inför Valet 2006." Last modified June 1, 2006. Accessed February 15, 2017. https://web.archive.org/web/20061014152559/http://etc.se/artikel/12699/raettsoevergreppen-frodas-naer-pirater-jagas-infoer-valet-2006.
Solberg, Janine. "Googling the Archive: Digital Tools and the Practice of History." *Advances in the History of Rhetoric* 15, no. 1 (2012): 53–76.
St. Clair, William. "Metaphors of Intellectual Property." In *Privilege and Property: Essays on the History of Copyright*, edited by Ronan Deazley, Martin Kretschmer, and Lionel Bentley, 369–396. Cambridge, UK: OpenBook Publishers, 2010.
Ståhl, Henrik. "EU-valet Avgörande för Piratpartiets Tillväxt." Last modified July 14, 2009. Accessed April 25, 2017. www.svd.se/eu-valet-avgorande-for-piratpartiets-tillvaxt.
Stallman. *Free Software, Free Society: Selected Essays of Richard M. Stallman*. Boston: Free Software Foundation, 2010. www.gnu.org/doc/fsfs-ii-2.pdf.
Stambaugh, Joan. "Introduction to" *On Time and Being*. Translated by Joan Stambaugh. New York: Harper and Row, 1972.
Steedman, Carolyn. *Dust: The Archive and Cultural History*. New Brunswick, NJ: Rutgers University Press, 2001.
———. "The Space of Memory: In an Archive." *History of the Human Sciences* 11, no. 4 (1998): 65–83.

Stewart, Angus. "The Social Roots." In *Populism: Its Meanings and National Characteristics*, edited by Ghita Ionescu and Ernest Gellner, 180–196. London: Weidenfeld and Nicolson, 1969.

Stuckey, Mary. "Presidential Secrecy: Keeping Archives Open." In "Forum on the Politics of Archival Research." Special issue, *Rhetoric and Public Affairs* 9, no. 1 (2006): 138–144.

Suber, Peter. "Open Access Overview." Accessed September 11, 2018. http://legacy.earlham.edu/~peters/fos/overview.htm.

Szydlowski, Nick. "Archiving the Web: It's Going to Have to Be a Group Effort." *The Serials Librarian* 59, no. 1 (2010): 35–39.

Taggart, Paul A. *The New Populism and the New Politics: New Protest Parties in Sweden in a Comparative Perspective*. London: Macmillan Press, 1996.

Taylor, Diana. *The Archive and the Repertoire*. Durham, NC: Duke University Press, 2003.

Tirabassi, Katherine E. "Journeying into the Archives: Exploring the Pragmatics of Archival Research." In *Working in the Archives*, edited by Alexis E. Ramsey, Wendy B. Sharer, Barbara L'Eplattenier, and Lisa S. Mastrangelo, 169–180. Carbondale: Southern Illinois University Press, 2010.

Tong, Judy. "Responsible Party—Brewster Kahle: A Library of the Web, On the Web." *New York Times*, September 8, 2002. www.nytimes.com/2002/09/08/business/responsible-party-brewster-kahle-a-library-of-the-web-on-the-web.html?pagewanted=1&register=google.

Tuman, Myron. *Wordperfect: Literacy in the Computer Age*. Pittsburgh, PA: University of Pittsburgh Press, 1992.

Tyerman, Barry. "The Economic Rationale for Copyright Protection for Published Books: A Reply to Professor Breyer." *UCLA Law Review* 18 (1971): 1100–1125.

Tynan, Dan. "30 Things You Didn't Know You Could Do on the Internet." *PCWorld*, July 2005, 76. www.pcworld.com/article/120784/article.html.

Ulmer, Gregory. *Internet Invention: From Literacy to Electracy*. London: Longman, 2003.

———. "Sounding the Unconscious." In *Glassary*, edited by John P. Leavey, 23–27. Lincoln: University of Nebraska Press, 1986.

Uncertain Commons. *Speculate This!* Durham, NC, and London: Duke University Press, 2013.

Vaidhyanathan, Siva. *Copyrights and Copywrongs: The Rise of Intellectual Property and How It Threatens Creativity*. New York: New York University Press, 2001.

Veyne, Paul. *Writing History: Essay on Epistemology*. Translated by Mina Moore-Rinvolucri. Middletown, CT: Wesleyan University Press, 1984.

Vico, Giambattista. *The New Science of Giambattista Vico: Unabridged Translation of the Third Edition (1744)*. Translated by Thomas G. Bergin and Max H. Fisch. Ithaca, NY: Cornell University Press, 1984.

———. *On the Study Methods of Our Time*. Translated by Elio Gianturco. Ithaca, NY: Cornell University Press, 1990.

Virno, Paolo. *A Grammar of the Multitude*. Los Angeles, CA: Semiotext(e) Foreign Agents Series, 2004.

Voight, Joan. "Meet Your Maker: Which Big Brands Are Courting the Maker Movement, and Why." *Adweek* 55, no. 11 (2014): 23. www.adweek.com/brand-marketing/which-big-brands-are-courting-maker-movement-and-why-156315/.
Wall, Derek. *The Commons in History: Culture, Conflict, and Ecology.* Cambridge, MA: MIT Press, 2014.
Wallace, Karl R. "*Topoi* and the Problem of Invention." *Quarterly Journal of Speech* 58, no. 4 (1972): 387–395.
Wark, McKenzie. *General Intellects: Twenty-One Thinkers for the Twenty-First Century.* New York: Verso, 2017.
Warnick, Barbara. *Critical Literacy in a Digital Era: Technology, Rhetoric, and the Public Interest.* New York: Routledge, 2001.
———. "Rhetorical Criticism of Public Discourse on the Internet: Theoretical Implications." *Rhetoric Society Quarterly* 28, no. 4 (1998): 73–84.
———. "Two Systems of Invention: The Topics in the Rhetoric and The New Rhetoric." In *Rereading Aristotle's Rhetoric*, edited by Alan G. Gross and Arthur E. Walzer, 107–129. Carbondale: Southern Illinois University Press, 2008.
Weber, Max. *The Protestant Ethic and the Spirit of Capitalism.* Translated by Talcott Parsons. New York: Charles Scribner's Sons, 1958.
Welch, Kathleen. *Electric Rhetoric: Classical Rhetoric, Oralism, and a New Literacy.* Cambridge, MA: MIT Press, 1999.
Wells, Susan. "Claiming the Archive for Rhetoric and Composition." In *Rhetoric and Composition as Intellectual Work.* Edited by Gary A. Olson, 55–64. Carbondale: Southern Illinois University Press, 2002.
Westlind, Dennis. *The Politics of Popular Identity: Understanding Recent Populist Movements in Sweden and the United States.* Lund, Sweden: Lund University Press, 1996.
Wheelwright, Philip. *Heraclitus.* New York: Atheneum, 1974.
White, Richard. "Nietzsche on Generosity and the Gift-Giving Virtue." *British Journal for the History of Philosophy* 24, no. 2 (2016): 348–364.
Wiles, Peter. "A Syndrome, Not a Doctrine: Some Elementary Theses on Populism." In *Populism: Its Meanings and National Characteristics*, edited by Ghita Ionescu and Ernest Gellner, 166–179. London: Weidenfeld and Nicolson, 1969.
Williams, Rosalind. "Afterword: An Historian's View on the Network Society." In *The Network Society*, edited by Manuel Castells, 432–448. Cheltenham, UK: Edward Elgar, 2004.
Wirten, Eva Hemmungs. *No Trespassing: Authorship, Intellectual Property Rights, and the Boundaries of Globalization.* Toronto: University of Toronto Press, 2004.
Woodmansee, Martha. "The Genius and the Copyright: Economic and Legal Conditions of the Emergence of the 'Author.'" *Eighteenth Century Studies* 17, no. 4 (1984): 425–448.
Worsley, Peter. "The Concept of Populism." In *Populism: Its Meanings and National Characteristics*, edited by Ghita Ionescu and Ernest Gellner, 212–250. London: Weidenfeld and Nicolson, 1969.
Yakel, Elizabeth. "Searching and Seeking in the Deep Web: Primary Sources on the Internet." In *Working in the Archives*, edited by Alexis E. Ramsey, Wendy B. Sharer, Barbara

L'Eplattenier, and Lisa S. Mastrangelo, 102–118. Carbondale: Southern Illinois University Press, 2010.

Zappen, James P. "Digital Rhetoric: Toward an Integrated Theory." *Technical Communication Quarterly* 14, no. 3 (2005): 319–325.

Zappen, James P., Laura J. Gurak, and Stephen Doheny-Farina. "Rhetoric, Community, and Cyberspace." *Rhetoric Review* 15, no. 2 (1997): 400–419.

Zilioli, Ugo. *Protagoras and the Challenge of Relativism: Plato's Subtlest Enemy.* Hampshire, UK: Ashgate, 2007.

INDEX

"Age of Steam," aesthetics of, 91
Albaih, Khalid, 59–60
Allemansrätten, 8, 102–3, 117, 122, 149n16, 188n64
ambiguity, 104
Apter, Emily, 171n89
archival commons, 70–72, 88–89; and the "allure of the archives," 74–75; and archival knowing, 72–78, 89, 181–82n112, 182n123; the archive as an illustration of epistemic power, 73–74; discourses concerning, 93–94; excesses of, 75, 93, 179–80n90; methods of access to, 77–78, 95–96; national archiving in France and Britain, 73; opposing qualities (ordinary versus mystical) of, 74–75; overwhelming excess of, 93; rise of the public archive with the rise of the nation state, 73; two forms of archival expertise, 75–76. *See also* digital archive
archival processing, 180n107
archivists/archival scholars, 76, 88, 94, 176n39, 181n109; and the gifts of archival work for scholars, 175–76n37
Arditi, Benjamin, 103, 113, 114, 186n40, 187n41
Areopagitica (Milton), 47
Aristotle, 17–18; on the definition of rhetoric, 34–35
Armstrong, Timothy, 67, 172n107
art/artists, 32–33, 168n62

attribution, individuation, and value, 56–58
Austin, J. L., 51
authorship, legitimacy of, 51–52

"Basic Course in Pirate Ideology" (Sjöman), 119, 120
being, acknowledgement of, 35
Being and Time (Heidegger), 30, 156n106
Benkler, Yochai, 6, 25, 152n52, 152n54
Bentham, Jeremy, 53
Biesecker, Barbara, 75
Bitzer, Lloyd, 10
Black Mirror, 118, 189n70
blogs, 49, 178n74
"Bloomington School, the" 12
Bollier, David, 10, 16; on historical industrialization, 13–14
Boon, Marcus, 1–2
Bourdieu, Pierre, 66, 140
Boyle, James, 16, 21–22; on information environmentalism, 149–50n23
British Museum, 91–92

Canovan, Margaret, 109
Carey, James, 154n68
Castells, Manuel, 3, 6, 22–23, 25, 26
Clinton, Bill, 23–24
collective knowledge production, 135, 167n61

209

colonialism, 74
commons, 10–11; classically conceived commonplaces (*koinoi topoi*), 17; digital commons, 14; as resources + community, 16, 149n12. *See also* archival commons; cultural commons; digital commons; infrastructural commons; natural commons
Commonwealth (Hardt and Negri), 150–51n34
Congressional Committee of Detail, 48
copia, 178–79n78; association of with knowledge, 139–40; as the most prevalent theme of the Creative Commons, 64–65, 72. *See also copia*, and productive retrieval
copia, and productive retrieval, 87–89; archival delivery and disposition of, 92–96
copyright, 44–45, 136, 143–44; capricious enforcement of, 53; copyright "pessimists," 164n29; and the term "own," 52, 161n15; two models of, 166–67n59. *See also* copyright "stuff," and structures of control
Copyright Act (1790), 48, 172n107, 173n6
Copyright Extension Act (1998), 7
copyright "stuff," and structures of control, 45–46; copyright policy debates, 49; developments concerning, 49–50; and incentivized creativity, 52–53; the origins and regimes of control, 46–47; two models of (Anglo-American [utilitarian] and French [natural]), 50–52; and the 'US "Copyright Clause," 47–49
Courant, Dean, 91
Creative Commons (CC), 3, 21, 44–45, 49, 125; access to, 127–30; attribution function of, 56, 167nn60–61; connotations of with genes/genetics, 63–64; and the construction of gifting as a matter of philanthropy, 135–36; and continuous regeneration, 88; and copyright law, 168n63; and copyright timing aspects, 65–68; critics of, 166–67n59; definition of, 170n86; gifting logos of, 53–54, 58, 59–60; kairos of, 45, 66–67, 98, 140–41; reasons for the support of, 60; termination provisions of, 67; three layers of code sustaining the Creative Commons, 63. *See also* Creative Commons (CC), tailored licenses of
Creative Commons (CC), tailored licenses of, 54–56, 59, 67–68, 132–33, 143–44; "Attribution-NoDervis" tag, 55; "Attribution-NonCommercial" tag, 55, 63; "Attribution-NonCommerical-NoDervis" tag, 55; "Attribution-NonCommerical-ShareAlike" tag, 55, 63; "Attribution-ShareAlike" tag, 55, 166n54, 171n98; "Attribution" tag, 55, 56, 66; and the "License Chooser," 61; rise of licensed materials (2006–2016), 64; success of due to copious growth, 138
cultural artifacts, 64–65
cultural commons, 15–19, 148n13, 149n19; and the concept of *doxa*, 18; definition of, 15–16
cultural production, 4, 45, 120, 123, 140, 172n101; as gifting, 182–83n124
cultural resources, 2, 10, 70, 95, 127; sustainable, 139

Davisson, Amber, 25
Dawes Act (1887), 148n5
Deazley, Ronan, 52, 67, 162n17
Dell Corporation, 84
digital archive, 78; access to, 77–78, 95–96; and the archive/data distinction, 85–86
Derrida, Jacques, 7, 27, 82, 157nn146–47; on "archive fever," 75; dispute with John Searle, 51–52; rejection of the concept of a gift by, 33–34
determinism, 25–26
digital commons, 19, 38, 44, 65, 86, 131, 141; gifting logos of, 65–66, 104; expertise in, 98–100; network infrastructure of, 22–26; resources of, 21–22; and the theory of multitude, 19–21, 26, 39; three components of, 26
Digital Millennium Copyright Act (1998), 49
digital populism, 106–7, 128, 129–30; and the articulation of the people, 110–12; political/populist discourses of, 106, 108, 110–11, 112; populist idealism, 110; and representative government, 112–14; and the rhetoric of antagonism, 107–9, 119–24; rhetorical approach to, 107; twenty-first century digital populists, 108–9

Eldred, Eric, 49, 162–63n22
Emerson, Ralph Waldo, 38
England, 46
ethics, Christian, 38
expertise, 86–87; in the digital commons, 98–100; digitally networked expertise, 4; and the gifting logos, 104–5, 145–46; Greek expertise and wisdom (as *haplous*), 94–95; invention of, 2–3; as the making of sense of something, 137, 145–46; two forms of archival expertise, 75–76
Eyman, Douglas, 25, 148n12

INDEX   211

Facebook, 170–71n88
Falkvinge, Richard, 101, 118–20
Farge, Arlette, 74, 76
Finnegan, Cara, 76
flânerie, 95–96, 182nn115–16, 182n123
Flickr, 171n94
Foucault, Michel, 51, 164n32, 165n35
Free Software Foundation, 50

Gaillet, Lynée Lewis, 76, 94
General Inclosure Act (1845), 11
general intellect, 10, 20–22, 151n40
general public license (GPL), 50, 171n95
Geschwandtner, Christina M., 38
gift/gifts/gifting, 27, 57; of archiving to digital archives, 179n80; cultural content of, 68; gift exchange as a struggle, 29–30; gifting as sharing, 58–61; as a rhetorical practice, 27; in rhetorical studies, 34–38; theories of, 57–58
gifting logos, 3–4, 5, 6, 37–38, 38–39, 68–69, 130; abundance of, 40–41; and the concept of charity, 63; and the concept of choice, 61–62; and the concept of time, 141–42; as cumulative, 64–65; and expertise, 104–5; as expertise in the digital commons, 98–100; future of, 146; intent and agency of, 61–62; kairos of, 45, 66–67, 98, 140–41; playful posture toward its "others," 41–42, 143–46; political implications of, 129–30; progressivism of, 41, 159n185; as a rhetoric of expertise, 145–46; and the theme of inheritance, 62–65; as time sensitive, 41. See also gifting logos, characteristics and functions of; pirate politics, and the gifting logos; Wayback Machine, and the gifting logos
gifting logos, characteristics and functions of, 131; abundance of the gifting logos, 137–40; the gifting logos assumes participants' awareness in order to function, 39–40, 132–34; the gifting logos assumes a rhetorically playful posture toward its "others," 143–46; the gifting logos derives rhetorical potency from tensions between artifice and nature, 40, 135–37; as time-sensitive and progressivist, 140–43;
Gilliat, Bruce, 78
Ginsburg, Jane, 52
Girkin, Igor, 84
"given," the, meaning of, 103–4
God, 35, 158n162
Gold, David, 75

Goldstein, Paul, 164n29
Google Picasa, 171n94
Governing the Commons (Ostrom), 12
government, representative, 112–14
Greene, Jody, 47, 165n35

Hardin, Garett, 11–12, 16, 149n8
Hardt, Michael, 16–17, 150–51n34
Harvey, David, 17
Heidegger, Martin, 5, 7, 27, 141, 156n106; on treatment of the gift and appropriation, 30–31
Henry VIII (king of England), 11
Heraclitus, 5–6, 172n109
Hess, Aaron, 25
Hobbes, Thomas, 20
Hoffman, Abbie, 62, 170n87
Hofstadter, Richard, 109
Homer, 36
homo mensura thesis, 2
Houck, Davis, 76
Hyde, Lewis, 7, 13, 27, 65, 157n147, 158n159; on artists, 168n62; on the concept of the gift and the relationship between art and artists, 31–33; on the distinction of gifts from commodities, 32–33; on the gift as a mystery, 32; on reciprocity, 158n162
Hyde, Michael J., 7; on acknowledgment as a moral action, 35–36; on the gift as rhetorical, 37

incentives, financial, 52–53
individualism, 46–47
"informationalism," 3
information environmentalism, 149–50n23
information society, emergence of, 119
infrastructural commons, 43–45
In Praise of Copying (Boon), 1
intellectual property, 161–62n16, 162n17; intellectual property rights, 117
Internet Archive (IA), 71, 72, 125, 138–39, 178n73; central function of, 97; considerations of storage and preservation, 181n108; and the dialectic of the traditional archive's bureaucratic function, 72; emphasis of on delivery, 92–93; gifting logos of, 95, 98; growth of facilitated by the Archive-IA initiative, 87–88; IA/Wayback machine as an archive, 89; institutional affiliations of, 79; as machine or archive, 89–92; motto of, 79, 94; origins of, 78–79, 81; preservation as the principal function of, 83–84; romanticism of,

Internet Archive (IA) *(continued)*
    83, 177n68; structure of, 94; urgency of
    IA's preservation, 142

jazz, improvisational, 1–2

Kahle, Brewster, 71, 72, 78, 79–82, 90, 138; as
    eccentric technophile, 144; genius of, 80; gift
    of to the commons, 91; and the gifting logos,
    80–82, 83–84; on historical research, 95; on
    libraries, 96; personal motives of, 177n53;
    transition of from entrepreneur to philan-
    thropist, 79–80
Kaltwasser, Cristóbal Rovira, 184n13
Karlsson, Bert, 116
Kennerly, Michele, 25
Kessinger, Berry, 82
Kostylo, Joanna, 46

Laclau, Ernesto, 111–12
language philosophy, 113–14
Lanham, Richard, 151n43
legein, 5–6
Lepore, Jill, 90
Lessig, Lawrence, 7, 22, 44, 49, 58, 60–61; on
    the architecture of the internet, 152n49; on
    "circumvention technologies," 151–52n44;
    and the founding of the Creative Commons,
    53–54
L'Estrange, Robert, 47
Library of Congress, 96, 144
Licensing Act (1662), 46, 47
Life-Giving Gift of Acknowledgement, The
    (M. J. Hyde), 35
Lindblom, Kenneth, 76
Linebaugh, Peter, 10
Lirsch, Gesa E., 75
literary culture, 162n19
Locke, John, 47
logos: layers of, 58–61; pre-Socratic, 5–6. *See also*
    gifting logos

Malaby, Thomas M., 189n76
Marklund, Liza, 120
Marvin, Carolyn, 154–55n69
Marx, Leo, 89
Mauss, Marcel, 6, 27, 31, 32, 65; and the functions
    of gifting for social order, 28–30; on gifting
    as political, 56
McAteer, John, 38, 168–69n66
McGill, Meredith, 48–49, 162n19

megethos, 178–79n78
Midsummer, 19
Mifsud, Mari Lee, 7, 18, 35; analysis of Aristotle's
    rhetorical theory by, 36–37; on the gift as a
    call from something Other, 36; on the gift as
    rhetorical, 37; on gifts as both material and
    "animistic," 37
Miller, Paul, 182–83n124
Milton, John, 47
mimesis, 1
Monsters Inc. (2001), 92
Mudde, Cas, 184n13
multitude, the, 6–7, 19–21, 145, 150–51n34,
    151n40; digital multitude, 39; networked
    multitude, 26, 39

National Archives (Paris), founding of, 73
natural commons, 10, 11–15; dialectical feature
    of, 14–15; distinction in between labor time
    and not-labor time, 13
natural/moral rights (*droit moral*), 50
natural resources, 8, 11, 136, 148n5, 149–50n23
Negri, Antonio, 16–17, 150–51n34
New Democracy (Ny Demokrati), 114–15
Nietzsche, Friedrich, 6, 59, 132; theory of the gift,
    27–28

open access movement, 7–8, 17, 19, 49, 50, 55,
    163–64n28; advocates of, 148n13; as an issue
    in national elections, 103; and the Swedish
    Pirate Party, 117, 120
open code/open source, 50, 163n25, 163n27
Ostrom, Elinor, 12–13
Ott, Brian, 21

Pasquino, Gianfranco, 115
Pfister, Damien Smith, 24, 25; 152–53n59
piracy, 101
Pirate Bay, 102
Pirate Party. *See* Swedish Pirate Party
pirate politics: and the gifting logos, 116–17; and
    the rhetorical exigence of a copyright crisis,
    117–19
plagiarism, 1, 62
poesis, 37
politics, 103–5
Polyakov, Sofya, 59, 169n72
popular commons, 101–6
populism, 115–16, 185n18. *See also* digital
    populism
Powell, Malea, 74, 76

Power of Open, The (Creative Commons report), 7, 44, 58, 168n64
producerism, 108, 185nn17–18
Protagoras, 2, 3, 147n4
pseudonyms, 56
Public Records Office (London), founding of, 73
Purdy, James, 179n80

Rancière, Jacques, 103, 130, 184n8
Real Story of Stone Soup, The (Compestine), 43, 159–60n1
republicanism, 48
resources. *See* cultural resources; digital commons, resources of; natural resources
rhetoric: digital rhetoric, 24–26; networked rhetorics, 24
Rhetoric (Aristotle), 17–18
rhetorical activities, 4–5
"rhetorical aggregate," 10
rhetorical scholarship, 5
Rice, Jenny, 178–79n78, 190n77
Rohan, Liz, 75
Rose, Mark, 46–47
Russia (Imperial Russia), agrarian territories of, 107

Schrag, Calvin, 158n162
scientific inquiry, rhetorical analysis of, 3–4
Scott, Robert L., 3
Searle, John, 51–52
second enclosure movement, 16–17, 21–22, 149–50n23
sharing, 58–61
"Signature, Event, Context" (Derrida), 51
Sjöman, Mika, 116–17
social hierarchies, 28
social media, 49, 170–71n88
software, commercial governance of, 49
Sonny Bobo Copyright Extension Act (1998), 49
source code. *See* open code/source code
Speculate This manifesto, 166n58
Spinoza, Baruch, 20
Stallman, Richard, 50, 171n95
Stambaugh, Joan, 31
State of the Commons, The (Creative Commons memorandum), 44, 59, 61, 170n86, 171n91
Stationers' Company, 46–47, 60
Statue of Anne (1710), 7, 47
Steal This Book (Hoffman), 62, 170n87
Steedman, Carolyn, 74, 82–83
Stewart, Angus, 185n18

"stuff," 44, 81–82, 151n43. *See also* copyright "stuff," and structures of control
Sweden Democrats, 114–15, 187n51
Swedish Pirate Party, 4, 8, 21, 101–3, 127–30, 136, 138; constituents of, 123; criticism of toward the international entertainment media, 122; digital populism of, 128, 129–30; endorsement of information technologies by, 118–19; and the open access movement, 117, 120; opponents of, 123–24; political/populist discourses of, 106, 108; political program of, 143; and popular rights to privacy and integrity, 124–27; "Program of Principles" of, 103, 105–6, 117, 119, 121, 122–23; public messages of, 105–6; second national election campaign of, 125; Swedish populism and party politics, 114–16, 128, 129–30; and the term *"personal data,"* 125. *See also* pirate politics, and the gifting logos
Sword in the Stone, The (1963), 15
symbols, 113
Szydlowski, Nick, 178n74

Taylor, Diana, 77, 88, 181–82n112
"Team Open" webpage, 59
technoliberalism, 189n76
technology, 22, 26; "circumvention technologies," 151–52n44; communication technologies, 154n68, 154–55n69
"textification," 74
Thus Spoke Zarathustra (Nietzsche), 27–28, 59, 155n77
time travel machine, 91
"Tragedy of the Commons, The" (Hardin), 11–12
tropes, 104–5, 129, 187n53
Twitter, 170–71n88
Two Treatises of Government (Locke), 47

United Sates of America, agrarian territories of, 107
US Constitution, 48
User, John, 48
Usher, John, 46

Venice, 161n9; and copyright privilege, 45, 46
verum factum principle, 2, 3
Vico, Giambattista, 2–3; epistemology of, 147n5
Virno, Paolo, 19–21. *See also* multitude, the
volonté générale (general will of the people), 108
von Speyer, Johannes, 45–46

Wachtmeister, Ian, 115, 116
walkabout, the, 13
Wayback Machine, 3–4, 41, 71, 72, 87, 141–42; ambivalence concerning the purposes of, 83; central function of, 97; discourses concerning, 93–94; as "humongous," 144; IA/Wayback machine as an archive, 89; as machine and archive, 89–92; origin of the name of, 90–91; purposes of, 82–87; ubiquitous language of its web page, 97; urgency of its efforts, 97–98; use of, 178n71. *See also* Wayback Machine, and the gifting logos
Wayback Machine, and the gifting logos, 78–79, 95; and Brewster Kahle, 79–82; legal contexts of, 84–85; and the romance of preservation, 83–84

Weber, Max, 74
Welch, Kathleen, 25, 154n63
Wells, Susan, 175–76n37
Westlind, Dennis, 115
"What Is This a Picture Of?" (Finnegan), 76
whisper networks, 153n61
White, Richard, 155n84
World Intellectual Property Organization, 49, 161–62n16
World Wide Web, 14, 45, 49, 54; design of as an end-to-end structure, 163n23; early years of, 86–87
Worsley, Peter, 116
Worth, Jonathan, 168n64

You-Tube, 166n47

Founded in 1893,
UNIVERSITY OF CALIFORNIA PRESS
publishes bold, progressive books and journals
on topics in the arts, humanities, social sciences,
and natural sciences—with a focus on social
justice issues—that inspire thought and action
among readers worldwide.

The UC PRESS FOUNDATION
raises funds to uphold the press's vital role
as an independent, nonprofit publisher, and
receives philanthropic support from a wide
range of individuals and institutions—and from
committed readers like you. To learn more, visit
ucpress.edu/supportus.

www.ingramcontent.com/pod-product-compliance
Lightning Source LLC
Chambersburg PA
CBHW030651230426
43665CB00011B/1039